TRAVELER

athens &
the islands

NATIONAL GEOGRAPHIC
TRAVELER

athens &
the islands

by Joanna Kakissis

National Geographic
Washington, D.C.

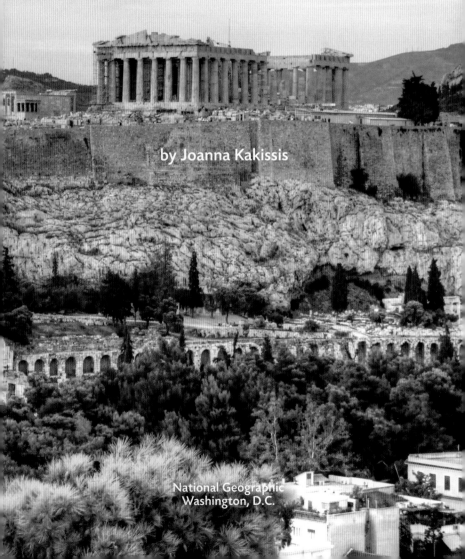

CONTENTS

Pages 2–3: The Acropolis, perched above Athens
Opposite: A morning view over Santorini Bay

TRAVELING WITH EYES OPEN

Alert travelers go with a purpose and leave with a benefit. If you travel responsibly, you can help support wildlife conservation, historic preservation, and cultural enrichment in the places you visit. You can enrich your own travel experience as well.

To be a geo-savvy traveler:

- Recognize that your presence has an impact on the places you visit.

- Spend your time and money in ways that sustain local character. (Besides, it's more interesting that way.)

- Value the destination's natural and cultural heritage.

- Respect the local customs and traditions.

- Express appreciation to local people about things you find interesting and unique to the place: its nature and scenery, music and food, historic villages and buildings.

- Vote with your wallet: Support the people who support the place, patronizing businesses that make an effort to celebrate and protect what's special there. Seek out shops, local restaurants, inns, and tour operators who love their home—who love taking care of it and showing it off. Avoid businesses that detract from the character of the place.

- Enrich yourself, taking home memories and stories to tell, knowing that you have contributed to the preservation and enhancement of the destination.

That is the type of travel now called geotourism, defined as "tourism that sustains or enhances the geographical character of a place—its environment, culture, aesthetics, heritage, and the well-being of its residents." To learn more, visit National Geographic's Center for Sustainable Destinations at *www .nationalgeographic.com/travel/sustainable.*

athens & the islands

ABOUT THE AUTHOR

Joanna Kakissis is a journalist currently based in Athens, Greece. She was born there but grew up in North Dakota, South Dakota, and Minnesota. Her work appears in many outlets, including the *New York Times, TIME,* the *Washington Post, Financial Times,* online travel magazine *World Hum,* and on National Public Radio. Kakissis has also taught journalism and essay writing at universities in North Carolina. Her stories have been distinguished by the American Association of Sunday and Feature Editors, the Society of Professional Journalists, and the North Carolina Press Association, and she is also the recipient of several writing awards and journalism fellowships. Kakissis has traveled extensively in Greece and has strong ancestral connections to Kyparissia in the western Peloponnese (her father's home) and Rethimno in central Crete (her mother's home).

Charting Your Trip

Visiting Athens and the Greek islands means planning well: There is so much to see that even a month may seem like too little time. That doesn't mean a well-rounded trip is impossible, however. You can combine ancient wonders with modern art, fine dining, and, of course, trips to the most beautiful beaches in the Mediterranean.

How to Get Around

Within the city of Athens there is an excellent public transportation system (see sidebar p. 11) and no shortage of taxis. Although Athens's traffic problems have eased recently, it's still not a great place to drive. Outside the city, however, renting a car (see Travelwise p. 239) is an excellent way to get around, especially if you are touring the Peloponnese or venturing north to Delphi. Greece has a fairly efficient rail system (see www.ose.gr), but as many sights are some distance from the large towns where the trains stop, it isn't particularly useful. A number of bus companies (see Travelwise p. 239) will take you directly to sites of interest.

Ferry trips (see Travelwise pp. 238–239) range from brief hops over to the islands in the nearby Saronic Gulf (which take about 30 minutes) to eight-hour cruises to the distant islands of Crete or Rhodes. On longer trips travelers can book cabins. Booking ahead is essential for most ferry trips except for hops to the near islands.

The more popular islands, including Crete and Santorini, have airports served by frequent flights from Athens. On the islands, most visitors find it easiest to get around on foot, occasionally using taxis or rental cars when they need to travel farther.

Athens & the Mainland

A visit to Athens is rewarding no matter how long you spend there—whether it's a week in the city or just an afternoon passed while waiting for a ferry. Although most people are familiar with the Acropolis and its monuments, the cultural riches of this city are by no means limited to the ancient past. Furthermore, you do not have to travel far out of the city to find yourself in a thoroughly different landscape, where you can spend a day exploring Mycenaean ruins or the narrow streets of a medieval fishing village.

Traditional black-figure decorated pottery

Ancient Athens: No trip to Athens would be complete without a visit to the **Acropolis.** The best thing to do is to visit when it first opens at 8 a.m. to see the Parthenon, the Erechtheion, and the Propylaia before the site gets too hot and crowded. Before leaving the Acropolis, walk down to the ancient theaters on its southern slopes, where the great works of ancient Greek drama had their first performances. From there, head over to the fabulous **New Acropolis Museum.** If you still have time after this, and still want to see more ancient relics, you can hop on the Metro at Acropolis station (across the street from the museum) and travel three stops north to Omonoia and the nearby **National Archaeological Museum,** which stays open until 7 p.m. on weekdays.

Modern Athens: Take a leisurely stroll into the center of town, find yourself a nice café, then sit and sip your *elliniko* (traditional Greek coffee) while the sellers at the **Monastiraki** markets set out their wares. Spend the morning exploring the strange and wondrous little shops that are scattered throughout the winding streets of Athens's historic core. Later, after lunch in a taverna, head over to **Gazi** and explore the playful (if sometimes rather odd) modern art exhibitions at the cultural center that occupies the former gasworks. After dinner in one of the hip restaurants nearby, take the Metro to Evangelismos and head up to the summit of **Lykavittos Hill** to see the lights of Athens glowing below.

Visitor Information

The **Greek National Tourism Organization** maintains a helpful website *(www.visitgreece.gr)* with a wealth of essential travel information for visitors.

In addition, the Greek Ministry of Culture hosts an online database called **Odysseus** *(http://odysseus .culture.gr),* which has pages on most historic sites in Greece. Each page usually has some historical information about the site, as well as practical details like opening hours and admission charges.

Day Trips on the Mainland: Many of the places that Athenians once considered distant are now close enough for a quick day trip. The most popular destination for excursions out of Athens is the sacred temple complex at **Delphi,** around an hour's travel northwest of the city either by taxi, rental car, or bus.

If You Have More Time: Although the northern towns of the **Peloponnese** are within day-trip distance of Athens, taking a few days to explore the area at a more leisurely pace can be very rewarding. On the first day, leave early and head west to

Cultural Etiquette

Athens is a relaxed and cosmopolitan city, but there are a few etiquette pointers to keep in mind:

- Men and women alike greet each other by kissing on the cheek.
- Because of the heat, Athenians usually eat dinner after 9 p.m.
- At a café, don't ever call *elliniko*—the thick, grainy coffee served in tiny cups—a Turkish coffee.
- Older Greeks still take a siesta between 3:00 p.m. and 5:00 p.m. every afternoon.
- If you're out to dinner with Athenians and they offer to pay, don't argue too forcefully or you will offend them. Just thank them and let them pay.
- When visiting someone's house, don't arrive empty-handed; bring flowers, a bottle of wine, or a box of pastries from a *zacharoplasteio*, or bakery.

the **Corinth Canal** and the ruins of **Ancient Corinth** before continuing south to **Mycenae.** In the evening, settle into a hotel in the charming harbor town of **Nafplio** and enjoy the town's famous seafood. The next morning, continue south to the beautiful coastal village of **Monemvasia.** The trip down there is a three-hour drive from Nafplio, assuming you resist the urge to stop along the way for a swim.

The Islands

For those tired of city life, a constellation of islands, large and small, awaits just a ferry ride away from the harbor at Pireas (near Athens). Even if you're short on time, there are plenty of nearby places that satisfy most people's desires for sun, sea, and sand.

The Near Islands: These islands are scattered just off the eastern and western coasts of the mainland, in the Aegean Sea and the Saronic Gulf. As their name would suggest, these Near Islands, which include **Evia** and **Egina,** are only about a 30-minute ferry ride from Pireas, and most can even be seen from the mainland on a clear day. During the summer (and particularly on sunny weekends), these islands are usually so packed with people that they feel like they might sink, but during the off-season they can be almost eerily quiet and make an excellent place to escape and relax for a day. A perfect example of this is **Idra,** where donkeys are still favored over cars.

The Cyclades: When you think of Greek islands, it is usually images of the Cyclades that spring to mind—whitewashed houses, clear blue seas, and dry, rugged landscapes. The principal inhabited islands of this chain include **Mikonos, Andros,** and **Siros.** Each of these islands has its own unique character, but all share the same lovely weather and relaxed attitude. All are within a morning's ferry ride of Pireas and worth a leisurely visit of a day or two. Some (particularly Andros) are surprisingly free from commercial development.

The Ionians: Alternatively, visitors can catch a short domestic flight from Athens airport to the Adriatic island of **Corfu,** the jewel of the Ionian chain. The character of these charming islands, which also include **Paxi, Kefalonia,** and **Ithaca,** is defined by the architectural and cultural legacy of 400 years of Venetian rule. Here you will find neat coastal villages of pastel-painted neoclassical houses, mighty Venetian fortresses, and, of course, stunning beaches. Be sure to check out the beautiful sunken Korissia Lagoon on Corfu.

A flag seller on an Athens street

If You Have More Time: It's well worth visiting the more far-flung islands in the Aegean Sea. Although very well trodden by European tourists, the island of **Santorini** (Thira)—around six hours on the ferry from Pireas—is still an unmissable destination, with its beautiful whitewashed houses clinging to the fractured remains of an exploded volcano. From Santorini, visitors can catch another ferry three hours south to the much larger island of **Crete** (or, alternately, take an overnight ferry or a one-hour flight from Athens). In addition to miles of pristine beaches, this island boasts unique Minoan ruins, picturesque mountain villages, and a fiercely independent tradition of food, song, and literature.

For more information on how to make your way to and between the various Greek islands, see Travelwise pp. 238–239.

Public Transportation

Athens has some of the world's best public transportation. Tickets ($) are good for an hour and a half on the Metro, buses, or trolleys in the city center.

The Attiko Metro is cheap, efficient, and well-designed. The bus and trolley system is also good, though they often slow down in the city's overwhelming traffic. The tram, which travels along some of the Athens shoreline, can take you to southern seaside suburbs such as Glyfada. The suburban railway goes to far-flung towns around Athens. Both the suburban railway and the Metro go to the airport; a one-way Metro ticket ($$) from central Athens to the airport is a good value. There are also express buses that go to the airport from Syntagma Square and other central locations.

See Travelwise p. 238 for additional information.

History & Culture

Elite *evzones* guarding the Tomb of the Unknown Soldier

Athens &
the Islands Today

Athens is really two cities, one imagined and glorious, the other immediate and daunting. Among the ruins of the ancient city lie fragments of Western civilization's founding society. The coexistence of old and new defines Athens, which has existed under the same name for thousands of years.

Modern Athens has never realized the accomplishments of ancient Athens, but its identity and ego are firmly attached to those past glories. The Acropolis and its architectural crown jewel, the Parthenon, loom high above the anarchic rows of tightly-packed apartment blocks and traffic-clogged streets. Athenians may criticize their city, but they are also very protective of it. They will deflect a visitor's harsh words with a simple wave to that ancient temple above the city, a symbol that Athens will always be far greater than it looks.

Though Athens derives much of its cultural identity from an incarnation of the city that existed 2,500 years ago, it also revels in its more recent history. There are Byzantine churches, Roman ruins, and Ottoman-era public baths and mosques. You do not have to search for long to find a statue of a noted Greek statesman or a hero of the Greek War of Independence overlooking one of Athens's public squares. Athenians do not wallow in their city's past though, however impressive it might be. Like the natives of any major city, Athenians tend to take great pride in the bewildering cacophony of their modern metropolis, enthusiastically taking part in the processions, cultural events, and, of course, protests, that define public life in Athens.

....

Athenians tend to take great pride in the bewildering cacophony of their modern metropolis.

....

The city went through a radical makeover for the 2004 Summer Olympic Games, adding a new state-of-the-art Olympic Stadium and other athletic venues, a cobbled walkway around the Acropolis, a Metro system, and a new airport. The makeover also saw the restoration of historic buildings and the redevelopment of many dowdy city squares, including Syntagma Square, across the street from the Parliament building. Much of central Athens is very walkable, which means a visitor can enjoy the longtime Athenian pastime of *peripato*, or strolling while talking. It's inspired by the Peripatetic School of Aristotle, who walked and talked philosophy with his students.

The Modern City

To be sure, Athens is not the whimsical, whitewashed Greece of travel brochures or poems. Though it's blessed with 300 days of sunshine a year and 75 miles (120 km) of coastline nearby, Athens is a growing, and sometimes growling, metropolis that seems to thrive on chaos. Although the new Metro system has

Inside the walkway that surrounds the Olympic Stadium

improved matters, traffic in the city still frequently descends into a cacophony of blaring horns and shouting, while the hubbub of a Saturday maketplace can be daunting.

More than a third of the Greek population lives in or around Athens, many of them young people from elsewhere in the country who come looking for work. In addition to being its largest city, Athens is also Greece's administrative, political, and economic center. These factors mean that now, as during the age of Pericles, Athens dominates the intellectual, social, and political culture of Greece.

Though it is known for its architectural masterpieces, Athens is blighted by poorly planned urban development. Much of its neoclassical architecture was razed in the 1950s, replaced by thousands of nondescript apartment buildings that helped house an influx of Greek refugees from Turkey and Egypt. Old World cafés filled with grandfathers and bearded priests sipping tiny, grainy Greek coffees or icy Nescafé frappes have been supplanted by sleek cafés catering to the smartphone set that specialize in iced espresso and French pastries. Athenians are also harried and all-business, much different from the rural Greeks who still welcome visitors with a shot of *tsipouro*, a strong distilled spirit, and a slice of syrupy walnut cake.

A few Athenian neighborhoods still cling to the past. Plaka, though touristy, feels like a Greek island, with pastel-painted neoclassical mansions and the tiny, Cycladic-style stone homes of nearby Anafiotika on the slopes of the Acropolis. Worn neoclassical buildings stand alongside bold 20th-century Bauhaus architecture in the neighborhoods of Metaxourgeio—a former silk factory center-turned-theater district—and Exarcheia, the lively neighborhood that's also a longtime base for Greece's restless political activists. Other neighborhoods, especially the suburbs, are notably modern. Kifissia, with its wide boulevards, giant homes, and manicured lawns, looks like an old-money American city. Glyfada, with its mansions and lofts along the seaside, has beach clubs and steakhouses. Marousi mixes apartment blocks and single-family-homes with stretches of cafés, shops, and the city's biggest shopping mall.

Athens is a rush for the senses: the harsh scent of cars and concrete dust mixed with sweet spring blossoms of bitter orange and jasmine; a soundtrack of honking taxis, the din of a thousand conversations, and the occasional wail of an old man singing along as he cranks up a burlesque tune on an ancient hurdy-gurdy. At night the city is at its most beautiful. Darkness cloaks its imperfections and the cool air relaxes Athenians, who love to go out. Bars, tavernas, and clubs are packed with people talking, smoking, drinking and, occasionally, dancing. At the popular *bouzouki* clubs, named for the signature lute that energizes *laika*, or Greek pop songs, singers both great and cheesy dance with fans who shower them with roses. Worldly intellectuals,

Protest

Athens's constant protests and demonstrations are the one aspect of city life that often makes international news. Violence or destruction of property is extremely rare and usually confined to battles between radicals in the Exarcheia neighborhood and the police. It is quite likely that you will witness a few protests during your time in Athens, but this isn't anything to worry about. Greeks simply have a cultural tradition of making their voices heard, often loudly. Demonstrations are triggered by anything from salaries to food prices. The people you see waving banners are far more likely to be kindergarten teachers than anarchists.

dreadlocked artists, and black-clad anarchists fill the bars of Exarcheia, occasionally spilling out onto the square to watch a movie on a makeshift screen or play foosball or ping-pong into the early hours. Gazi, the former site of the city's gasworks, has in recent years exploded into the hottest neighborhood for live music and trance and electro-punk clubbing.

A Changing City

The royal family fled in 1967, after a coup by the Greek army. The military junta itself fell in 1974, partly because of a strong uprising by student activists at the National Technical University of Athens, which Greeks call the Polytechnio. Since 1974, only democratically elected parliamentary governments have run the country. Athenians love discussing politics, especially as it relates to the two main parties running Greece, the Panhellenic Socialist Movement (PASOK) and the conservative Nea Dimokratia (New Democracy) party. They both idolize and ridicule political dynasties like the Papandreous, who have produced three prime ministers and are often likened to the Kennedy or Bush families in the United States.

These days, the city's changing cultural face is also a hot political topic. Until about 20 years ago, most of the people who lived in Athens were Greeks who identified themselves as Greek Orthodox Christians. Since then, a wave of new immigrants from

The Gazi neighborhood is the new cool place to be in Athens after the sun goes down.

Mothers and daughters in elaborate traditional costumes for a Holy Week event

Eastern Europe, South Asia, and Africa has arrived, bringing new religions and cultural traditions. As many as 10 percent of Athenians are now immigrants, according to various census figures.

The Islands

The question *"poia einai i katagogi sou?"*—which roughly translates as "where are you from?"—is a staple of Athenian small talk. Despite the size of the city, it is rare to hear anyone say "Athens" in response, even among those who were born there. Many will instead identify themselves with some tiny island village out in the Aegean Sea—a place, they will say, of beautiful sunsets, tight-knit communities, and endless white beaches.

These first- or second-generation Athenians often idealize the islands as much as any excited tourist. The islands are often places they know only from vacations and childhood memories, forever associated with the summer sun. In reality, even the liveliest and most popular islands, like Santorini, can be lonely places in the winter, lashed by storms and severe winds, emptied of their summer crowds. During school holidays the populations of many islands swell with the arrival of residents' grandchildren, but most of the time there is a conspicuous absence of young people on the islands.

For those who continue to reside on the islands, their relationship with Athens is a difficult one. As in ancient Greece, Athens exerts a strong influence on the economy, culture, and politics of the islands, but, just like in Pericles's time, it is also dependent on them. More than anything else, it is images of the islands' sunny beaches, blue seas, and whitewashed villages that attract tourists to Greece. Without the islands, one of Athens's most important industries would shrink dramatically.

Many islanders have mixed feelings about the expansion of the tourist industry on the islands. They welcome the income and the jobs that will keep at least some of the younger generation around, but they worry about the impact on their culture and society. Many islands are now striving to achieve the often elusive goal of sustainable, responsible development, moving away from the monolithic resort industry of the 1980s and 1990s. Islands now seek tourism on a smaller scale and pay more attention to maintaining the tranquility and natural beauty that attracts visitors in the first place.

The relationship between Athens and the islands is not just economic, however. For many Athenians, the islands are a symbol of the ideals that drove the early 20th-century *Megali Idea*—the dream of a greater Greece (see p. 35). Recently, when some German political commentators suggested that Greece sell a few of its islands to relieve its debts, the public reaction in Greece was one of horrified outrage. Although they may appear small and insignificant on any map of Greece, the islands still occupy an important place in the Greek national consciousness. ■

> **For many Athenians, the islands are a symbol of the ideals that drove the early 20th-century *Megali Idea*—the dream of a greater Greece.**

EXPERIENCE: Exploring Ancient Athens

Athens benefited from many improvements and renovations in preparation for the Olympics, but few have had as dramatic an impact as the creation of the **Grand Promenade.** This pedestrianized zone links Hadrian's Arch and the Temple of Olympian Zeus with the Acropolis, Ancient Agora, and Kerameikos Cemetery. The Grand Promenade has transformed what was once a loose collection of archaeological sites separated by noisy, congested roads into a unified national landmark.

One interesting consequence of this project has been the growth in popularity of guided tours through the historic core of Athens, made possible by the pedestrianized routes. Such tours can be organized through companies such as **Athens Walking Tours** (*tel 210/884 7269, www.athenswalkingtours.gr*) or through the hundreds of licensed and highly knowledgeable private guides that can be contacted through the **Tourist Guides Union** (*Apollonos Street 9a, Plaka, tel 210/322 0090, www.tourist-guides.gr*).

Food & Drink

People from all over Greece end up in Athens, so the city's restaurants, cafés, and bars serve dishes from every corner of the country. You will find tavernas that specialize in food from the islands of Crete, Santorini, and Kefalonia; from the mainland provinces Epirus, Macedonia, and Thrace; and even from Istanbul, where many Greeks lived until the 1950s.

The ancient Athenians were not known as great foodies, but it seems they enjoyed eating as much as their modern counterparts. Their staple food was barley bread, which they dipped in wine or sweetened with thyme honey from Mount Hymettus. Larger meals featured sardines and anchovies, broad beans, lentil soup, olives, and, of course, more wine. Like other ancient Greeks, they also drank a savory beverage called *kykeon,* which mixed barley gruel, water, herbs, and grated goat's cheese. Dessert was usually dried figs or pomegranates.

Although you'd be hard pressed to find kykeon anywhere today, many of those same foods—fish, figs, pulses, legumes, cheese, and olives—are still staples of Athenian tables. Baked sardines and marinated anchovies, for instance, are the mainstay of meze platters, or tapas-style meals. But the Athenian palate has also incorporated foods from later years, especially the Ottoman period. Some of the most famous Greek dishes, including baklava, a phyllo-based pastry of ground nuts and syrup, have their origins in the imperial kitchens of Constantinople. Other popular Near Eastern-inspired foods include the baked eggplant-and-spiced beef casserole called moussaka, the roasted eggplant dish called *imam bayaldi,* and the spicy, saucy meatballs called *soutzoukakia.* As new immigrants have arrived in Greece in the last 20 years, Athenians have also added new cuisines to the table, including Ethiopian, Indian, Chinese, and Mexican.

Greeks are not enthusiastic about early starts, nor, by extension, do they much care for breakfast, so it's hard to find restaurants serving it. For those who can't do without, however, some hotels and tourist-focused cafés will offer fried English breakfasts and the muffins, eggs, and pancakes of American breakfasts. Greeks usually have a simple morning meal of coffee and a *tyropita,* or cheese pie. For decades, when an afternoon siesta was incorporated into the workday, the biggest meal was lunch, eaten at around 2 p.m. and featuring a family-style spread of salads, dips, and bread as well as *mageirefta,* or casserole dishes such as moussaka, *gemista* (stuffed tomatoes and peppers), and *kotopoulo lemonato me patates* (lemony chicken baked with potatoes). Now that Athenians work much longer hours, sometimes at two jobs, they often eat fast food such as gyros or sandwiches on the run or at their work desks. Dinners are usually platters of appetizers called meze or small meals of salad, yogurt, and omelettes.

Greek-style Meze

Meze are a collection of small dishes and appetizers served family-style and usually with wine or drinks such as the anise-flavored ouzo, the pomace brandy *tsipouro,* or raki, also called *tsikoudia* in Crete, which is a strong distilled liquor made from grape must. Meze-style dining is popular throughout the Mediterranean and Middle East.

Meze dishes, including *dolmadhes* and roasted eggplant, at a taverna in Plaka

Although the style of meze eaten today has its origins in the Ottoman Empire (the word "meze" is thought to derive from the Persian word *maze,* meaning "snack"), the ancient Greeks ate similar dishes in the form of the dried figs, chickpeas, and plates of grilled chestnuts they served to accompany a jug of wine. Nowadays, modern Greeks eat their biggest meals at lunch, so at night they opt for the same light meal of meze and wine (or spirit) of their forebears. Sharing meze with friends is a bonding ritual in Greece and especially in Athens, where urban life has grown increasingly hectic. Friends invite each other over for homemade meze, enjoyed on a breezy balcony with a carafe of wine, or they meet at the city's many eateries for a night of lively conversation, drinks, and dining.

Athenians also love coffee, or rather, the opportunity to have long, lingering conversations while drinking coffee.

Most tavernas offer a *poikilia,* or a platter that holds a variety of meze dishes. Diners can choose from seafood, meat, vegetarian, or a combination of meze platters. There are also restaurants and cafés, called *mezedopoleia,* that specialize in meze exclusively. These establishments typically serve both hot and cold dishes and include staples such as *melitzanosalata, taramosalata, saganaki,* sausages, olives, cheese, and *bekri meze,* the "drunken meze" made of pork stewed in wine. Some *mezedopoleia* are even more specialized: *Tsipouradika* specialize in meze that go well with *tsipouri, Ouzadika* tailor their menus to ouzo, and *Rakadika* to raki. Some *mezedopoleia* or tavernas have *krasomezedhes,* which literally means "meze for wine."

Greek dining isn't all about small dishes and delicate flavors, however. Many hard-working Athenians still enjoy a hearty soup dish called *patsas,* which is sold in tavernas

Menu Reader

Avgolemono: *A sauce made with egg (avgo) and lemon (lemono) that's used to flavor everything from soups to meatballs.*

Barbouni: *Red mullet, usually served fried and doused with fresh lemon juice.*

Bifteki: *A grilled hamburger patty usually spiced with Greek oregano.*

Dakos: *A traditional Cretan salad that's also a staple of Athenian tavernas, comprising barley rusks, tomatoes, onions, feta cheese, olive oil, and Greek oregano.*

Dolmadhes: *Grape leaves stuffed with lightly spiced rice.*

Gavro Marinato: *Marinated anchovies.*

Gemista: *Tomatoes and peppers stuffed with herbed rice, doused with olive oil, and slow-cooked.*

Gigantes: *Giant broad beans slow-cooked in a savory tomato sauce.*

Gyros: *Strips of either roasted pork or chicken rolled into a grilled pita with onions, tomatoes, fried potatoes, and dollops of yogurt or tzatziki, a garlicky yogurt dip.*

Horiatiki: *A traditional Greek salad with tomatoes, cucumbers, onions, feta cheese, and green peppers. All doused in olive oil.*

Melitzanosalata: *A dip made from roasted and creamed eggplant.*

Moussaka: *A baked casserole of spiced beef and eggplant topped with bechamel.*

Pastitsio: *A baked casserole of spiced beef and pasta, topped with bechamel and a sharp, hard white cheese called kefalotyri.*

Saganaki: *Fried sheep's milk cheese.*

Souvlaki Kalamaki: *Grilled pork kebabs spiced with Greek oregano and fresh lemon juice and served with either grilled pita or hunks of crusty white bread.*

and cafés throughout the city. Although primarily a working-class dish, it is popular with a wide segment of Athenian society, largely thanks to the fact that patsas kitchens stay open all night. Go into a patsas restaurant after the clubs have closed for the night and you'll see a fascinating cross-section of Athenian society, from well-heeled Kolonaki kids to cement-covered construction workers.

Patsas is credited with almost miraculous properties by older Athenians, who say it will cure hangovers, drive away illness, and make you strong. Few visitors ever find out if this is true though, as a brief description of the dish puts most people off. The main ingredient is boiled tripe (stomach and intestines, usually from pigs), but sometimes other parts of the animal will be thrown in for flavor. The result is a thick, incredibly filling soup, with a strong flavor and powerful odor. It is very fatty, so if you do order some, remember to eat it quickly, before it congeals.

Athenians, like most Greeks, love wine and spirits. At tavernas, the best

A traditional Skopelos cheese pie, made with goats' milk

wine is often the *hima,* or the house barrel wine. Of the bottled wines, the best whites tend to come from the island of Santorini, the best reds from the northeastern region of Drama. Ouzo, the famous anise-flavored spirit, and the strong Cretan distilled liquor called raki are favorite aperitifs. Wine, ouzo, raki and the pomace brandy called tsipouro also accompany platters of meze.

Athenians also love coffee, or rather, they enjoy the opportunity to have long, lingering conversations while drinking coffee. Athens has a few surviving old-style coffeeshops, called *kafeneia,* which are filled with grandfathers playing backgammon and arguing about politics. The drink of choice here is the *elliniko,* the strong traditional coffee made by grinding the beans into a fine powder. Other drinks include the *nes* (hot instant coffee served with evaporated milk) and the frappe, a frothy combination of instant coffee, sugar, ice, and evaporated milk. Nowadays, though, most modern cafés specialize in freddo espressos and freddo cappuccinos—iced versions of the Italian coffee drinks. A few tea shops serving everything from Japanese green tea to traditional Cretan sage tea have also opened in the capital, but Athenians still prefer coffee to tea. ∎

History

Although a glorious imperial city during the era of Pericles, Athens was neglected by many of its subsequent rulers. In the 20th century, the city reclaimed its former role as the economic, political, and creative center of modern Greece and the wider region.

Mythic Roots

The city of Athens has been continuously inhabited for more than 4,000 years, and the area was probably inhabited by hunter-gatherers as early as 10,000 years before that. The graves and wells of Neolithic settlers have been found on the slopes of the Acropolis. Since so little is known about these founding settlers, Athenians have embraced the city's mythic origin stories. The most colorful of these asserts that the city's founder, Cecrops, was a half-man, half-serpent, demi-god.

According to the ancient Greek historian Strabo (63/64 B.C.–A.D. 24), Cecrops's city was coveted by two gods: the sea-god, Poseidon, and the goddess of wisdom, Athena. Both wanted to become patron of the city, so they held a contest to see who could most impress Cecrops.

> **Since so little is known about these founding settlers, Athenians have embraced the city's mythic origin stories.**

Poseidon struck the rock first with his trident, producing a well rushing with water. Athena hit the rock with her spear and produced an olive tree. Cecrops deemed the olive tree a more suitable gift, as it provided wood, oil, and food. Athena was made protector of the city, and a temple was built in her honor. Early Athenians were called Cecropidae for their serpent king, but nowadays, thankfully, the city and its people are named for their goddess.

The Mycenaeans & Minoans

Between 1600 and 1100 B.C., Athens became a major city in Mycenean, or Bronze Age, Greece. Named for the archaeological site in the northeastern Peloponnese some 55 miles (90 km) from Athens, Mycenean Greece was the setting for much of ancient Greek poetry and myth, including the epic poems of Homer. Historians don't know why Mycenean culture declined; it could have been an invasion by the Dorians, infighting among the Myceneans, natural disasters, or climate change. Whatever the case, Athens, like all of Greece, descended into a dark age that lasted from 1050 to 750 B.C.

By the time the Mycenaeans rose to prominence on mainland Greece, another even older culture, known as the Minoan civilization, was already thriving on the islands. From their cities on Crete, Santorini, and Kithira, the Minoans built a powerful trade empire that stretched from the Black Sea to Egypt. They were technologically advanced for their time and had a highly developed artistic culture.

Despite their apparent prosperity and power, the Minoans are something of a mystery. Their civilization went into an abrupt and terminal decline around 1400 B.C., but no one is sure why. Beyond a few garbled and ambiguous references in Greek myth, there is no evidence that the ancient Athenians were aware that the Minoan civilization had ever existed. The Minoans were not rediscovered until the palace of Knossos, Crete, was excavated in 1900 (see pp. 188–189).

Epidavros Theater, a symbol of the technical and cultural achievements of ancient Greece

From the Dark Ages to a City-State

Athens had likely started recovering by 900 B.C. since Iron Age burials in the ancient cemetery of Kerameikos show signs of wealth. By 800 B.C., Athens had begun bringing neighboring towns in Attica under its administration in a process called *synoikismos* (bringing together into one home). Thus, the city-state was born. In the city-state structure, power was supposed to be shared, but due to ingrained social traditions that favored the elite, only the wealthy and privileged had any real power. Athens replaced monarchy with oligarchy; its leaders belonged to the landowning aristocrats called the *eupatridai* (or, the well born), who met on the stony hill called the Areopagus to appoint the city-state's top officials *(archons)* and a commander *(polemarch)*. Yet this was a time for intellectual and artistic renewal throughout ancient Greece. Greeks developed a written alphabet, new military strategies, a central banking system, and coinage. Their colonies reached western Europe, North Africa, and the Black Sea.

A bronze frieze depicting Pericles orating on the Acropolis

Athenian Democracy

The elitist city-state system left most Athenians—especially the poor and slaves, who had no rights at all—feeling ignored and abused. The first refinements to the system were made by an archon named Draco (who ruled in the mid-seventh century B.C.), who put together a set of written laws that any literate Athenian could understand. Although they were an improvement on the old system in many ways, the new laws were notoriously harsh. Draco thought that the most trivial of crimes—such as idleness or petty theft—should be punishable by death, and he lamented the fact that there was no worse punishment possible for more serious offenses.

In 594 B.C., the statesman Solon (638–538 B.C.) repealed Draco's laws and created a new code. He gave common Athenians the power to vote and hold elected officials accountable. According to Aristotle, Solon pushed for all citizens to be admitted to the *ekklesia*, an assembly of Athenian citizens, and allowed to vote. He created four classes of Athenian society based on agricultural wealth; all but the lowest class, the *thetes*, were eligible to run for some form of public office.

Solon's laws failed to take root, however, and after two decades of unrest, one of his cousins, Peisistratos, seized power. Peisistratos is known as a tyrant, but he was actually a very popular leader. In ancient Greek, the word *tyrannos* meant "one who seizes power by force," rather than a cruel leader. Under Peisistratos, Athens flourished as a military and economic power, with a powerful navy and trade connections throughout the known world. This prosperity was undermined by the cruel rule of his sons, Hipparchus and Hippias, who took over on his death in 527 B.C. Hipparchus was assassinated in 514 and his brother overthrown, with help from the Spartans, four years later.

From the chaos emerged Cleisthenes, the man known by historians as the "father of Athenian democracy." Cleisthenes reformed the constitution in 508/507 B.C. and restored Solon's reforms. With broad support from common Athenians, he embarked on a series of wide-ranging changes. Cleisthenes also created an assembly where all Athenian citizens could vote on public policy. Although it is idealized as the world's first democracy, the political system of ancient Athens doesn't measure up well to most modern states. Women, slaves, freed slaves, people with unpaid debts, resident foreigners, and those born of non-Athenian parents were barred from voting, meaning that only about 10 percent of the population had a say in politics.

Athens at War

Persian King Darius I invaded Greece in 492 B.C. At the time, he was ruler of an empire that stretched across much of the Middle East and Central Asia. After taking the north of the country, Darius stopped his army of around 30,000 men

Pericles and the Athenian Golden Age

The quiet, studious son of influential Athenian parents, Pericles (495–429 B.C.) grew up to be the city-state's most famous leader. He was a skilled military strategist and populist politician who expanded the democratic system in ancient Athens. Under Pericles poor citizens, who comprised the majority of the Athenian military at the time, gained the right to vote. A brilliant orator, Pericles was described by the historian Thucydides as "carrying the weapons of Zeus" when delivering speeches.

Pericles ruled Athens from 461–429 B.C., a period known as the Golden Age of Athens or the "Age of Pericles." He promoted arts and literature and began a massive public works project on the Acropolis, commissioning the construction of the Parthenon and beautifying the city. He also imposed Athens as leader of the Delian League, an assembly of 183 city-states. This move triggered the Peloponnesian War (431–404 B.C.) between Athens and Sparta.

His closest friends were the Sophist philosopher Protagoras, the cosmological theorist Anaxagoras, and his companion, Aspasia of Melitus. Aspasia was a controversial figure in ancient Athens, at least as portrayed by some ancient writers and comic poets, who claimed she was a brothel-keeper. She was apparently very well-educated and was thought to be part of the *hetaerae*, or the group of intelligent, independent courtesans who were the closest thing to liberated women in Athens. Pericles had a son with her, Pericles the Younger, who became his father's heir after his older sons from his first marriage died in a plague in 430 B.C. (Pericles the Younger was executed after the Battle of Arginusae in 406 B.C.)

Pericles had not cultivated a strong successor, so after he died, Athens fell into political turmoil, run by demagogues who tried to mimic Periclean populism. After Pericles, Athens would never again experience the same kind of political, military, and cultural glory.

A modern illustration depicts the Battle of Salamis (480 B.C.). Ancient naval battles were chaotic affairs, won by boarding, burning, and ramming enemy ships.

on the plain of Marathon to gather their strength before the attack on Athens. To meet this threat, Athens and a few other city-states mustered an army composed of 10,000 hoplites (heavily armored foot soldiers) and a few thousand auxilliaries.

In the battle, the rigorously drilled and trained hoplites, who fought in a tightly organized phalanx formation, crushed the Persian invaders with few losses of their own. It was seen as proof that a massive army assembled by a tyrant was no match for a force of free citizen-soldiers.

After Darius's death in 486 B.C., his son Xerxes took over Persia. Three years later, he too invaded Greece. Xerxes's vast army plowed through northern Greece and defeated

King Leonidas of Sparta at the Battle of Thermopylae. Although defeated, the Spartans were able to hold off the Persians long enough for Athens to be evacuated. When Xerxes reached Athens and found an abandoned city, some accounts say he flew into such a rage that he burned the city to the ground. Many historians doubt this story however, and argue that, if it happened, the fire was probably set by the Athenians as they left the city. Whatever the case, the rumor that the Persians had destroyed one of the crown jewels of Greek civilization united the Greek city-states against Xerxes. Soon after the capture of Athens, the Athenian general Themistocles tricked Xerxes's vast navy into attacking the Greek fleet in the narrow straits of Salamis. Without the navy to keep his huge army supplied, Xerxes retreated north with the majority of his troops, leaving a smaller occupying force behind in Greece. In 479 B.C., the Athenians and Spartans led the defeat of that Persian army at the Battle of Plataea.

The Golden Age

Following the defeat of the Persian invasion, Athens flourished as a center of commerce, art, and philosophy. This period has come to be known as the Athenian Golden Age. The height of the Golden Age was marked by the rule of the statesman Pericles (r. 461–429 B.C.; see p. 27) who was responsible for the creation of many of ancient Greece's great monuments, such as the Parthenon, Erechtheion, and Propylaia at the Acropolis; the Temple of Hephaistos, nearby; and the Temple of Poseidon at Cape Sounion.

During the Athenian Golden Age, the dramatists Aeschylus, Aristophanes, Euripides, and Sophocles ruled the city's ancient theaters. (Pericles introduced the *theorica,* state money which gave poor Athenians access to the theater.) The philosophers Socrates, Plato, and the Macedonian-born Aristotle taught and debated in the city. The era also gave rise to the historians Herodotus (484–425 B.C.), Thucydides (460–395 B.C.), and Xenophon (430–354 B.C.); the lyric poet Pindar (c. 522–c. 438 B.C.); and the sculptor Phidias (480–430 B.C.).

The Delian League's contributions were spent glorifying Athens and fighting territorial wars with other mainland city-states.

For the islands, however, the Golden Age was a less glorious time. In 477 B.C., a few years after the defeat of the Persians, the islands joined Athens in an organization called the Delian League. The smaller island states pooled their wealth and resources with Athens to create a powerful military force that could repel another Persian attack. Over time, however, the Delian League came to be dominated by Athens. A series of Athenian leaders—most notably Pericles (see p. 27)—misappropriated the funds given by the island states. The Delian League's contributions were spent glorifying Athens and fighting territorial wars with other mainland city-states. Several of the temples on the Acropolis—including the Parthenon—were paid for with money that was supposed to be spent on the islands' defense.

Though Athens and Sparta were allies during the wars against the Persians, they resumed their rivalry soon after Xerxes's defeat. Between 440 and 404 B.C., Athens and Sparta were locked in a prolonged cold war that was punctuated by periods of vicious fighting. Neither side could gain a decisive advantage: Athens's great naval power was little use against a landlocked city-state, while Sparta's mighty army could not penetrate

Athens's huge city walls. Pericles maintained a defensive, cautious strategy that avoided large scale confrontations with Sparta but failed to do anything to resolve the standoff.

Pericles died in 429 B.C. during a great plague—probably typhoid fever—that swept through Athens and killed up to one-third of the population. With Pericles gone and the Athenians weakened by disease, Athens began to falter. After Pericles died, few Athenian leaders showed much intelligence in military strategy—they launched a series of ill-considered military expeditions that ended in devastating defeats. They also refused Sparta's offers of peace. Sparta finally defeated Athens in 404 B.C., reducing the once mighty power to an impoverished shadow of its former glory.

The Macedonians and the Empire

Although the Spartans emerged victorious, the war would soon take a heavy toll on their wealth and military capability. Soon after the fall of Athens, one of Sparta's rivals, the northern city-state of Thebes, invaded Sparta's territory. Athens didn't play much of a role in this conflict, but the economic turmoil that this new war created hampered its efforts to rebuild. Athens also tried to restore its sea power by forming the Second Athenian Confederacy, a collection of Aegean and Ionian island-states. But it didn't have the cohesion of the Delian League and thus failed.

An ancient depiction of Alexander the Great and his father hunting a stag

Herodotus and Thucydides

Much of what we know about the history of ancient Greece comes from the two great historians of the Athenian golden age: Herodotus (484–425 B.C.), known as "the father of history," and Thucydides (460–395 B.C.). They both lived in Athens for most of their lives, but that is about all they have in common.

Herodotus's *The Histories* is the older of the two works. It focuses on the background and causes of the war between Persia and Greece. Herodotus's account relies on local legends and the memories of old men, with any gaps filled in with his own speculations. Herodotus was undeniably well traveled, and he provides detailed descriptions of the peoples of Persia and Greece. Herodotus seemingly wrote down everything he heard, reproducing it without comment on its plausibility or value. This means that while he provides fascinating insights into ancient daily life, he also includes some bizarre errors, like his description of the giant ants (larger than foxes but smaller than dogs, apparently) that mine for gold in India.

Thucydides, by contrast, usually wrote from personal experience and selected from multiple sources when recording events he didn't witness. His style is very dry and serious, with none of the anecdotes and digressions that enliven Herodotus's work. There are almost no women in Thucydides's work, nor gods. History for Thucydides was solely about men fighting, arguing, and wielding political power.

Although it is the more intellectually rigorous work, Thucydides is undeniably less fun and established an extremely narrow focus for the field of history. It is only recently that historians have returned to the style of Herodotus, with its focus on the lives of ordinary people (although they're usually a little less credible).

As the Greek city-states squabbled, King Philip II (382–336 B.C.) of Macedonia plotted to expand his empire. The Athenians tried to negotiate a peace with the Macedonians, against the warnings of the orator and statesman Demosthenes. After Philip reneged on the deal, the Athenians declared war on the king. In 338 B.C., Philip's army defeated the Athenians in Chaironeia in central Greece. Philip's son, Alexander (known to later generations as Alexander the Great, 356–323 B.C.), traveled to Athens to return the ashes of the Athenian dead and ask the city to ally itself with Macedonia. In 337 B.C., Philip formed the Corinthian League, a council with representatives from all the Greek city-states except Sparta and with Philip as the hegemon, or leader. After Philip was murdered at his daughter's wedding, his cunning son Alexander ascended and expanded his father's empire from Greece to Afghanistan while he was still in his 20s. Though Alexander was taught by Aristotle and loved Greek literature—he is said to have slept with a copy of Homer's *Iliad* under his pillow—he was no champion of the Greek people. Athenians danced in the streets when they learned that the young king had died in 323 B.C. of a mysterious disease.

After Alexander's death, the city fell into chaos, and its despotic leaders abolished democracy. The city was restored in 307 B.C. by Demetrios I of Macedon. Alexander's death and Demetrius's reign heralded the Hellenistic era, during which Athens behaved not as an inward-looking city-state but as a center of a massive empire. Philosophy and the arts reflected this new engagement with the world at large. Demetrius's son Antigonos kept the empire under Macedonian rule until 229 B.C.

Roman and Byzantine Athens

While Alexander's great empire broke apart and Athens declined, a new power was rising in the west. The Romans soon began threatening the weakened Macedonian empire, and by 86 B.C. they had taken over the whole of Greece. The Roman general Sulla occupied Athens, destroyed its walls and plundered its treasures. After this initial conquest, however, there began a period known as the *Pax Romana*, during which Athens became the intellectual and cultural capital of the Greco-Roman world. Roman emperors modified the Acropolis and added a spectacular stairway to the Propylaia, the Acropolis Gate. The ardent Philhellene Emperor Hadrian (r. A.D. 117–138) loved Athens and strove to make it the cultural capital of the Roman Empire. He commissioned the construction of many elaborate structures, including Hadrian's Library, east of the ancient Agora and the Temple of Olympian Zeus. The temple was a long-stalled project that he pushed to completion. Hadrian also repaired the Parthenon after a devastating fire and built a reservoir on the slopes of Lykavittos Hill, the city's highest point, that collected water from channels at Mount Parnes.

Later, in A.D. 161, the rich Greek aristocrat and Roman senator Herodes Atticus built a theater named after himself on the slopes of the Acropolis. The Odeon of Herodes Atticus still stands today and hosts performances from international performing arts stars. In A.D. 267, the Romans could no longer withstand the constant attacks by Germanic nomads called the Heruli, who stormed Athens and destroyed its buildings. The Athenians fled north of the city and built walls from the broken marble of their crushed architecture.

During this time, Christianity was gaining strength in the Roman Empire. In A.D. 52, St. Paul arrived in Athens and was shocked to find a city filled with idols depicting pagan gods. He spoke to the Areopagus council about the Gospels and tried, unsuccessfully, to convert the Athenian philosophers and politicians. In 313, Emperor Constantine I (272–337) issued the Edict of Milan, declaring religious tolerance for Christians. Constantine himself converted to Christianity and moved the empire's capital from Rome to the

Athens's Archaeological Institutes

During the second half of the 19th century, Athens witnessed what can be best described as an archaeological goldrush. Enticed by stories of buried cities and long-lost wonders, scholars from all over Europe and North America descended on the city. They established archaeological institutes to coordinate their efforts and house their research collections. The first institute to be established was the École Française d'Athènes (1846), which was soon followed by other institutes, including the **American School of Classical Studies at Athens** (*Souidias Street 54,*

Kolonaki, tel 213/000 2400, www.ascsa .edu.gr) and the **British School at Athens** (*Souedias 52, Kolonaki, tel 211/102 2800, www.bsa.ac.uk*).

In addition to carrying out archaeological excavations and research projects, these institutions act as intellectual embassies for their home countries—working with local universities and providing guidance to visiting scholars. Both the British and American schools offer summer study programs to students and teachers with an interest in Greece but competition for places is intense.

Greek city of Byzantium (present-day Istanbul) on the shores of the Bosphorus. Constantine re-christened the city Constantinople.

With Constantinople now the empire's centerpiece, Athens fell into obscurity. Weakened by barbarian raids and a string of plagues and earthquakes, the city suffered a prolonged dark age. Emperor Justinian closed Plato's Academy in 529; the Parthenon, Erechtheion, and Temple of Hephaistos were converted into churches; and the city's most prominent artwork was taken to Constantinople. Justinian even removed columns from Athenian temples to use in the building of the Hagia Sophia in Constantinople.

Some notable churches were built during this period: the Kapnikarea, named for the Byzantine chimney-tax collectors, as well as the churches of Saint Catherine, Saint Theodore, and the Holy Trinity. From 797 to 802, a native Athenian, the noblewoman Irene Sarantapechaina (752–803) managed to seize control of the city and become empress. She was overthrown in a coup, exiled to the Aegean island of Lesvos, and died there the following year.

The Tower of Winds in the Roman Agora

From the Ottomans to King Otto

Athens was in sorry shape by the 13th century, as a changing cast of invaders, including the French and the Venetians, took over. The city was impoverished, neglected, and virtually forgotten by the rest of the world. Between 1394 and 1402, the Venetians and Ottoman Turks fought over the city. The Ottomans finally captured the Acropolis in 1456, three years after they captured Constantinople. Two years later, Sultan Mehmet II, a philhellene who spoke fluent Greek, galloped into Athens to admire its architecture and sculptures. Despite Islam's strict prohibition of representations of the human form, Mehmet threatened to execute anyone who damaged or stole the city's sculptures. The Ottoman Turks ruled Greece for nearly four centuries.

The city had mixed fortunes under the Turks. Though the Ottomans tried to build Athens up, it remained parochial, much like a village. Athenians were not Muslim, so they didn't have the same rights as Ottoman citizens, though a few Greeks enjoyed privileged bureaucratic positions in the Ottoman Empire. And while Mehmet may have liked the city's monuments, the other Ottoman Turk leaders didn't consider them so precious. A harem was housed in the Erechtheion, for instance, and the Parthenon—already converted to a church during Byzantine times—became a mosque and a storage space for gunpowder. The ammunition-packed Parthenon was badly damaged during a 1687 battle between the Venetians and the Ottomans.

In 1801, the British ambassador to the Ottoman Empire, Lord Elgin, hacked off some 50 pieces of sculpture from the Acropolis, including the Panathenaic frieze and one of the six caryatids from the Erechtheion. Elgin took the pieces back to England, where they remain to this day, a source of ongoing tension between the two countries (see sidebar p. 59).

While the Ottomans sold off chunks of their heritage, Greek rebels were strategizing a war of independence. In addition to Greek patriots, philhellene intellectuals from western Europe, such as the English poet Lord Byron, encouraged and even joined the Greeks in their fight. The war against the Ottomans lasted from 1821 to 1833, when the Ottomans finally withdrew from Athens. The ambassadors of the United Kingdom, France, and Russia met on the island of Poros and drafted a protocol that created a Greek state led by a monarchy. In 1832, they appointed the Bavarian prince Otto of Wittelbach, then just 17, to lead Greece, but without consulting the Greeks on the matter. At the time, Athens was nearly deserted; only about 4,000 people lived in the city, just below the north slope of the Acropolis. In 1834, Athens took over from the city of Nafplion as the capital of the modern Greek state.

The young King Otto decided to remake the impoverished city. He commissioned neoclassical buildings and landscaped boulevards. Philhellene archaeologists such as the German Heinrich Schliemann also began restoring the buildings on the Acropolis, stripping away centuries of modifications from the Franks and the Ottomans. The Greeks never warmed to Otto, and he was expelled in 1862, but the Danish prince George I took his place in 1863 and ruled until 1913, when he was assassinated. King George I ruled during the 1896 Olympics in Athens, the first international staging of the Games since antiquity, and during the rise of the shipping port of Pireas. Completed in 1893, the

The Philhellenes

In the early 19th century, many European intellectuals were troubled by the apparent failure of the utopian revolutionary movements that had swept Europe in the 1790s. Disillusioned with contemporary politics and culture, these intellectuals began to idealize ancient Greece. They became active supporters of the Greek independence movement, hoping that an independent Greece might herald a rebirth of the ancient culture they idealized. These intellectuals called themselves "philhellenes" (from the Greek *philos*, which means friend, and *hellene*, which means Greek). Some prominent philhellenes, such as the British poet Lord Byron, traveled to Greece to fight the Ottomans.

The Panagia Kapnikarea in Athens is an example of the city's Byzantine heritage.

Corinth Canal connected the Gulf of Corinth with the Saronic Gulf in the Aegean Sea. This made shipping routes more accessible.

Modern Athens

Though the new Greek state was still fragile, its leaders and supporters had big ambitions. The *Megali Idea*, or "great idea," was wrapped around the notion of creating a Greek empire from the ruins of the Ottoman Empire. In 1923, not long after the First World War ended, the Greeks tried to invade Smyrna in Asia Minor; the incursion resulted in catastrophic defeat. Turkish nationalist forces, led by the charismatic Mustafa Kemal (later known as Atatürk), drove the Greeks out of Turkey. In 1924, the Treaty of Lausanne—drafted by the League of Nations—ordered the exchange of minority populations as a rather crude way of preventing mob violence and persecutions. Some 400,000 Muslim Turks left Greece and another 1.5 million Christians, mostly Greeks, left Asia Minor.

The 1930s were marked by increasingly tense relations with Italy. Gripped by his

continued on p. 38

The Great Athenians

Modern Athenians like reminding visitors about their city's glory days in the fifth century B.C., when Pericles ruled, Socrates taught, and Thucydides and Herodotus recorded it all. Ancient Athens produced some of the West's intellectual, artistic, and political leaders, and their influence is still felt today.

Statues of Socrates and Apollo outside the 19th-century Academy of Athens

The philosopher Socrates (469–399 B.C.) invented the Socratic Method, a form of question-and-answer debate that stimulates critical thinking among people with divergent viewpoints. The Socratic Method is still used in law schools around the world. Socrates was put on trial and sentenced to death after clashing with Athenian politicians. His student, Plato (427–348 B.C.), recorded Socrates's teachings, trial, and eventual execution. Plato went on to be one of the world's most influential philosophers and founded the Academy of Athens, the first higher education center in the Western world.

The politician Pericles (495–429 B.C.) marshaled resources to build the Parthenon and other iconic temples on the Acropolis (see sidebar p. 27). But the creative credit went to the architects Iktinos and Kallikrates, who designed the Parthenon, and the sculptor Phidias, who designed two statues of the goddess Athena there: the Athena Parthenos (Virgin Athena), a gold and marble statue that stood inside the Parthenon, and the Athena Promachos (Athena who fights in the front lines), a gigantic bronze statue that stood between the Parthenon and the Propylaia—the gateway to the Acropolis.

The historian Herodotus (see sidebar p. 31) was born in what is now modern Turkey but later emigrated to Athens, where his influence grew and his work was both lauded and criticized. Thucydides (see sidebar p. 31), a native Athenian, followed in Herodotus's footsteps and wrote the History of the Peloponnesian War detailing the epic war between Sparta and Athens.

Prominent Modern Athenians

Athens has produced some notable figures since the ancient Golden Age, including artists, architects, and a Kennedy-like political family.

Painter Nikos Hadjikyriakos-Ghikas (1906–1994) deconstructed Greece's rich landscape and beautiful light into geometric shapes and linked, connected planes. He went on to become a leading Cubist artist. His former house at Kriezotou Street 3 in Athens has been converted to a museum gallery run by the Benaki Foundation.

The architect Dimitris Pikionis (1887–1968) inaugurated a new era of contemporary Greek architecture that melded the past with modern shapes and functions. Born in Pireas, he studied civil engineering at the National Technical University of Athens and in Paris and Munich. The historian and diplomat Sir Michael Llewellyn Smith calls Pikionis an "ascetic visionary" who landscaped the area around the Acropolis, turning a forgotten area into a peaceful park interspersed with ancient ruins and native Greek shrubs.

And in modern Greece, no political family looms quite like the Papandreous, a father, son, and grandson who all became prime ministers. None were born in Athens, but they rose to prominence here. George Papandreou Sr. (1888–1968) was born in western Greece, governed Greece for short periods in the 1940s and 1960s, and died under house arrest during the military dictatorship in 1968. He is still known to many Athenians as the "old man of democracy."

His son Andreas (1919–1996), born on the island of Hios, became a leading politician in Athens before the 1967–1974 military dictatorship and surged in prominence afterward. A Harvard-trained economist who spoke like a populist firebrand, Andreas founded the Pan-Hellenic Socialist Party (PASOK) and was prime minister throughout most of the 1980s and some of the 1990s. Andreas's son George, born in St. Paul, Minnesota in 1952 to an American mother, was elected prime minister in 2009. Quiet and cerebral, George inherited a heavily-indebted Greek state and is facing an epic battle to save it from bankruptcy.

Demosthenes and the Ancient Greek Orators

Greeks had admired the art of oratory at least since the eighth century B.C., when Homer likened the warrior to a "speaker of words" in his epic work, the *Iliad*. In the classical era (fifth to fourth century B.C.), the ten greatest logographers (speechwriters) were known as the Attic orators. They included Antiphon, Lykourgos, Aeschines, and the great Demosthenes.

Demosthenes is especially revered nowadays because his speeches are a window into the politics and culture of ancient Greece. Orphaned at seven, he was said to have a speech impediment that he eventually overcame by working hard on his diction and gestures. At 20, he delivered his first effective judicial speech and won what remained of his family's inheritance. Later, he worked as a logographer and lawyer to pay his bills. He sparred bitterly with fellow orator Aeschines, who accused Demosthenes of pederasty.

Demosthenes idealized Athens and detested the Macedonians and their leader, Philip II. He called on Athenians to rebel against Philip and, later, his son Alexander the Great, but the revolution fizzled. Rather than be arrested by one of Alexander's deputies, Demosthenes instead committed suicide by drinking poison. The Athenians erected a statue that honored him, engraved at its base with the words: "Had you for Greece been strong as wise you were, the Macedonian had not conquered her."

A man looks at a wreath hung outside the Polytechnio in memory of the 1973 student uprising.

own imperial ambitions, the Italian leader Benito Mussolini (1883–1945) was constantly looking for a pretext for war with Greece. In 1940, he gave up on finding a plausible reason and invaded Epirus. Athens was a long way from the front line during the Greco-Italian war of 1940–1941. The Greek army fought off the Italian attack then counter-attacked into Albania. Though successful, this defence of northern Greece left Athens and eastern Greece almost completely undefended. When Nazi forces invaded from Bulgaria in 1941, the Greek army was cut off and the capital overrun in weeks.

Hitler's troops cut off food and supplies to Athenians. Many of the city's residents died of starvation during the especially harsh winter of 1941–1942, and many others left the city to join the resistance. The Hotel Grand Bretagne, a landmark on Syntagma Square (see Travelwise p. 243), was a headquarters for the Germans. When they retreated from the country, the city changed hands to the British and Greeks. But just as Greece was emerging from World War II, it was also fighting a battle within its own borders. In the absence of a shared enemy, the conservative government and the primarily communist resistance groups turned on each other. The Greek Civil War, which lasted from 1946 to 1949, pitted conservatives against communists and also families, neighbors, and friends against each other. More Greeks died during the Civil War than during World War II.

The conservatives won, and the Greek state outlawed communism until 1962. But the schism between left and right, and the wounds of the civil war, remain to this day. In 1967, a right-wing military dictatorship supported by the United States seized power and ran Greece until it was toppled in 1974. The colonels lost power partly because of a powerful group of young student-activists at the National Technical University of Athens, also called the Polytechnio. The students transmitted anti-junta messages via clandestine radio stations and held a sit-in protest in November 1973. The colonels sent tanks to overrun the university grounds, killing at least 24 people and wounding hundreds. Greeks were outraged and turned on the colonels.

Today, between four and five million people live in or around Athens. Since the 1950s, rural Greeks who didn't emigrate abroad often moved instead to Athens to find work. This migration, as well as the influx of refugees from Turkey in the 1920s and 1950s, created a housing shortage in the city. A flurry of unregulated building ensued, and thousands of hastily-constructed apartment blocks shaped like cigarette boxes went up. There was little or no planning involved in these new developments, and by the 1960s, the city had expanded far beyond what its infrastructure was designed to handle. With very little public transport and poorly designed roads, Athens became one of the most traffic-congested cities in the world. Thanks to an unusual microclimate, the noxious yellow smog generated by this traffic hung over the city for weeks on end.

Thanks to the 2004 Olympics, the city underwent a massive face-lift that eased traffic, opened a magnificent Metro system, added expressways, and restored smog-stained monuments. The city was made more attractive and welcoming than it had been in years. The Olympics also left the country billions of euros in debt, however, adding to a ballooning deficit that pushed the country to near-bankruptcy in 2009. Athens hasn't looked so good in years, but now it has to pay the bill. ■

The Olympic Games

Once every four years, the city-states of ancient Greece sent athletes to the Olympic games, a great tournament held in the town of Olympia, in the western Peloponnese. The games were not revived until the 1890s, when a group of philhellene intellectuals decided to hold a new olympiad, this time in Athens.

The games attracted 241 athletes from 14 nations, who competed in 43 different events in nine sports. Some of these were revivals of the events of the original olympics—like the discus throw, long jump, and wrestling—while others were modern additions—like cycle racing, shooting, and tennis. Conversely, some traditional events were left out, such as chariot racing, *hoplitodromos* (a 400-yard run with bronze armor and shield), and *pankration* (anything-goes hand-to-hand combat), which were all considered unsuitable for a modern event.

The United States won the most gold medals (which were made of silver at the time), with the Greeks winning the most medals overall. The first modern marathon race was won by a Greek water carrier named Spiridon Louis.

Although it submitted numerous bids, the city wouldn't host the Olympic games again for another 108 years. By the time it won the right to host them again, the games had become a much larger event, drawing more than 10,000 athletes from more than 200 countries and an army of reporters and TV crews. Constructing the facilities for the 2004 Summer Olympic Games cost Greece more than $11 billion. Despite worries about security and the city's readiness, the games were held without a hitch. They included 301 medal events in 28 different sports. That August, everything in Athens revolved around the games. The 2004 Olympics were one of the most celebrated on record. IOC president Jacques Rogge pronounced them to have been an "unforgettable dream Games."

Arts

The impact of Athenian culture on the modern world is so enormous that we tend to take it for granted. Everything from the neoclassical architecture of Washington D.C. to the high emotion of a dramatic new play owes its existence to the artistic tradition of ancient Athens.

Ancient Greek Literature

The development and style of Greek literature has been profoundly affected by the work of its first great writer, Homer. The two surviving works attributed to him—the *Iliad* and the *Odyssey*—are great historical epics, poems that stretch to many thousands of lines, intertwining history, legend, and myth. The world they depict, with its arrogant kings, squabbling gods, and brave warriors, shaped Greek culture and, to an extent, all subsequent Western cultures.

Curiously for such an influential writer, almost nothing is known about Homer—it's not even known for sure if he existed. The ancient Greeks wrote of him as if he were a famous historical figure, but in reality they knew no more about him than we do. He is traditionally thought of as a brilliant individual whose works outlasted any memory of his own life, but some assert that he was a group of authors writing many decades apart, or perhaps an individual who compiled and edited preexisting oral traditions.

For many centuries the forms we know as epic and lyric poetry were the dominant literary forms in ancient Athens. Poets like Hesiod, Sappho, and Pindar wrote poetry that spoke of the gods, love, and nature. Many of these poems would have been originally performed at cultural or religious festivals, read out loud to a large crowd.

> The development and style of Greek literature has been profoundly affected by the work of its first great writer, Homer.

Ancient Greek theater has its origins in these poetry readings. In its earliest recorded forms, the play was a *dithyramb,* or an ancient Greek hymn sung in honor of Dionysos, the god of wine and fertility. Ancient Greek theater flourished between 550 B.C. and 220 B.C., when Athens held the Dionysia, a festival which honored Dionysos, at which contests were held for poetry and drama.

The greatest playwrights of the ancient world—including Aeschylus, Sophocles, and Euripides—competed to come up with ever more complex and emotionally powerful tragedies. Aeschylus's *The Persians,* which won the first prize for tragedy in 472 B.C., is the oldest surviving play in the world. It is focused on the defeat of the Persians at Salamis and the tragic arrogance of their king, Xerxes. Other well-known plays include Sophocles's *Oepidus the King,* a harrowing story of murder, incest, and madness. Originally the contest was strictly for tragedies, but in later years a parallel contest for comedies was introduced. The most famous writer of comedies was Aristophanes, whose plays were filled with dirty jokes, scatological humor, and biting political satire. Many of his plays are still performed today, particularly his riotous proto-feminist work *Lysistrata,* in which the women of Athens refuse to sleep with

Modern Greek pottery from the island of Rhodes, depicting a couple relaxing

Ancient Drama

In ancient Greece, plays were performed on a semicircular space, called the orchestra, which held the chorus. The orchestra was at the foot of a hill, the slope of which held the *theatron* (place where you watch), where the audience sat.

Thespis of Icaria, who lived in the sixth century B.C. and sang stories about mythology called *dithyrambs*, is also described by Aristotle as the first ancient Greek playwright. Thespis created the first play by using a singer or actor to perform the dialogue of a character in a dithyramb and so created a protagonist. Thespis won the first documented Dionysia festival, held in Athens, and inaugurated a new style of drama called tragedy (which loosely translates as "goat song"). Tragedy focused on narratives of human suffering. Actors still call themselves thespians in honor of Thespis.

their husbands until they agree to end the Peloponnesian War. Another hugely influential comic playwright was Menander, whose style—known as "New Comedy"—was peppered with foul language and insults directed at wealthy Athenians, political figures, and religious authorities. Sadly most of his plays were lost in the Middle Ages, but fragments are occasionally found among ancient manuscripts.

Thanks, in part, to the performative aspect of Greek cultural contests, elements of oratory and storytelling creep into all Greek written works. For example, although they are traditionally considered to be historical texts, the work of Herodotus and Thucydides (see sidebar p. 31) have as much literary merit as factual. Herodotus constantly breaks from the narrative of his history to tell interesting tales he has heard on his travels or myths associated with certain places. Even Thucydides, who liked to think of his work as objective and matter-of-fact, couldn't help but get carried away when transcribing the half-remembered speeches of Pericles, creating beautifully composed works of oratory that are probably as much his work as they are that of his subject.

Modern Greek Literature and Film

During the centuries of Byzantine and Ottoman rule, most literary energies were directed into religious writing; scholarly religious tomes and books of philosophy represented most of the empire's written work. The intellectual center of the Byzantine world was at Constantinople, not Athens, so the city's literary tradition declined.

Since the modern Greek state was founded in 1833, several notable writers have emerged from Athens, which once again became a center for intellectual and artistic development. Athens was also home to Greece's first Nobel laureate for literature (1963), George Seferis (1900–1971). A poet and diplomat, Seferis gave voice to the dichotomy of modern Hellenism by juxtaposing ancient Greece's metaphors against the stark, craggy realism of the modern country. Seferis, born Giorgos Seferiadis, moved to Athens in 1914 and attended university at the Sorbonne in Paris. The son of a lawyer who was a respected poet in his own right, Seferis went on to become an accomplished diplomat who was stationed in England and Albania. Though he spent chunks of time abroad, Seferis spent much of the rest of his life in Athens.

Sixteen years later, a contemporary of Seferis, the poet Odysseas Elytis (1911–1996), won a Nobel prize by using sensual, surrealist lyricism to describe the uneasy existence of past and present in Greece. Elytis, born Odysseas Alepoudhelis, was descended from a well-established industrial family with roots in the Aegean island of Lesvos. He moved to Athens as a child and attended university there, inspired and encouraged by Seferis to write poetry. His landmark work, "To Axion Esti" (Worthy It Is), shows how he tried to construct a modern mythology for present-day Greece. He spent much of his later life in the well-to-do central Athens neighborhood of Kolonaki.

Another notable Athenian writer is the political journalist and novelist Vassilis Vassilikos (b. 1934). Vassilikos is best known for his political novel, *Z* (1967), the story of a political assassination and its aftermath. Based on a true story, *Z* was later made into a movie by the Greek-French director Costa-Gavra. The politically-infused work of the poet Jenny Mastoraki (born 1949) is representative of the writers who emerged in the 1970s after the *metapolitefsi,* or the fall of the 1967–1974 military dictatorship.

The first cinema opened in Athens in the early 20th century. The first Greek film, *Gynaikes pou Klotoun* (Women Weaving), was made in 1905 by Yiannakis and Miltos Manaki, who were born in an Aromanian village in what is now northern Greece. Most of the first films were short comic productions by Spiros Dimitrakopoulos, though a feature-film love story, *Golfo,* was released in 1915. Many early Greek movies were historical adaptations of novels. *Dafnis and Chloe,* a 1931 film by the director Oreskis Laskos is adapted from a pastoral novel written in the second century A.D. It chronicles the love story of two shepherds (a boy and girl) in ancient Lesvos and features the first nude scene in European film history.

> **The first Greek film, *Gynaikes pou Klotoun* (Women Weaving), was made in 1905 by Yiannakis and Miltos Manaki.**

A busker playing the bouzouki in the old Plaka district of Athens

The iconic Greek actress—and later politician—Melina Mercouri in *Never on Sunday*

The 1950s and 1960s are generally viewed as the golden age of Greek cinema. Directors drew on a wealth of home-grown talent including the actresses Ellie Lambeti, Irene Papas, Melina Mercouri (see sidebar p. 45), and Katina Paxinou. In 1960, the American director Jules Dassin released *Never on Sunday*, which was mostly filmed on location in Pireas. It explores the conflict between ancient and modern Greece as personified by Ilya, a prostitute portrayed by Melina Mercouri.

In the last two decades, a few notable Greek films have been made, including *Safe Sex*, a popular 1999 film that satirized modern Greece's relationship to sex; *Politiki Kouzina* (A Touch of Spice), a 2003 film about a Greek man's return to the home in Istanbul he was forced to flee as a boy in the 1950s; and *Nyfes* (Brides), the story of a Greek mail-order bride who has set sail to meet her husband-to-be in Chicago.

Music

Music was an integral part of ancient Greek culture and still is today. The word "music" has its origins in "muses," the word for the daughters of Zeus who inspired creativity in ancient mortals. The most common ancient Greek instruments were the two-stringed lyre, the kithara (a more complex lyre played by mostly professional musicians), the *aulos* (a double-reed instrument that resembled an oboe), the pan pipes, the *pandoura* (a long-necked ancestor of the modern bouzouki), and the *hydraulis* (an ancient organ that used an ingenious and highly complex system of pumps, valves, and water reservoirs to push compressed air through the pipes).

In ancient Athens and throughout all of ancient Greece music infused almost every aspect of cultural life—from the songs of the choruses in ancient Greek theater to the chants used in religious ceremonies, marriages, and funerals. In myths, some of the greatest heroes were also masters of music; Orpheus, for instance, could tame the wildest enemies with the beautiful songs he played on his lyre.

The Romans adopted Greek musical techniques, but by Byzantine times the Greek style had been absorbed into musical traditions from other cultures. The eastern liturgical chant of the Byzantines combines the artistic discipline of classical Greece with Jewish and early Christian music, while the Acritic (frontiersmen) songs of the ninth century are epic poems of the soldiers who guarded the eastern edges of the Byzantine empire. During the Ottoman era, Greek-language songs influenced by Near East traditions flourished in the *cafe-santan* (music cafés) of Constantinople and Smyrna.

In post-Ottoman times, the Peloponnese and Thessaly were the epicenters of musicians specializing in *palaia dimotika,* or old traditional songs. *Nisiotika,* or island songs, mainly from the Aegean, were also popular during this era. In Pireas and Athens, many singers specialized in *rembetika,* or Greek blues. A prominent performer of rembetika and *laika* (popular) modern Greek songs was Stelios Kazantzidis (1931–2001), an Athenian singer whose textured, aching voice is still admired today. Athenian singer Mariza Koch revived interest in *nisiotika* during the 1970s and 1980s, while Athenian vocal artist Savina Yannatou reinterpreted enduring Greek songs from the Byzantine, Ottoman, and post-Ottoman eras. Yannatou is also credited with reviving interest in the Ladino ballads of Thessaloniki's Sephardic Jews, most of whom were murdered by the Nazis during World War II.

Melina Mercouri

An actress, singer, and politican, Melina Mercouri was born in Athens in 1920, the granddaughter of prominent Athenian mayor Spyros Mercouri. An energetic and elegant woman with a smoky voice and wide, intense eyes, Mercouri began her acting career in theater but got rave reviews for her first film, *Stella* (1955). Her iconic role as Ilya, the prostitute in the port of Pireas, came five years later, in *Pote Tin Kyriaki* (Never on Sunday; 1960), a film directed by her second-husband and mentor, American director Jules Dassin. At Cannes that year, she won the award for Best Actress.

Mercouri became a political activist during the 1967–1974 military dictatorship in Greece. She despised the colonels, whom she called fascists, and traveled the world denouncing them. In 1977, three years after the colonels were overthrown, she became a member of the Greek parliament. In 1981, she became Greece's first female Minister of Culture and conceptualized the idea of a rotating European Capital of Culture, an annual title in which the host city hosts artistic events. The European Union has since adopted the idea.

Mercouri was also instrumental in creating momentum for building a new Acropolis museum to house the Parthenon marbles, whisked out of Greece by Lord Elgin in the 19th century. She campaigned for their return to Athens until her death in 1994. After her death, Jules Dassin set up the Athens-based Melina Mercouri Foundation to work toward the return of the marbles and the construction of the new museum. The New Acropolis Museum opened in 2008 to great acclaim, though the marbles are still at the British Museum in London. Near the New Acropolis Museum, in a small square along busy Amalias Street, there's a bust of Mercouri.

Since the 1980s, Athens has been a hub for discos and *bouzoukia,* the clubs named after the long-necked, mandolin-like instrument that's the core of modern Greek music. The bouzouki has a storied place in modern Greek music; it's the centerpiece of songs by Melina Mercouri in the hit movie *Never on Sunday* and for the composers Manos Hadjidakis and Mikis Theodorakis. But it's also a symbol of *skyladika,* the clubs that loosely translate as "place of the dogs," since some of the worst singers there sound like howling dogs. At *skyladika,* the focus isn't on the music, but on the experience: dancing on the tables, drinking overpriced whiskey, and letting go of the day's troubles.

Art & Architecture

The earliest examples of Greek art come from the prehistoric Cycladic and Minoan civilizations, which thrived on the islands of the Cyclades and Crete, respectively, from around 2500 B.C. The visual arts developed much earlier among

The "History Lost" exhibition at the Benaki Museum examines the impact of the global trade in smuggled or stolen antiquities, a major problem for Greek archaeologists.

these island cultures than they did in Athens and mainland Greece. Minoan art, for example, progressed from abstract patterns to detailed representations of people and animals almost 1,000 years before similar advances were made in Athens.

During the Greek dark ages, however, these artistic traditions were forgotten, as were the societies that created them. The cultural development and artistic fashions of later island communities were roughly in step with the rest of the Greek world. The islands did maintain their own distinctive visual styles, however, and many had some area of specialization, such as bronze working, pottery decoration, or sculpture. Sculptors and masons from Tinos and Paros, for example, were renowned throughout the Greek world.

The visual arts developed much earlier among . . . island cultures than they did in Athens and mainland Greece.

Ancient Greek art is usually broadly divided into four periods, associated with a particular style or technique. The geometric era (1000–700 B.C.) roughly coincides with the Greek dark ages. It is named for the elaborate geometric motifs that the people of the time put on their pottery, one of the few surviving artifacts of

their culture. The most distinctive features of geometric art are meanders—twisting borders made with a continuous line shaped into a recurring pattern—which remain a distinctive and instantly recognizable feature of Greek design. Over time these borders were supplemented by other abstract patterns, and later by heavily stylized representations of horses, mythical beasts, and people.

During this time, similarly abstracted depictions of the human form were common in sculpture. Small terra-cotta figurines of women—known as "bell-idols" for their peculiar conical torsos and extremely long necks—were made throughout Greece, as were cast bronze animals given as offerings to the gods.

As Greek art transitioned into what we know as the Archaic period (700–480 B.C.), the realism of thse small figurines increased, developing into *kouros* (male) and *koure* (female) figures. These statues depicted idealized human figures with slim bodies, elegant braids, and noble, if somewhat impassive, faces. The Peplos Koure, found on the Acropolis, was made around 530 B.C. and shows a young woman in a peplos, or simple robe.

During the Archaic period the decoration of Athenian pottery became increasingly popular. By 550 B.C., Athenian pottery dominated exports throughout the Mediterranean. Athenian vases showed painted narratives of life at the time: funerary rites, athletics, religious rituals, myths, warfare, food, and love. Most Attic pottery was painted using black figures and was exported to Etruria (now central Italy), where it was discovered later in Etruscan tombs.

Ancient Athenian art reached its zenith during the Classical era (480–323 B.C.), when Athens itself flourished intellectually, economically, and politically. Decorated pottery—such as the famous "Muse on Mount Helikon," which depicts a muse playing a lyre—became increasingly naturalistic and subtle. The sculptor Phidias created the Parthenon frieze, a stunning set of relief-sculptures that show the story of classical Athens and the gods of Olympus. Meanwhile, the Athenian sculptor Praxiteles made the famous nude "Aphrodite of Knidos." Most sculpture before the fifth century B.C. showed the female form draped. Although classical scholars were originally horrified by the idea, most now accept that Greek scuptures from this period were all originally painted in bright, eye-catching colors.

It was also during the Classical era that architecture fused with art, with beautiful results. The ancient architects Iktinos and Kallikrates designed the Parthenon, the temple to Athena on the Acropolis that is still considered an architectural jewel. The architects designed the columns using meiosis (tapering) and entasis (a slight swelling so the column could hold the weight of the entablature) that creates an illusion of movement in the marble. Meanwhile, the Erechtheion followed an Ionic style and featured a porch supported by maidens called caryatids. The draping of the caryatids' robes reflects the folds of Ionic columns. According to legend, the Erechtheion marks the spot where Athena and Poseidon fought over the city.

Hellenistic art (323 B.C.–31 B.C.) moved from idealizing the human form to expressing the range of human emotions. Hellenistic art was expressive, dynamic, and full of movement. The most famous example of Hellenistic sculpture is the "Nike of Samo-

EXPERIENCE: Visit a Famous Sandalmaker

Few things are handcrafted in Athens any more, but the sandals made at the **Poet Sandalmaker** (Agios Theklas St. 2, Monastiraki, tel 210/321 9247, www .melissinos-poet.com) are still made the traditional way. Stavros Melissinos inherited the shoe shop in 1956 from his father, Georgios, who had been running it since 1927. That first shop made rubber-soled shoes for workers and hunters and was financially ruined after World War II. Stavros took it over just as tourists were starting to trickle into the city. He started making handmade sandals inspired by ancient and neoclassical designs and featuring iconic names such as Aeolian, Aristotle, and Maria Callas.

With his feathery halo of white hair, grandfatherly smile, and creative sandal designs, Stavros Melissinos became a celebrity of sorts in Athens. He made sandals for international celebrities such as the Beatles, Jacqueline Kennedy Onassis, and actresses Sophia Loren and Ursula Andress. He also wrote poetry ranging from a meditation on wine called Rubayat (1959) to a reinterpretation of Aesop's Fables (2003).

Melissinos's children now carry on the sandal-making tradition. His son Pantelis, an artist and craftsman, runs **Melissinos Art** (www.melissinos-art.com) from the store next door. There he makes sandals based on his father's designs as well as his own updated versions. Stavros's daughter, Olgianna Melissinos, runs **Athena's Sandals** (Normanou St. 7, Monastiraki, tel 210/331 1925, www .melissinos-sandals.gr) where she also makes traditional but stylish Greek sandals based on her father's designs.

An exhibition of contemporary Greek art in the Gazi Factory in Gazi

thrace," the statue of the winged goddess of victory that is now on prominent display at the Louvre in Paris. It was discovered on the northeastern Aegean island of Samothraki in 1863. Roman sculpture was inspired by the art of ancient Greece, and Byzantine art shows the ancient Greek humanistic ethic replaced by a Christian ethic. Though Greek art has never attained the glory of ancient times, modern Greece has produced notable Athens-based artists such as the cubist painter Nikos Hadjikyriakos-Ghikas and the architect Dimitris Pikionis.

Today Athens is the home of several notable art museums and galleries, including the various branches of the Benaki Museum, which feature Greek, Islamic, and modern artworks, as well as the Goulandris Museum of Cycladic Art, the National Art Gallery, the Museum of Greek Folk Art, and the Center for the Study of Traditional Pottery. ■

athens

Iconic monuments, seemingly around every street corner—
reminders of the origins of Western civilization

Old Athens

Pages 50–51: The Acropolis's Erechtheion temple
Opposite: A quiet street in the old part of Athens

Old Athens

From the heights of the Acropolis to the low stelae of Kerameikos cemetery, old Athens is packed with so much character, culture, and history that few visitors get to see it all. Rushing from one sight to another, however, is not the Athenian way. Be slow and selective, and don't worry about missing some of the sites.

Walking the streets of Athens's old town, you're rarely out of sight of the Acropolis. This ancient fortress has dominated the Athens skyline for thousands of years. According to myth, it was here that the first king of Athens—the half-man–half-serpent Cecrops—had his palace, and where Athena and Poseidon had their contest to see who would be the city's patron (see p. 24). The Acropolis is also where the city had its more mundane birth as a small but prosperous Bronze Age settlement.

The monumental temples here have always attracted pilgrims, from women praying for the intercession of Artemis Brauron to European aristocrats doing the "grand tour" to the camera-laden tourists of the present day. Thousands of pictures are taken of the Parthenon and its surrounding buildings every day, but nothing compares to standing in the presence of these ancient masterpieces. In addition to the site itself, the New Acropolis Museum, located to the south, is a must-see.

The City Center

There is far more to old Athens than just the Acropolis. Beneath the walls of the fortress lie the maze-like streets of Plaka and Monastiraki, which, for many centuries, were all there was to see of Athens. From the Acropolis visitors can see the neat domes of the neighborhood's Byzantine churches and Ottoman mosques peeking out from between the neoclassical buildings.

To the northwest, a swath of green space marks the enormous archaeological site at the ancient Agora, where teams of excavators have uncovered the remains of the old city's commercial heart. Beyond it stand the ancient monuments of Kerameikos cemetery, where the city's dead, both great and humble, were buried.

Farther west, you will see the curious juxtaposition of the ancient Temple of Hephaistos on the edge of the Agora—which has survived 2,500 years almost completely intact—and the soot-stained 19th-century buildings of Thissio and Gazi, where the shells of Athens's industrial past have been taken over by artists and restaurateurs.

Hills & Temples

Arranged around the Acropolis to the south and east are the rocky hills of the Pnyka, Areopagus, and Filopappou, as well as

GAZI

PIREOS

Technopolis

THESSALONIKI

Melina Mercou
Cultural Cente

THISSIO

DIMOFONTOS

Theater c
Filopappo

Area of map detail

the spectacular ancient theaters of Herodes Atticus and Dionysos. These were the places where Athenians would gather for debates, religious ceremonies, and elaborate theatrical performances.

To the north and east stand the districts of Omonoia and Syntagma. Though not ancient by the standards of Plaka or Monastiraki, these neighborhoods have been at the heart of the country's more recent history and are home to many of Greece's great historical and cultural institutions, where the treasures of the city's heritage are displayed for all to see. ■

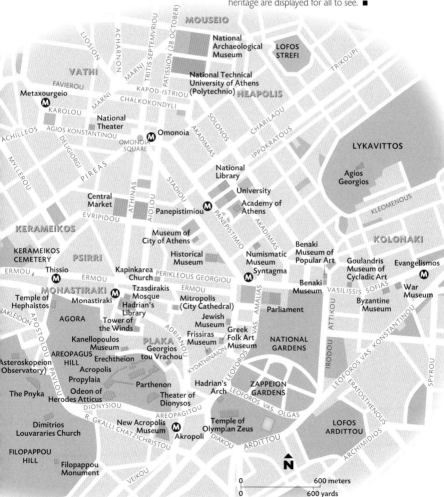

The Acropolis & Around

This ancient citadel was first settled in prehistoric times and earned its iconic status during the reign of Pericles. In later centuries it became a stronghold for Byzantine Christians and Ottoman Turks before beginning its long road to restoration after the modern Greek state gained independence. Despite the rapid development of Athens, the Acropolis is still the city's most prominent and recognizable landmark.

A small section of the Parthenon frieze

Acropolis

- 55
- Akropoli
- (210) 321 0219
- $$$ (includes the Agora, Kerameikos, Temple of Olympian Zeus, & Theater of Dionysos)
- Akropoli

The Acropolis

The Acropolis stands on a huge limestone outcrop that rises 490 feet (150 m) over the center of Athens. Surrounded by steep cliffs and accessible only from its western end, the Acropolis is a natural fortress. The Mycenaean settlement built here around 3,500 years ago formed the core of what was later to become Athens.

Beginning in the sixth century B.C., the Acropolis was transformed

from a fortress to a place of worship. The structures visible on the site today date from the Athenian Golden Age (see pp. 29–30). This period saw the construction of the Temple of Athena Nike, the Propylaia, the Erechtheion, and the Parthenon.

By the third century A.D., the threat of barbarian invasion saw the Acropolis returned to its original role as a fortress. It would serve as the cornerstone of Athens's defenses for the next

INSIDER TIP:

On August's full-moon night, the Acropolis stays open late; it's well worth a nocturnal visit to see the Parthenon bathed in moonlight, the Caryatids erect in a lunar glow.

—KATHLEEN CROMWELL
Travel writer and author

1,500 years, while its ceremonial and religious role was largely forgotten. Since the foundation of the modern Greek state in 1830, the site has been carefully restored and maintained as a symbol of Greece's heritage.

Located high above the center of the city, the Acropolis isn't a hard landmark to find. In the past, however, it could be a tough landmark to get to, especially if you were coming from the outskirts of town. Today, this historic site and its environs are served by a fittingly impressive **Metro station,** positioned a short distance to the south of the Acropolis, close to the New Acropolis Museum (see p. 63). This station is something of an attraction in itself, as it houses a fascinating exhibition of artifacts uncovered during its construction, as well as reconstructions of the Parthenon's sculptures.

The entrance to the Acropolis is located at the western end of the site, set within several acres of landscaped parkland. Wheelchair access is provided by an elevator (constructed for the 2004 Paralympic Games) that runs up the cliffs on the northern side. There are numerous ticket kiosks on the paths leading up to the main entrance. Acropolis tickets grant access to several of the city's ancient monuments and are valid for four days.

The first structure you see on reaching the Acropolis is the **Beule Gate.** The gate was built by Flavius Septimius Marcellinus, a Roman, in A.D. 280. It was assembled using salvaged stones as a last-ditch defense against barbarian raids. There is an inscription over the doorway recording the victory of a flute player called Pantaleon, revealing that many of the stones were salvaged from old choregic monuments.

From the Beule gate it is a steep climb to the **Propylaia,** which was the entrance to the Acropolis during the Athenian Golden Age. On your right as you climb, perched on a 26-foot-high (8 m) stone platform, is the small **Temple of Athena Nike** (see p. 64). On the left, below the north wing of the Propylaia, there's a large pedestal that has held a number of different statues over the years, including a Pergamene king in a chariot and Agrippa, the son-in-law and military advisor of the emperor Augustus.

The Propylaia: At the top of the steps is the monumental gateway known as the Propylaia. This imposing structure was constructed in the fifth century B.C. as part of the massive building program initiated by the great Athenian leader Pericles.

Designed by the ancient Greek architect Mnesicles, the Propylaia is the most elaborate secular structure from this period. It had a hexastyle facade (six columns wide) with a series of grand interior chambers. The main gateway functioned as a security checkpoint, preventing fugitives (who could claim asylum in the sacred precinct) or the ritually unclean from entering.

Mnesicles also envisioned two wings extending alongside the entryway. These wings were never finished, however, because the Athenian treasury was emptied by the cost of the Peloponnesian War midway through construction. Evidence of this can be seen on some of the Propylaia's walls, which are still dotted with the stone lugs that ropes were tied to during construction (these were

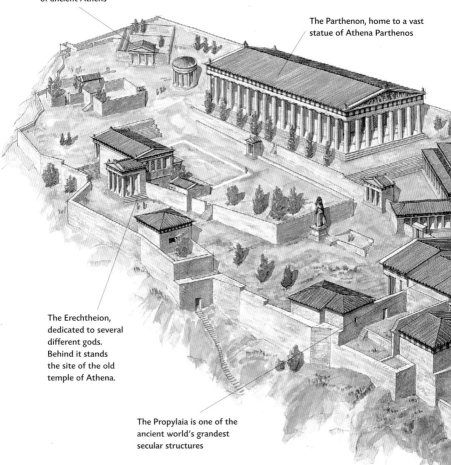

The Sanctuary of Pandion, dedicated to a mythical ruler of ancient Athens

The Parthenon, home to a vast statue of Athena Parthenos

The Erechtheion, dedicated to several different gods. Behind it stands the site of the old temple of Athena.

The Propylaia is one of the ancient world's grandest secular structures carefully removed and smoothed over on finished buildings).

Centuries later, the Ottomans used the Propylaia as a garrison, and it was badly damaged during the Venetian siege of 1687. The Greek government is now carrying out a long and painstaking restoration. Every few years there are brief periods when the structure is not covered by scaffolding (usually for a few weeks during a pause in the reconstruction work), but it is unlikely that the building will be permanently free of scaffolding for a long time.

The Parthenon: Named "chamber of the maidens" for the priestesses of its patron goddess, Athena Parthenos, this architectural masterpiece symbolizes both the glory of golden-age Athens and its enduring

The Sanctuary of Artemis Brauron, protector of women during childbirth

The Temple of Athena Nike, which commemorates the Greek victory against the Persians

The Elgin Marbles

In 1801, Lord Elgin, a British diplomat and collector, obtained a *firman* (royal warrant) that allowed him to study the Acropolis. The firman gave Elgin's men permission to make plaster casts of sculptures, excavate ruins, and recover any interesting artifacts they found. The wording of the document is vague, but it is doubtful that they were given permission to remove anything from the buildings. Elgin's assistant, Philip Hunt, interpreted the firman very broadly, however, and decided to chisel off around a third of the Parthenon frieze. The fragments were shipped to the British Museum in London, where they remain to this day. The Greek government has campaigned for the return of these sculptures since the 1980s, but it doesn't seem likely that they will be returned any time soon.

stamp on modern Greek culture. As part of his great building program, the Athenian leader Pericles recruited the sculptor Phidias and architects Iktinos and Kallikrates to design the building we see today. Their brilliant designs were realized between 447 and 438 B.C. using the finest Pentelic marble, which was hauled in 16 miles (26 km) from Mount Pendeli.

The Parthenon is considered to be the finest Doric temple ever built. The beauty of the design is the result of both artistic genius and engineering expertise. Although at first glance the temple appears to be composed entirely of straight lines and right angles, it is actually much more complex. Firstly, the base has a slight curve to it, sloping down toward the edges. To compensate *(continued on p. 62)*

A Walk Around Ancient Athens

In a city with such a dazzling abundance of ancient structures and spectacular ruins, it is easy to forget that even Athens's lesser sites would be the definitive must-see attraction of almost any other city in the world. This walk will take you on a tour of some the amazing places that stand within sight of the Acropolis.

A good place to start is the **Akropoli Metro station ❶**. Like several other stations on the network, the concourse here has a compact exhibition space that showcases the fascinating finds unearthed in the station's construction. On exiting the station, head north (toward the Acropolis) up Makygianni Street. This street is home to the gleaming modern edifice of the New Acropolis Museum (see p. 63). At the end of the street, go right onto the broad, pedestrianized Dionysou Areopagitou Street, and continue straight across Leoforos Vasilissis Amalias Avenue to the **Temple of Olympian Zeus ❷**.

Although only a few columns remain, the sheer scale of the site hints at the extravagant generosity of its Roman patron, the emperor Hadrian. At the site's northwest corner stands another testament to Hadrian's generosity—a triumphal arch thought to have been erected by his Athenian admirers.

After carefully going back across the eight busy lanes of Amalias Avenue, walk up Lysicrates Street (directly opposite Hadrian's Arch) to the small public square at its western end. Here you will see the **Choregic Monument to Lysicrates ❸**, an often-imitated icon of ancient Greek design. This monument has survived thousands of years of weather, war, and even the attentions of Lord Elgin (who wanted to add it to his collection; see sidebar p. 59). Cross the square and continue up the steeply sloping Epimenidou Street, with its lovely adobe houses, toward the Acropolis.

Around the Acropolis

At the end of Epimenidou Street turn left and then bear right onto the broad walkway that runs along the southern side of the

INSIDER TIP:

The admission ticket to the principal sites of the Acropolis is valid for four days, so you can schedule your visits to different buildings over time and not be rushed.

—CLIVE CARPENTER
National Geographic contributor

Acropolis. The path cuts through the ruins of the Odeon of Pericles before reaching the gigantic ancient **Theater of Dionysos ❹**. It was here that the legendary Athenian Dionysia was held every year, a spectacular cultural and religious festival that attracted playwrights, poets, actors, and singers from across the Greek-speaking world. Today visitors can walk around the ruined theater and sit on the stone benches.

Farther along, the path runs above the ruined **Stoa of Eumenes ❺**, a long promenade where ancient Athenians came to see and be seen. About halfway along the Stoa, take the path on the right that goes up the hill. Although the path is well maintained, and the steps even, this can still be a pretty tiring climb, especially in the summer heat, so stop off halfway to admire the **Odeon of Herodes Atticus ❻**. From up here you can see down the rows of seats to the stage. The next part is probably the steepest bit of the climb, as the path winds its way up past the entrance to the Acropolis before continuing down to the pedestrianized Theorias Street.

Directly opposite the Acropolis is the enormous slab of stone known as the

NOT TO BE MISSED:

Temple of Olympian Zeus • Theater of Dionysos • View from the Areopagus Hill • Ruins of Hadrian's Library

Areopagus 7 (Ares's Hill). The top of the Areopagus provides an amazing vantage point for photographing the Acropolis and historic Athens. It is from here that the Apostle Paul is reputed to have discussed his faith with local intellectuals. If you continue to follow Theorias Street as it passes along the north side of the Acropolis, it will take you into the heart of **Plaka 8**, where you can stop and relax in one of the area's many lovely cafés and tavernas.

Alternatively, you can turn left and walk down the stepped Aretousas Street, which runs alongside the excavated ruins of the ancient Agora (see pp. 70–71). From this vantage point you can see the ruined Roman defensive wall and the almost perfectly preserved Temple of Hephaistos in the distance.

The street winds down the hillside until it reaches the ruins of the **Roman Agora 9**, where a grand Roman archway still stands at the entrance to the old marketplace. Near the grand arch, Areos Street heads north past the imposing rear wall of **Hadrian's Library** and the neat Ottoman architecture of the Tzasdirakis Mosque. It ends at **Monastiraki Square 10**, with its bustling market and Metro station.

- See area map pp. 54–55
- Akropoli Metro Station
- Around 2 hours
- 1.25 miles (2 km)
- Monastiraki Square

Some of the ancient statues in the New Acropolis Museum

New Acropolis Museum

⚑ 55

✉ Dionysiou Areopagitou 15

☎ (210) 900 0900

💲 $$

🕐 Closed Mon.

🚇 Akropoli

www.theacropolis museum.gr

for this, the pillars are inclined slightly inward and are very subtly curved. The columns also bulge slightly as they rise, an effect called entasis. Those who have studied the Parthenon say that Phidias and the architects approximated the aesthetically-pleasing golden ratio when designing the temple.

Sadly, the most impressive sculpture in the Parthenon—one created by Phidias himself—does not survive today. The colorful, 36-foot-tall (11 m) chryselephantine (overlaid with gold and ivory) statue of Athena Parthenos originally stood inside the *naos* (inner chamber) but is thought to have been destroyed by a fire in the fifth century A.D.

Some of the 92 **metopes** (or marble panels) have also been removed or have been destroyed by time. Designed by the sculptor Kalamis, the metopes depicted historical and mythic events in

high relief. The most distinctive surviving artwork is the Parthenon **frieze,** a low-relief sculpture that once adorned the upper part of the inner chamber of the Parthenon's temple. A little over a third of the frieze is at the British Museum in London (see sidebar p. 59), while about half is still in Greece. The remaining portions are located in smaller museum collections around the world.

In addition to its function as a temple, the Parthenon served as a treasury for the Delian League from 454 to 404 B.C. Christians converted it to a church devoted to the Virgin Mary in the sixth century A.D., while the Ottoman Turks converted it into a mosque in the 1460s.

Centuries of weathering have taken their toll on the structure but the Parthenon's present-day state is largely the result of a single, relatively recent event. In

New Acropolis Museum

It was nearly 30 years in the making, but since its opening in spring 2009 Athens's New Acropolis Museum has become one of the city's cultural highlights. This striking modern building accommodates a huge collection of statues and artifacts from the Acropolis and around, a collection that grows with each new excavation.

With its elegant, sweeping structure and high-tech construction, the museum is something of an anomaly in Athens's historic center. Indeed, the construction of such a large and ambitious building was fraught with setbacks and controversies.

It was decided as long ago as 1976 that the city needed to replace the smaller, older building that then served as the Acropolis museum. Although repeatedly extended, it had long since become unable to properly display the riches recovered from the site, and its condition was often cited by foreign museums as a reason for not returning Greek antiquities.

Architectural competitions were held in 1976, 1979, and 1989, but none of the designs chosen were ever built—the first two because funds ran out, the last because the discovery of a large Roman settlement beneath the site necessitated a dramatic change of plans.

The Museum Today

The structure that stands on the site today was chosen in 2000. It incorporates the Roman ruins into the museum, with viewing platforms and glass floors allowing visitors to look down on the ruins underneath. It has won many international architectural awards and is frequently described as one of the finest museums in Europe. Its stellar reputation has been slightly soured among the locals by the government's attempts to demolish several historic buildings near the museum to improve its view of the Acropolis.

Visitors enter the building from a long covered terrace, which is pierced by openings that reveal the ancient ruins of Makriyianni beneath. The floor slopes upward from the entrance,

INSIDER TIP:

The New Acropolis Museum presents the Parthenon's sculpture in a manner that far surpasses the British Museum's. It subtly screams for the repatriation of the Elgin Marbles.

—THOMAS STRASSER
National Geographic grantee

leading visitors past a collection of artifacts recovered from the slopes of the Acropolis. These include a variety of votive offerings, some small statues, and a collection of black-figure pottery. The second floor is dedicated to the earliest period of the Acropolis's known history. This includes the intriguing remains of the Hekatompedon—the Parthenon's predecessor—and four largely intact sculptures that once adorned the archaic temple of Athena. The top floor is devoted to sculptures and and decorative details from the Parthenon. Some of these were removed from the structure in modern times (to preserve them from the elements), while others were dislodged over the last 2,500 years by war, weather, or earthquakes.

Going back down through the building, visitors pass through an exhibition of material dating from the Athenian Golden Age, including the original Caryatids from the Erechtheion (see pp. 65–66). A tour of the museum finishes with a gallery of votive offerings and sculptures from the Hellenistic and Roman periods, where visitors come face to face with a youthful but imposing Alexander the Great.

1687, a Venetian army attempted to capture Athens from the Ottomans. The Venetians bombarded the Acropolis, partially destroying the Propylaia and damaging many other buildings on the site. The worst damage, however, occurred when a shell penetrated the roof of the Parthenon and detonated an Ottoman gunpowder store inside. The explosion collapsed the roof and brought down many of the massive pillars, scattering priceless sculptures and architectural details that had survived for more than 2,000 years. To add insult to injury, looters picked over much of the debris when the Venetians finally took the city.

Temple of Athena Nike: This striking temple, located on a bastion in front of the Propylaia, is tiny by comparison with its monumental neighbors. Designed by the architect Kallikrates (who also worked on the Parthenon), it was built between 427 and 424 b.c. after the Persians destroyed the previous temple. It has four Ionic columns on each portico end and bas-reliefs on the surrounding parapets. A portion of this relief, "Nike Unfastening Her Sandal," is displayed at the New Acropolis Museum (see p. 63). The British Museum in London also has pieces of this frieze.

The temple's patron goddess, Athena Nike, represented the combined attributes of Athena and Nike (the personification of victory and a minor goddess in the Greek pantheon). At one point, a cult statue of Athena Nike stood inside the inner temple. The travel writer Pausanias noted that the statue was made of wood and held a helmet in one hand and a pomegranate in the other. Though most statues of Nike had wings, such as the famous Nike of Samothrace (on display at the Louvre in Paris), the Athena Nike did not. This prompted Athenians to call the statue *Nike Apteros* (Wingless Victory).

The Acropolis by Moonlight

On the night of the August full moon, the city of Athens opens the gates of its historic sites and lets visitors in for free. This annual tradition began in the mid-20th century and has become enormously popular both with tourists and locals. It should be remembered, however, that the Acropolis sits in the center of a brightly lit city, so you're not likely to see many stars.

In recent years many other sites in the country have followed suit (although not always on the same night), so it's worth asking around if you're in Greece near a full moon. At the **Temple of Poseidon** on Cape Sounion (see p. 132), 28 miles (45 km) southeast of Athens, you can watch the moon shimmering over the Aegean Sea from between the site's towering columns.

The Sanctuary of Artemis Brauron: On your right as you walk through the Propylaia are the remains of the Sanctuary of Artemis Brauron, also known as the Brauroneion.

In the form of Artemis Brauron, the usually fierce hunter-goddess revealed a gentler face. Artemis Brauron was the protector of women during pregnancy

On clear days, the view south from the Acropolis reaches as far as the island of Egina.

and childbirth, and it is thought that many expectant mothers made the long and difficult climb here in order to leave offerings and pray for the goddess's help.

Although today the sanctuary is little more than a set of foundations cut into the bedrock, it originally consisted of a colonnaded stoa with two enclosed wings that contained shrines and statues.

A little farther up the hill from the Brauroneion stood the **Chalkotheke,** a building used to house votive offerings and donations to the temples on the site. Although archaeological investigations suggest that the now ruined structure was relatively large, most ancient sources refer to it as an unremarkable storage building, if they mention it at all.

Erechtheion: A short distance to the north of the Parthenon lies the Erechtheion, a temple that was dedicated to several different gods. In the open space between the two buildings visitors can see the outlined foundations of the **Old Temple of Athena**—the Parthenon's smaller predecessor—that was destroyed during the Persian wars. Very little is known about this structure, but the New Acropolis Museum (see p. 63) houses some carvings and statues thought to have once adorned its pediment.

The Erechtheion was completed in 406 B.C. It is not known exactly how this temple was used in ancient times—the name "Erechtheion" was coined by the travel writer Pausanias in the second century A.D.—but it is thought

**Theater of
Dionysos**

🅰 55

✉ Dionysiou
Areopagitou

☎ (210) 322 4625

💲 $; free with
Acropolis ticket

Ⓜ Akropoli

that the different chambers of
this irregularly shaped building
probably once held altars to different gods and legendary figures.
These are known to have included
Erectheus, a legendary king of
Athens; Athena Polias (protector
of the city); and Hephaistos (the
god of blacksmiths and fire).

The most distinctive part of
this temple is the **Caryatid Porch**
The porch is supported on the
heads of six maidens (called Caryatids), though the ones you see
are copies. Five of the originals are

into a café and exhibition space,
but this scheme has not yet
been carried out. At the farthest
end of the Acropolis there is a
defensive tower that provides a
wonderful vantage point looking
toward the National Gardens.

South of the Acropolis

Below the eastern end of the
Acropolis is the **Theater of
Dionysos,** the best-preserved
portion of the ancient Sanctuary
of Dionysia. It is here that the
great Dionysian festival was once

EXPERIENCE: Athens Segway Tours

Established in summer 2010, **Athens Seg-
way Tours** (Aischinou Street 9, Plaka, tel
210/322 2500, www.athenssegway
tours.com, $$$$$) has already proved to be
a big hit with visitors to Athens. Their
electric personal transporters allow you
to glide effortlessly and quickly between
the sights of old Athens, and their guides

provide knowledgeable commentary on
the history of the area. The **Acropolis
Tour** allows visitors to see all the major
sights of old Athens (including the
Acropolis, Filopappou Hill, the Odeon of
Herodes Atticus, and the ancient Agora)
in just two hours—ideal for those with a
boat or plane to catch.

---

displayed in the New Acropolis
Museum. The sixth, removed
by Lord Elgin in the early 19th
century (see sidebar p. 59), is at
the British Museum.

The Eastern Acropolis:
Beyond the Erechtheion and
the Parthenon there are a few
ruined shrines, mostly from the
Roman period, but nothing to
compare with the western half
of the site. The low, modern
building located to the east
of the Parthenon is the old
Acropolis museum. When the
old museum closed, plans were
made to convert the building

held (see p. 40), and its stage
saw the first performances of
the works of great dramatists
including Aeschylus, Sophocles,
and Euripides. In the sixth and
early fifth centuries B.C., during
the golden age of Athenian
drama, plays were likely performed in a makeshift wooden
amphitheater. The orator and
politician Lykourgos (390–324
B.C.) commissioned the first
stone theater on the site, which
was subsequently added to and
rebuilt by the Romans a few
centuries later.

Across the pedestrianized Dionysiou Areopagitou Street stands

the gleaming glass structure of the **New Acropolis Museum** (see p. 63)–Athens's grandest public building. The design and placement of this structure was the cause of a major controversy in Athens. The original plans called for several nearby buildings—including fine examples of neoclassical and art deco architecture–to be demolished, igniting a fierce debate about whether the preservation of Athens's ancient history should be allowed to come at the expense of its more recent past.

A short distance west of the Theater of Dionysos, very close to the main entrance to the Acropolis, stands a more recent, and better preserved, theater: the **Odeon of Herodes Atticus** (sometimes called the Herodeon).

Herodes Atticus was a Greek aristocrat and sophist who also served as a Roman senator. He paid for the construction of the Herodeon between 160 and 170 A.D. Although it does not have the illustrious history of its neighbor, the Herodeon's excellent condition makes it the favored venue for modern cultural events, including the Athens & Epidavros Festival (see p. 129). Originally there was a colonnaded *stoa* between the two theaters, where wealthy Athenians would gather before performances. It was built into the Byzantine defenses in the 11th century, but parts of it can still be seen.

Areopagus

Just outside the main entrance of the Acropolis is the Areopagus, a giant limestone rock named either for Ares, god of war, or Arae, goddess of vengeance. The Areopagus was the site of the Athenians' supreme judicial court. Some legendary

Odeon of Herodes Atticus

🅰 55

✉ Herodeon, Dionysiou Areopagitou, Akropoli

☎ (210) 321 0219

💲 $$; free with Acropolis ticket

🚇 Akropoli

Areopagus

🅰 55

🚇 Monastiraki

Using personal transporters to get around the Acropolis

Built in the 2nd century A.D., the Odeon of Herodes Atticus is still in use today.

The Pnyka

🅰 55

🅑 Thissio

Asteroskopeion

🅰 55

🅑 Thissio

www.astro.noa.gr

trials took place here, including the trial of Orestes for the murder of his mother, Clytemnestra.

Today, however, it is best known as the place where Saint Paul spoke to the Athenians about the new religion of Christianity. According to the New Testament account, he converted the senator Dionysos, who later became the first bishop of Athens, but largely failed to win over the skeptical audience. Nowadays, it's a popular spot for tourists taking panoramic photographs of the ancient Agora. The rocks are very slippery, so it's best to take the metal steps to avoid a painful fall.

The Pnyka

The word *pnyka* means "crowded" in Greek. This name has its origins in the gatherings of Athenian citizens that began to take place here after

the tyrants were banished from ancient Athens. What initially began as a place to discuss governance and municipal issues gradually developed into the Athenian *ekklesia* (assembly), the world's oldest democracy.

As more citizens met here over the years, the area on the smooth saddle of the hill was organized into a flat upper level, a semicircular sloped second level, and a central area, the *lithos*, set aside for an assembly speaker. Lithos speakers included the statesmen Aristides and Pericles, the noted orator Demosthenes, and many others. There was no roof to offer protection from sun and rain, so the assembly met very early in the morning and adjourned during downpours.

Compared with the Acropolis or Agora, however, the Pnyka looks like just a typically scrubby and rocky Greek park. You need a little imagination to conjure up its ancient glory. In 2001, archaeologists uncovered a nearby cave sanctuary dedicated to Pan, the god of shepherds, flocks, mountains, and rustic music. Pnyka also has the remains of an ancient fountain, the **Kallirhoe,** that was part of a water-trap system that may have been connected to the giant water supply works of Athens, established under Peisistratus.

On a nearby hill is the neoclassical **Asteroskopeion** (Observatory). Designed by the Danish architect Theophilus Hansen, it was completed in 1846.

INSIDER TIP:

Take in a sunset at the Filopappou monument for a romantic view of the Acropolis and the environs of Athens.

—THOMAS STRASSER
National Geographic grantee

Filopappou Hill

In the early 19th century, archaeological excavations led primarily by German archaeologist William Dorpfeld uncovered a sanctuary of Zeus Hypsistos and an ancient but complex water system on Filopappou Hill. You can enter the Filopappou site from a stone-paved road at the end of Dionysiou Areopagitou Street. Inside, you will see a dirt road that leads to a structure cut in the rock that is known, dubiously, as "Socrates's prison."

The most famous landmark here is the **Filopappou Monument,** built on top of the Hill of the Muses. The monument is dedicated to the Syrian Prince Gaius Julius Antiochos Filopappou, grandson of the last king of Commagene of Upper Syria. Because he was a generous benefactor of Athens, he got to build his burial monument here. In antiquity, the hill was called Mousaion and was named for either Musaios, the poet-disciple of Orpheus, or the Muses themselves.

On the south side of the paved road to Filopappou Hill stands the Byzantine **church of Dimitrios Louvararies,** dedicated to the military saint Dimitrios, who is said to have protected the church from a bombardment by the Turkish general Yusuf. A few yards away is **Kimon's Tomb,** a large, rectangular rock-cut monument said to commemorate Kimon the Elder, father of the Marathon soldier Miltiades, and Kimon the Younger, Miltiades's son. The monument is also said to honor the historian Thucydides, one of their relatives.

Across from Kimon's Tomb, the paved roads to Filopappou and the neighboring hill of Pnyka meet. At that point, part of an ancient road runs about a third of a mile (0.5 km) to the **Church of the Metamorphosis of Christ.** This is part of the so-called **Koile Road,** which used to be the shortest road from Athens and Pireas and the safest road to transport goods, as it was protected by the length of the city's Themistoclean Long Walls, a pair of ramparts that ran all the way from ancient Athens to Pireas. ■

Filopappou Hill
🅰 55
🚇 Akropoli

Church of Dimitrios Louvararies
✉ Dionysiou Areopagitou
🚇 Thissio

Church of the Metamorphosis of Christ
✉ Theorias
🚇 Monastiraki

North of the Acropolis

Sheltered beneath the walls of the Acropolis, the neighborhoods of Plaka, Monastiraki, and Anafiotika form the historic core of Athens; the area has been continuously inhabited since around 1400 B.C. To the east of these neighborhoods you will find the ancient Agora and the marketplaces of the Roman Agora standing right next to medieval Byzantine churches, ornate Ottoman mosques, and 19th-century neoclassical architecture.

A relief from the Agora on display at the Stoa of Attalos

Ancient Agora &
Stoa of Attalos

🚇 55

✉ Adrianou 24

☎ (210) 321 0185

💲 $; free with 4-day Acropolis ticket.

🚇 Monastiraki

The Ancient Agora

Occupying a large site to the west of the city center, the ancient Agora is one of the largest and most important archaeological sites in the world. Excavations began here in the spring of 1931, when the American School of Athens was given permission to demolish the Ottoman-era neighborhood that stood on the site. The ancient structures that still stood in the area, including the miraculously well-preserved Temple of Hephaistos, hinted at the riches that

might be found if the site could be properly excavated.

Though many were sad to see the picturesque old neighborhood go, the demolition of the houses (which were mostly made from architectural salvage) yielded many fascinating artifacts—pieces of statue embedded in walls, ancient ruins used for foundations—before the archaeologists had even begun to dig. When the site was finally cleared a few years later, the archaeologists were faced with a site of such complexity and richness that, even after 80 years of excavations, new discoveries are still being made all the time.

A selection of this vast hoard of archaeological finds is displayed on the site in the **Stoa of Attalos,** a painstaking reconstruction of a building that once stood here. Dedicated by the Pergamene King Attalos II (r. 159–138 B.C.) the Stoa of Attalos consisted of a long walkway lined with Doric and Ionic columns and 20 chambers that are thought to have once held shops. Today, these rooms house display cases filled with pottery, statues, and other artifacts from the site. The most fascinating of these are the small fragments of broken pottery with names scratched on them, which were used as ballots in ostracism votes (in which politicians thought to be too power-hungry were chosen for ten years of exile).

Visitors to the site can tour the ruins of the various temples and public buildings that have been revealed by years of excavation. In the center of the site, the ruins of the **Odeon of Agrippa** demonstrate the scale of the buildings that once stood here. Constructed

INSIDER TIP:

Teams of archaeologists descend on the ancient Agora every summer, so some parts of the site are likely to be cordoned off.

—SALLY MCFALL
National Geographic contributor

in 15 B.C., the Odeon once housed a large roofed auditorium with 18 rows of seats. It remained in use until the Germanic Herulians destroyed it in A.D. 267.

To the south of the site stands a potent symbol of ancient Athens's final decline: the **Roman defensive wall.** This fortification was erected in the third century A.D., after the city was partially destroyed by the Herulians. It comprises two stone walls that were crudely assembled from the rubble of destroyed monuments. Ornately carved pediment blocks were stacked with pieces of ionic columns, grave markers, and statue bases in a desperate attempt to protect the city from further attacks.

The Agora's highlight, however, is undoubtedly the fifth-century-B.C. **Temple of Hephaistos,** or Hephaisteion. This masterpiece of Doric classical cult architecture was dedicated to the god of fire and metallurgy, Hephaistos. The temple has sculptures depicting the heroic deeds of Hercules on the front, of Theseus on the sides, and, on the back, a battle between Greeks and centaurs. At night, the Hephaistion is lit up and serves as an epic backdrop to the numerous cafés lining Thissio.

The Roman Agora

The other major archaeological site north of the Acropolis is the Roman Agora, also called the Market of Caesar and Augustus, which lies east of the ancient Agora and was once connected to it by a colonnaded street.

A notable monument is the Doric portico on the west side, the **Gate of Athena Archegestis** (Leader of the Tribe), that dates from around 10 B.C. Nearby is the **Tower of the Winds** (Horologion of Andronikos), an octagonal marble structure that housed a water clock. The clock, which was finished by Andronikos of Kyrrhos, operated via a system of pipes that connected it to reservoirs on the slopes of nearby hills. Outside the tower, the eaves show reliefs of the winds blowing from each direction. Each of the winds has a name—Boreas (north), Kaikias (northeast), Apeliotes (east), Euros (southeast), Notos (south), Lips (southwest), Zephyros (west), and Skyron (northwest).

Roman Agora

- ✉ Pelopida
- ☎ (210) 324 5220
- 💲 $$; free with 4-day Acropolis ticket
- Ⓜ Monastiraki

Tower of the Winds (Horologion of Andronikos)

- ✉ Horologion, Markou Aureliou
- ☎ (210) 324 5220
- 💲 $; free with 4-day Acropolis ticket
- Ⓜ Monastiraki

Plaka

🅰 55

🚇 Syntagma or Akropoli

Anafiotika

🚇 Monastiraki or Syntagma

Sholarhio Ouzeri Kouklis

✉ Tripodon Street 14, Plaka

☎ (210) 324 7605

www.sholarhio.gr

The Christians used the tower's waters to baptize converts.

Also near the Roman Agora is **Hadrian's Library,** built during the philhellene emperor Hadrian's reign. The library used to be enclosed by a high wall and had an entrance on the west side, which faced the ancient Agora. The entire complex likely served as more than a library; there's evidence that it had a lounge for Athenian intellectuals and also a room for the emperor's cult.

INSIDER TIP:

While in Plaka, visit Sholarhio Ouzeri Kouklis. Enjoy grilled eggplant, sausages, and fried cheese washed down with a Mythos beer or a house *krasi* (wine).

—JAMES V. BULLARD
National Geographic Expeditions

Plaka

Probably the loveliest neighborhood in Athens, Plaka extends from the slopes of the Acropolis north to Ermou Street and eastward to Amalias Street. Though the neighborhood is filled with too many tourist shops and souvlaki shacks, its neoclassical houses and tiny, whitewashed streets are a welcome break from the disastrous, traffic-clogged urban development that defines most of Athens.

The neighborhood went through a dreary period in the 1950s and 1960s, when it was nightclub central. But history-minded architects, scholars, and city planners banded with local residents to kick out the loud clubs and restore the neighborhood to its 19th-century glory.

Anafiotika: Anafiotika is an area in the upper part of Plaka along the northeastern slope of the Acropolis. In the 1840s, a huddle of tiny whitewashed houses was built here by stonemasons from Anafi, a small island in the Cyclades east of Santorini. They had come to Athens to work on the Royal Palace and other public projects during the reign of King Otto (r. 1833–1862). The homesick stonemasons built the Cycladic-style houses into the steep slope because it reminded them of the cliffs of their home island.

The settlement was poor; there were about 100 houses, all of them lacking utilities, with outdoor kitchens and toilets. Though city officials considered demolishing the settlement in the 1970s, they decided to keep and preserve the houses, which are still inhabited today. Curious visitors often peer into the windows of the stone houses or stop to admire gardens of blooming jasmine and roses. As with the settlements on Tinos (see pp. 167–168), even the humblest of homes are enlivened with ornate carved or painted decorations, added by their original artisan owners.

You can enter Anafiotika at the end of Statonos Street, near the 17th century church of **Agios Georgios tou Vrachou** (St. George of the Rock). The church is small and filled with simple Byzantine icons, like many whitewashed chapels in the Greek islands. The marble for the church was taken from an ancient temple.

Choregic Monuments: For the most part, the fabric of Plaka dates from the 18th and 19th centuries, but in places fragments of the ancient city can still be seen. The finest examples of this are the Choregic monuments—constructed to commemorate the winners of choral competitions.

Of those surviving monuments, the most spectacular is located in the south of Plaka, near the pedestrianized Dionysiou Areopagitou Street. It is dedicated to Lysicrates, the *choregos* (or producer), whose chorus won the top prize in 334 B.C. The inscription on the monument says, in translation: "Lysicrates of Kikyna, son of Lysitheides, was choregos; the tribe of Akamantis won the victory with a chorus of boys; Theon played the flute; Lysiades of Athens trained the chorus; Euainetos was archon."

In the Middle Ages, the monument was called the "Lantern of Demosthenes" because of a mistaken belief that the fourth-century-B.C. orator composed his speeches there. Between 1669 and 1821, the monument became part of a French Capuchin convent.

Agios Georgios tou Vrachou (St. George of the Rock)

⊠ Statonos Street, Anafiotika

🕒 Open for services only.

🚇 Monastiraki or Syntagma

One of the many traditional tavernas on the pedestrianized Kydathineon Street in Plaka

Whitewashed houses crowd a narrow lane on the north slope of the Acropolis.

Mitropolis
🅰 55
✉ Plateia Mitropolis, Monastiraki
☎ (210) 322 1308
Ⓜ Monastiraki

Panagia Gorgoepkos
✉ Plateia Mitropolis, Monastiraki
Ⓜ Monastiraki

Plaka's Churches: As one of the great intellectual centers of the Greek Orthodox faith, it is no great surprise that Athens has always had many churches and monasteries. Nowhere is this more apparent than Plaka, where the low, domed structures of medieval Byzantine churches compete with the less humble creations of the 19th century. These contrasting traditions can be seen most clearly in Mitropolis Square, where there are two churches—the 19th-century Mitropolis (City Cathedral) and the 12th-century Byzantine chapel of Panagia Gorgoepkos.

The larger and newer of these two buildings, the **Mitropolis,** is the seat of the Greek Orthodox Archbishop of Athens and one of the city's best known landmarks. Its construction was begun in 1843 under the supervision of Theophilus Hansen (see pp. 84–85) whose plans were, as always, neoclassical. His design was only built up to the height of the first set of windows, however, before another architect, Dimitrios Zezos, took over and completely changed the design. The project would change hands once more before it was finally completed in 1862. Although not an ugly building by any means, the result is a rather strange mixture of architectural styles, especially when compared to the neat simplicity of its older neighbor.

The cathedral's exterior and interior have been undergoing a massive renovation for years now. The scaffolding makes it hard to really enjoy the church's details, though the beautiful Byzantine icons and painted columns inside can still be enjoyed.

During Easter Holy Week, when the services are especially memorable, the church is packed with Athenians singing "Christos Anesti" (Christ is Risen). The crowd often spills onto Mitropolis Square, where you'll see a statue of the Byzantine Emperor Constantine Palaiologos, the last Hellene to rule before the empire fell to the Ottomans.

The lovely 12th-century chapel of **Panagia Gorgoepkos** sits on the site of a church built by the Byzantine Empress Irene (a native Athenian) in the eighth century. The empress built her church on the ruins of an ancient temple devoted to Eileithyia, the goddess of childbirth. The "Little Mitropolis," as it's also known, is considered one of the most beautiful churches in Athens. It's dedicated to Panagia Gorgoepkos (All Holy Virgin who quickly grants prayers) and to St. Eleutherios.

Instead of the bricks used in most Byzantine churches, the Panagia Gorgoepkos is made entirely of marble. Its outer walls are covered with reliefs of animals and figures from the classical and Byzantine period, as well as zodiac signs and the ancient calendar of feasts. Inside, people pray for miracles at the painting of the Virgin, which dates to between the 13th and 14th century.

Museums: Although none of the city's giant cultural institutions are located in Plaka, there are many small museums dotted around the neighborhood.

The **Jewish Museum** on Nikis Street gives a historical narrative of Jewish history in Greece from the Hellenistic period to the holocaust. It makes excellent use of oral and personal history in describing life for the Hellenized communities of Romaniote Jews in Ioannina and Sephardic Jews in Thessaloniki. The museum also functions as a memorial to the Jewish community of Athens, almost all of whom were killed during the Holocaust.

The **Frissiras Museum,** which opened in December 2000 in two restored neoclassical buildings, houses paintings, sculptures and sketches by modern Greek and foreign artists. The collection belonged to the museum's founder, the lawyer Vlassis Frissiras. The **Kanellopoulos Museum,** housed in a 19th-century neoclassical building, has art and

Jewish Museum
- 55
- Nikis 39, Plaka
- (210) 322 5582
- $$
- Closed Sat.
- Syntagma

www.jewishmuseum.gr

Frissiras Museum
- Monis Asteriou 3, Plaka
- (210) 323 4678
- $$
- Closed Mon.–Tues.
- Monastiraki

www.frissirasmuseum.com

Kanellopoulos Museum
- 55
- Theorias, Monastiraki
- (210) 321 2313
- $$
- Closed Mon.
- Monastiraki

Dora Stratou Dance Theater

A cultured Athenian from a high-class family, Dora Stratou (1903–1988) frequented royal balls and studied piano under the tutelage of Dimitris Mitropoulos, who later became conductor of the New York Philharmonic Orchestra. In 1952, after watching the performance of a Yugoslav folk ensemble, she was inspired to create a group that would perform Greek folk dances. She threw herself into the project, studying dances, songs, costumes, and folk jewelry from villages all around the country. She auditioned and assembled Greece's top dancers and musicians. Soon, the group was performing internationally.

In 1964, then-prime minister Constantinos Karamanlis commissioned the building of a special theater for the Dora Stratou Dance Group on the side of Filopappou Hill. The **Theater of Greek Dances** (tel 210 324 4395, www.grdance.org) still hosts Greek folk dance performances.

By the time Dora Stratou died in 1988, she had written three books on traditional Greek dances and recorded 50 albums of traditional Greek songs—one of the largest catalogues of folk music in the world. "I write what my eyes have seen, what went through my mind," she wrote in her 1979 book *Greek Traditional Dance*, "and what my soul fell in love with."

The Fethiye Mosque

At a glance, the small stone building at the corner of Panos and Pelopida Streets, at the northern end of the Roman Agora, seems like an unlikely cause for controversy. A closer look, however, reveals that this building—which is currently used as a storage shed—is an old Ottoman mosque. The Fethiye Mosque, as it is known, is in fact the oldest mosque in Athens, built by Mehmed II in 1458. In a city with a Muslim population of 200,000 but no mosques, the building's current state makes many people angry.

Some Muslim community leaders hope that it can be restored but have so far struggled to get much political support. Their proposal received a boost in 2010, however, when it emerged that the Turkish government was pressing for the restoration of the mosque as part of a deal that would see several properties in Turkey returned to the Orthodox Church.

Greek Folk Art Museum

- 🅰 55
- ✉ Kydathineon 17, Plaka
- ☎ (210) 322 9031
- 💲 $
- 🕐 Closed Mon.
- 🚇 Syntagma

Museum of Greek Popular Musical Instruments

- ✉ Diogenous 1–3, Plaka-
- ☎ (210) 325 0198
- 🕐 Closed Mon.
- 🚇 Monastiraki

Monastiraki

- 🅰 55
- 🚇 Monastiraki

artistic artifacts from prehistoric to modern times. On Kyda-thinaon Square, the **Greek Folk Art Museum** has an impressive collection of works dating as far back as 1650, including beautifuly embroidered traditional costumes, crafts, and artifacts of a bygone age. Near the Roman Agora is the **Museum of Greek Popular Musical Instruments,** which also has an excellent catalogue of rembetika.

Monastiraki

Monastiraki takes its name from the *monastiraki* (or little monastery) of the Pantanassa, or the Virgin Mary, an aisled basilica dated to the 10th century and located on the square between Athinas and Mitropoleos Streets.

But Monastiraki also sits next to the ancient Agora, so it's no surprise that the area is wholly devoted to commerce and tourism. Souvenir shops fill the side alleys, carrying strange and often rude T-shirts, as well as knock-offs of Greek art and traditional outfits. It's not all cheap, lowbrow fare, though; you can find well priced, Greek-made embroideries at Kedima, and there are several shops selling handmade jewelry, organic olive oil products, and flowing goddess dresses.

One of the main streets on the square, **Pandrossou,** used to be part of the Turkish bazaar. Ottoman remnants still stand, including the former **Tzasdirakis Mosque** (which today houses the Greek Folk Art Museum's pottery collection). Vendors will try to lure you in with elaborate stories that explain their high prices, but feel free to bargain. The market here gets very busy and overpriced in the summer, but it's also open late and on weekends.

When the weather is good, which is most of the year, street performers take center stage on the square, which has recently been remodeled. They include musicians such as Balkan brass bands and Peruvian flutists; pantomimes dressed as Socrates and Atlas (carrying a giant inflatable "Earth" on his back); and young Greeks practicing *capoeira,* the Afro-Brazilian martial art. That's when the food and drink vendors show up, too, with cotton candy (known as *mali tis yrias,* or old-lady hair), popcorn, and the winter favorite *salepi*—a drink made from the dried tubers of orchids.

Just off the square on Mitropoleos Street are a cluster of kebab shacks. The best (and best-priced) one is **O Thanasis** *(Mitropoleos St. 69, Monastiraki, tel. 210/324 4705)*, which serves juicy, well-spiced kebabs with roasted tomatoes on grilled pita bread. Order your kebab with tzatziki for the full experience. O Thanasis (the first name of the founder) gets very busy on weekends and in summer, so you may have to wait a bit for a table.

Abyssinia Square near the Monastiraki bazaar is a center of antique treasures, which are pricey despite the humble location. Stroll through and see furniture dealers restoring antique chairs, tables, and bookshelves as well as a range of antiques ranging from framed family portraits to tubas. During the week, you will see store owners playing backgammon during slow stretches or having a thick Greek coffee in the sunlight. On Sunday, scores of vendors and junk dealers converge on the square, spilling onto the surrounding area. Some of the merchandise is decidedly weird (unless you're hankering for a Soviet-era diving suit or a worn photograph of someone's Cretan grandfather), but it's a great place to browse. ∎

Bargains aplenty can be picked up at the Monastiraki flea market.

Kerameikos & Thissio

Full of lively cafés and *ouzeris*, the Thissio neighborhood offers some of the best views of the Acropolis. The main area is the Nileos pedestrian area across from the ancient Agora and along the cobbled promenade that's lined with artists, musicians, and popcorn and cotton candy vendors on weekends. Nearby Kerameikos holds one of the most fascinating, yet least visited, historic sites in Athens—the ancient cemetery.

Some tombs in Kerameikos Cemetery date back more than 4,000 years.

Looking down from the Acropolis, the neighborhoods of Thissio, Gazi, and Kerameikos can be seen as a maze of 19th-century buildings west of the Agora. This was once the metalworking and pottery district of Athens, where everything from swords to urns would have been hammered or molded into shape. Throughout the centuries, and the many changes that swept through Athens, the area kept its working-class character—complete with workshops and small factories.

It was not until the later decades of the 20th century that the forces of commerce began to replace those old workshops with cafés and bars. Today, Thissio is an exciting neighborhood, where visitors can get a taste of Athens away from the dense crowds of the other historic districts.

Kerameikos

At the northern end of the ancient Agora (see pp. 70–71) lies **Kerameikos Cemetery**—a hallowed site that has been used by Athenians as a burial place for around 4,000 years. The name Kerameikos, which is also applied to the surrounding neighborhood, comes from the ancient potters who worked in the area. This was once a marshy

INSIDER TIP:

Kerameikos Cemetery is a wonderful place to experience in winter or spring, when it is filled with wildlife and transformed by a carpet of lush greenery.

—CLIVE CARPENTER
National Geographic contributor

area divided by the Eridanus River, which marked the northwest border of ancient Athens.

Archaeological excavations have uncovered evidence of burials from the area dating from the Mycenaean era. During the Athenian Golden Age, burial sites in this area became the preserve of the city's wealthiest families. They built grand and eleborate monuments to their dead relatives, some of which survive to this day. The ones you see in the cemetery today are modern reproductions, however, as the originals have long since been moved to the National Archaeological Museum (see pp. 94–97) for safekeeping.

Walking around the site today you will see these grand tombs, alongside the simpler cylindrical ones that became mandatory in later centuries. At the southwest edge of the ancient cemetery are the remains of the **Dipylon Gate,** Athens's main entrance and the largest gate in ancient Greece. According to Thucydides, it was here that Pericles (see pp. 29–30) gave his famous funerary oration

at the *demosion sema* (public burial monument) in honor of the dead from the first year of the Peloponnesian War. Kerameikos also has an excellent **museum** displaying funerary art from the site, including pottery, dozens of moving monumental inscriptions, and a giant intact kouros—a statue of a young man.

On the southeast side of the site is the **Sacred Gate,** through which priestesses passed on their journey along the Sacred Way to Eleusis. At Eleusis, they would perform ancient Greece's most important religious rites: the Eleusinian mysteries of Demeter, the goddess of agriculture, and her daughter, Persephone, queen of the underworld. The cult of Demeter kept these rites secret in the hopes of uniting the worshippers with the gods and finding divine power in the afterlife.

Thissio

The area to the south of Kerameikos is known as Thissio, for the popular name of the nearby Temple of Hephaistos (it was believed to hold the remains of Theseus). The main commercial area in this district runs along **Nileos Street,** which begins opposite the Agora's entrance. This broad throughfare was recently pedestrianized and is now an excellent place to start exploring the area. Many of the neoclassical houses in Thissio have been converted to fancy cafés or eateries, but others are still homes quietly tucked away on side streets. Businesses here are generally less tourist-

Kerameikos

⚠ 55
🚇 Monastiraki

Kerameikos Cemetery

✉ Ermou, Kerameikos 148
☎ (210) 346 3552
💲 $; free with 4-day Acropolis ticket
🕐 Closed Mon.
🚇 Thissio or Kerameikos

Thissio

⚠ 55
🚇 Thissio

Benaki Museum of Islamic Art

- ✉ Agion Asomaton 22, Kerameikos
- ☎ (210) 325 1311
- $ $$
- 🕐 Closed Mon.
- 🚇 Thissio or Kerameikos

www.benaki.gr

Melina Mercouri Cultural Center

- ✉ Iraklidon, Kerameikos 66
- ☎ (210) 345 2150
- $ $$
- 🕐 Closed Sat.–Sun.
- 🚇 Thissio or Kerameikos

Maria Callas Museum

- ✉ Pireos 100, Technopolis, Gazi
- ☎ (210) 346 1589
- 🕐 Closed Sat.–Sun.
- 🚇 Thissio

oriented than those in Monastiraki or Plaka, giving visitors a calmer shopping environment and more interesting variety of stores. It does, however, mean that English is less frequently used on menus and shop signs, so it can help to know a few key words and phrases in Greek.

Museums: Although it is a little off the beaten path for many visitors, Thissio is not without cultural and historical attractions. One of the gems here is the **Benaki Museum of Islamic Art,** which is on a side street that straddles the Thissio and Psirri neighborhoods. This showcase of Islamic art is considered one of the best in the world. The museum is located in two restored neoclassical mansions on a side street not far from Thissio Metro station.

The restrained exteriors of these elegant old buildings give few clues that inside they hold a large and exotic collection of art and design. Antonis Benakis, founder of the original Benaki Museum in Kolonaki, had collected the art during his many years living in Egypt. The collection is featured on four floors and spans from the early years of Islam to the 19th century. The geographical range of the artifacts is also diverse, from Islamic Spain to India. Don't miss the carved doors from eighth-century Mesopotamia, a 14th-century universal astrolabe, and the 19th-century Iranian daggers resting in jewel-encrusted cases.

Another highlight in Thissio is the **Melina Mercouri Cultural Center,** which is housed in a restored building that was once the Poulopoulou hat factory. The museum features a painstaking reproduction of a 19th-century Athenian street, complete with stores and homes filled with artifacts from the period. In addition to this interesting exhibit, the cultural center also hosts temporary exhibitions by young Greek artists

The History of Gazi

A French company opened the city's gasworks here in 1857, on the invitation of King Otto. The complex grew quickly, and the surrounding area soon filled with rows of tiny homes for the company's workers. The neighborhood became known as Gazohouri, or Gas Lands (later shortened to Gazi). Many of the gasworks staff were Muslims from Thrace who came to Athens at the turn of the 20th century.

Gas was produced here by burning coal in special ovens, a process that generated a massive amount of foul-smelling smoke. For more than a century, the plant supplied Athens with light and heat but, at the same time, stained most of the city's great buildings black with a thick layer of soot. Faced with a notorious air-pollution problem, the city closed the gasworks in the 1980s, and the area fell into obscurity. In the late 1990s, however, the city resurrected the gasworks as a multipurpose arts space called **Technopolis** (see p. 81). Remnants of its industrial-age, working-class past remain, but today it's a hangout for artists, hipsters, and local television stars who linger at the trendy neighborhood tavernas.

Traditional dresses on display at the Melina Mercouri Cultural Center

and examples of traditional Greek entertainments.

Gazi & Technopolis

A short distance away from Kerameikos Cemetery, on the other side of the always-busy Pireas Street, stands the recently regenerated area of Gazi. What was once a smoke-belching gasworks (see sidebar, p. 80) has been transformed into an exciting young neighborhood, complete with restaurants, bars, and trendy modern art galleries.

The heart of this neighborhood is the **Technopolis** complex, which is housed in the buildings of the old gasworks. The only permanent exhibit here is the **Maria Callas Museum** (*Andreas Embirikos Hall, Pireas St. 100, tel 210/346 1589, closed Sat.–Sun.*), which has a collection related to the life and work of the famous opera singer (who was born Mary Anna Kalogeropoulou and spent much of her early career in Athens). The buildings and grounds of Technopolis also play host to a fantastic range of temporary exhibitions, art installations, and cultural events—so it's well worth a visit even if you have little or no interest in Greece's favorite opera singer.

Since Gazi's renaissance began in 1998, restaurants, bars, cafés, and galleries have gone up all around Kerameikos Square and the other streets around the old gasworks. The best of this new generation of Athenian restaurants includes **The Butcher Shop, Mamacas,** and **Sardelles** (*Persefonis 15, tel 210/347 8050, $$$*) all within sight of the Metro station. New bars and restaurants are popping up in the area everyday, however, so there's no shortage of excellent options. A few streets away from the square is the **New Benaki Museum,** an excellent venue for contemporary art, photography, and modern Greek history. ∎

The Butcher Shop
- ✉ Persefonis 18, Gazi
- ☎ (210) 341 3440
- 💲 $$$
- 🚇 Kerameikos

Mamacas
- ✉ Persefonis 41, Gazi
- ☎ (210) 346 4984
- 🕐 Closed Mon.
- 💲 $$$$
- 🚇 Kerameikos
- **www.mamacas.gr**

New Benaki Museum
- ✉ Pireas 138, Gazi
- ☎ (210) 345 3111
- 🕐 Closed Mon. & Aug.
- 💲 $$
- 🚇 Kerameikos
- **www.benaki.gr**

Syntagma & Around

Syntagma has been the seat of power in Athens since the days of the Roman emperors. It's also a gathering spot for demonstrators, café philosophers, tourists, and, on weekdays, smartly-dressed Athenian powerbrokers filing in and out of the Parliament building and the many banks around the square.

Once the royal palace, the Parliament building has also housed refugees.

Syntagma

 55

 Syntagma

Although the Acropolis is the spiritual and historical center of Athens, **Syntagma Square** is its most important hub, where roads to every part of the city meet. From a starting point under the broadleaved trees that shade the square, visitors can easily find their way to all of Athens's landmarks.

Directly ahead of you, and rather hard to miss, is the massive neoclassical **Parliament building,** originally built as a royal palace. To your right, the Leoforos Amalias curves south around the edge of Plaka, passing the Temple of

Olympian Zeus and Hadrian's Arch, before merging with Dionysiou Areopagitou Street. To your left, two roads branch off from the northeast corner of the square: Panepestimou Street will take you north, past the Numismatic Museum and the old University, before ending in Omonoia Square. Alternatively, Leoforos Vasilisis Sofias (Vasilissis Sofias Avenue) extends east through wealthy Kolonaki and its many excellent museums.

Behind you and to the left, Stadiou Street will take you to the **Historical Museum of Greece**

INSIDER TIP:

At Syntagma's Metro station, stratified excavations brilliantly reveal layers of Athenian civilization, from Byzantine to classical Greek.

—KATHLEEN CROMWELL
Travel writer and author

and the **Museum of the City of Athens**, while the pedestrianized Ermou Street, opposite the Parliament building, goes into the heart of Monastiraki.

The Parliament Building

After the Greek people won their independence from the Ottoman Empire, the great powers of 19th-century Europe decided that the new state of Greece needed a king. They chose Otto I of Bavaria, a 15-year-old prince from what is now southern Germany.

One of the first matters of business for the new king was the construction of his palace. It had originally been suggested that it be built on top of the Acropolis, but, thankfully, this idea was rejected. The building was designed by architects of the Bavarian court and completed in 1843. The architects envisioned a building that paid homage to Greece's past; they used a neoclassical design and built a Doric porch of Pentelic marble.

The building made its first appearance in the annals of Greek history only a few months later.

Greeks resented their young king, and many saw his rule as just another period of foreign occupation. When he turned against the outspoken heroes of the war of independence, the people erupted into open rebellion. The public unrest only ended when Otto stood on the balcony of his palace and proclaimed a new national constitution (the Syntagma) to the angry mob occupying the square. A landmark moment in Greek politics, this constitution returned many of his autocratic powers to the Greek people.

For the rest of the 19th and early 20th centuries, the palace continued to function as the royal residence, although the political and social importance of the king had dwindled away to nearly nothing by the outbreak of the First World War. In 1922, it housed thousands of Greek refugees who fled Asia Minor after Greece's failed campaign to claim that territory from Turkey. The royal family left the building when Greece became a republic in 1924. By the end of 1929, the Greek parliament had moved in, a move that symbolized the transfer of power from the king to the people. The building was remodeled to serve as a single-chamber council for the parliament. Today, most of the building is closed to the public, but the library is open to researchers.

The National Gardens

Behind the Parliament building are the National Gardens, a

(continued on p. 86)

Parliament Building

✉ Plateia Syntagma, Syntagma

🚇 Syntagma

The National Gardens

🅰 55

✉ Leoforos Vasilissis Amalias, Syntagma

☎ (210) 721 5019

🚇 Syntagma

Neoclassical Athens

Although the neoclassical style has its roots elsewhere in Europe, few cities have ever adopted it with the same enthusiasm as Athens in the 19th century. For the city's leaders and prominent citizens, neoclassicism provided a symbolic link between their new city and the ancient city that came before.

The Academy of Athens building is Athenian neoclassicism at its best.

Architects first began to revisit the ideas of ancient Greek architecture in the 16th century. Famous figures like Andrea Palladio (1508–1580) were attracted to the symmetry and simplicity of classical design. The work of these early architects developed into a new style, known as neoclassicism, that was defined by the application of ancient Greek architectural principles, strict symmetry, and (by the standards of the time at least) restrained external decoration. Although neoclassical buildings are often visually similar to the buildings of ancient Greece, they incorporate modern structural techniques and rarely adhere precisely to the very rigid rules of ancient architecture, where everything from the proportions of the columns to the angle of the roof was fixed.

When the Greek people regained their independence in 1832, Athens was little more than a village. In order to accommodate the institutions of a national capital, the city had to be expanded rapidly and rebuilt. The sheer scale of the necessary construction was one of the reasons the city was chosen—it gave the new Greek state a chance to start with a blank slate in a place relatively unchanged since its ancient heyday. The neoclassical style was the obvious choice for the many new public buildings of the new nation. Unfortunately, centuries of Ottoman rule had left the Greeks with little expertise with this type of architecture, so the government had to hire two Danish architects, Theophilus Hansen (1813–1891) and his brother Hans Christian (1803–1883), to realize their grand plans.

The Old University

The centerpiece of neoclassical Athens is the city's old university campus on Panepistimiou Street. The three huge public buildings located here—the Academy of Athens, the National and Capodistrian University, and the National Library—are often admiringly described as Athens's "neoclassical trilogy." The university was designed by Hans Christian Hansen, while the Academy and the Library were the work of Theophilus Hansen—although his assistant, the young German architect Ernst Ziller (1837–1923) also played an important role in their design. The Hansen brothers studied the buildings of the Acropolis before they began and even went so far as to incorporate some features, such as the colorful decoration on the pediments and friezes that, although authentic, had long since faded from the Acropolis. All three men would go on to design numerous public and private buildings around the city.

The building that stands in the center of the site, the **National and Capodistrian University,** was the first to be constructed, with building work taking place between 1839 and 1864. By comparison with its neighbors, this earlier building is a simpler, more practical affair. Ionic columns are used only on the entrance porticos, with solid walls or simpler square-section columns used elsewhere. The back wall of the colonnade is decorated with an enormous fresco that depicts ancient Greek scholars and teachers.

Today, the university system has grown so large that departments are housed in various buildings around Athens, with very little activity taking place in the central campus. The 1842 building is now called the "neoclassical university building" and is used mainly for major events such as graduation ceremonies and conferences.

In 1859, the **Academy of Athens,** designed by Theophilus, was built next to the university and served as a center for arts, science, and humanities study in the spirit of Plato's academy. The building consists of a rectangular central structure flanked by two symmetrical wings. The central structure is designed in the style of an Ionic temple, and loosely modeled on the Parthenon. A tall column topped by a statue stands on either side of the entrance. The one on the left is Athena, the ancient goddess of wisdom, while the one on the right is Apollo, god of light. Athena also appears on the pediment, which holds a depiction of her birth from the head of Zeus. The building's two wings are shorter than the central structure but are constructed in the same grand style. The interior of the building houses a large assembly hall, where conferences and meetings of the Academy are held.

The last of the three buildings to be constructed was the **National Library.** This building was also designed by Theophilus but with significant contributions by Ernst Ziller. The main entrance is modelled very closely on the Temple of Hephaistos but with the addition of pair of sweeping curved staircases up to the entrance (a feature you definitely wouldn't have seen on an ancient Greek temple).

INSIDER TIP:

The National Theater of Greece, near Omonoia Square, has a grand neoclassical facade and an even more lavish interior.

—SALLY MCFALL
National Geographic contributor

The two wings that run parallel to the main building hold the bulk of the library's collection, while the large central building houses the reading rooms (open to the public). These reading rooms are lit by a massive central skylight and surrounded by large Ionic columns. Most of the interior columns are decorated with the kind of multicolored paintwork that was common in ancient times.

Botanical Museum

- ✉ Leoforos Vasilissis Amalias, Syntagma
- ☎ (210) 721 5019
- 🕓 Closed Mon.
- 🚇 Syntagma

Temple of Olympian Zeus

- ⓐ 55
- ✉ Leoforos Vasilissis Olgas, Syntagma
- ☎ (210) 922 6330
- 💲 $; free with 4-day Acropolis ticket
- 🚇 Syntagma

Zappeion Gardens

- ⓐ 55
- ✉ Leoforos Vasilissis Olgas, Syntagma
- 🚇 Syntagma

Aigli Cinema

- ✉ Zappeion Gardens
- ☎ (210) 336 9370
- 🕓 Closed mid-Sept.–mid-May
- 🚇 Syntagma

verdant oasis in this densely packed city. The main entrance is located on Leoforos Vasilissis Sofias. It was initially planted in 1839 as a private sanctuary next to the Royal Palace (now Parliament). Greece's first queen, Amalia, commanded the cultivation of more than 15,000 domestic and exotic plants from Genoa, the coastal town of Sounion, and the island of Evia. Some of the original planting survives today.

INSIDER TIP:

Zappeion is a grand place to indulge in the pleasures of Aigli summer cinema. Athenians come here to catch a movie under the stars.

—KATHLEEN CROMWELL
Travel writer and author

The National Gardens are full of winding paths with trellised promenades. There's also a **Botanical Museum,** duck ponds, a playground, a café, a small zoo, and a children's library.

To the south, the lush greenery of the National Gardens gives way to the neatly manicured **Zappeion Gardens,** which surround the **Zappeion** exhibition hall. The Danish architect Theophilus Hansen built the hall in 1881. The entrance recalls an ancient temple, but the rest of the building is contemporary Mediterranean.

The Zappeion was the first headquarters of the 1896 Olympic organizing committee and also hosted journalists during the 2004 Olympics. It's a popular spot for conferences, exhibitions, and other public events. During elections, Greek politicians come here to make victory or concession speeches. The area in front of the building hosts outdoor concerts and events. The **Aigli café** (*Zappeion Gardens, Leoforos Vasilissis Amalias, Syntagma, tel 210/336 9363*), right next to the hall, has long been a popular meeting spot for politicians, power-brokers, and celebrities. There's also an outdoor cinema and a summer-only nightclub.

Hadrianopolis

On the southern side of busy Leoforos Vasilissis Olgas Avenue stands the remains of two major construction projects undertaken by the philhellene Roman Emperor, Hadrian (A.D. 76–138). The centerpiece of this part of the ancient town was the **Temple of Olympian Zeus,** a gigantic temple whose ruins still stand today. The construction of this building began in 515 B.C., but until Hadrian arrived, no ruler could raise the funds needed to finish the colossal structure. When finally completed, the temple was dedicated to Zeus and Hadrian (who, like many Roman emperors, considered himself to be partly divine) and used as the city's main temple until its destruction in a Herulian raid.

Only 16 of the original 104 columns stand today, but it's still a magnificent site surrounded by

Underground Galleries in the Metro

The construction of the Athens Metro spurred the greatest archaeological excavation the city had seen in decades. More than 50,000 artifacts were discovered during the Metro works, which began in 1869. Many of those artifacts are now on display in six Metro stations: Syntagma, Kerameikos, Monastiraki, Akropoli, Evangelismos, and Panepistimio.

Excavations for the first three yielded most of the finds. The Syntagma station features artifacts from the classical, sub-Mycenaean, and Byzantine eras, as well as portions of Roman baths, the Peisistratus Aqueduct, the bed of the Eridanus River, and a fragment of an ancient road. Kerameikos Metro station has artifacts from two burial grounds dating to the beginning of the Peloponnesian War, as well as the western wall of the Kerameikos Cemetery and the remains of ancient ceramic workshops. Monastiraki station has finds dating to the Geometric era and includes marble sculptures, mosaic floors, frescoes, pots, coins, and objects made from metal and bone.

Akropoli Metro station has finds dating to the third millennium B.C., while Evangelismos and Panepistimio stations have artifacts from ancient cemeteries.

---

the huge Peribolos Wall, which is made of squared blocks of Pireas stone. The temple itself is made of Pentelic marble, and it once housed a chryselephantine (or, ivory- and gold-covered) statue of Zeus, as well as a colossal statue of Hadrian. One corner of the temple survives reasonably intact, and another pair of columns still stands on the southern side. Between the pair of columns on the southern side there is a third that lies on the ground where it fell during a storm in 1852.

On the northwestern corner of the temple stands **Hadrian's Arch,** which was built around the same time as the Roman additions to the temple. Although its origins are not clear, it is thought that the arch was constructed by locals to commemorate the generosity of Hadrian, rather than by Hadrian himself. The arch bears two simple but enigmatic inscriptions. On the side that faces the Acropolis, the inscription reads "This is Athens, the ancient city of Theseus," while the other side, facing toward the Temple of Olympian Zeus, reads "This is the city of Hadrian, not Theseus." The arch may have marked the boundary between the Roman settlement of Hadrianopolis and the city of Athens, but no archaeological evidence has been found to prove this.

Museums and Galleries

Past the entrance to the National Gardens, Vasilissis Sofias Avenue passes along the southern edge of the wealthy neighborhood of Kolonaki (see pp. 103, 106–107), where many of Athens's major museums are located.

Walking up from Syntagma, the first of these you will see is the **Benaki Museum,** opposite the National Gardens. This museum is the oldest and largest of the numerous museums and

Hadrian's Arch

- 🅰 55
- ✉ Leoforos Vasilissis Olgas, Syntagma
- Ⓜ Syntagma

Benaki Museum

- 🅰 55
- ✉ Leoforos Vasilissis Sofias, Syntagma
- ☎ (210) 345 3111
- 🕐 Closed Tues.
- 💲 $$
- Ⓜ Syntagma
- www.benaki.gr

Goulandris Museum of Cycladic Art

- 🅰 55
- ✉ Neofytou Douka 4, Leoforos Vasilissis Sofias, Kolonaki
- ☎ (210) 722 8321
- 🕐 Closed Tues.
- 💲 $$
- Ⓜ Evangelismos

www.cycladic.gr

Byzantine Museum

- 🅰 55
- ✉ Vasilissis Sofias 22, Kolonaki
- ☎ (210) 721 1027
- 🕐 Closed Mon.
- 💲 $$
- Ⓜ Syntagma

www.byzantine museum.gr

galleries in Athens founded by Antonis Benakis (1873–1954). Today it houses artifacts related to the history of Greece, including paintings, sculptures, and tokens of everyday Greek craftsmanship from Mycenaean times to the mid-20th century. Other collections, including a treasure trove of Greek photography, Islamic art, and Chinese art, have been relocated to smaller satellite museums dotted around Athens.

If you head about 100 yards (91 m) north up Koumbari Street you will reach the cool shade of **Kolonaki Square** (see pp. 103, 106–107), one of the most exclusive addresses in Athens. Here the rich and famous gather in the outdoor cafés and bars, sipping coffee and reading in the shade of the square's many trees. It's not the cheapest place in Athens to go

for a coffee, but it's a great place for people-watching.

A short distance farther down the road is the **Goulandris Museum of Cycladic Art.** This museum showcases an amazing collection of art and sculpture from the mysterious Cycladic culture (which existed from 3000–2000 B.C.) and ancient Cyprus, as well as a collection of classical Greek and Roman art.

The beautiful, highly stylized figurines made by the Bronze Age Cycladic and Cypriot cultures represent a fascinating and little-understood period of ancient Greek history and culture. With their clean, smooth lines and modern-looking simplicity, they're the perfect antidote for those who feel like they've had enough classical sculptures for one trip.

A little farther along the

Shoppers enjoy a late afternoon coffee in the cafés of Ermou Street.

road, close to the Evangelismos Metro station, is the **Byzantine Museum,** one of the finest ecclesiastical museums in the world. Founded in 1914, the museum moved to this renovated mansion in 1930. It has expanded in recent years, adding a wing for temporary exhibits.

The museum traces the history of ecclesiastical art in Greece from the 4th to the 19th century and has an impressive collection of icons, sculptures, wall paintings, religious art, vestments, and scrolls. Some notable items include an 11th-century marble sarcophagus originally unearthed near Adrianou Street in central Athens, a 12th-century copy of the Gospel of John from a monastery in Serres, and a 17th-century icon depicting the life of the Prophet Ilias.

In a rather strange bit of juxtaposition, the building right next to the Byzantine Museum houses the **War Museum,** where everything from ancient chariots to fighter jets bristle with deadly weaponry.

Ermou Street

If you head west from Syntagma Square, away from the Parliament building, you find yourself on Ermou Street, a leafy shopping district with numerous excellent cafés. At the far end of Ermou Street there is a tiny chapel, the **Church of Panagia Kapnikarea.** It's often overlooked by the crowds, although tired shoppers like to rest just outside it. Kapnikarea was once called the "Church of the Princess," due to a legend

Café Culture

A Greek coffee break can last for hours, hence the packed Athenian cafés at nearly all hours of the day. In the old days, men at old-style cafés called *kafenia* would dissect the day's social problems over an *elliniko* (the grainy coffee that's known as Turkish coffee in most other countries) or a frappe (cold, frothy instant coffee) and perhaps a game of backgammon. These days, the cafés are as sleek as the patrons in sunglasses sipping espressos. In the mornings, however, you witness a different scene: For many Athenians, especially young ones, a large coffee is regarded as an adequate breakfast, so the cafés fill with people stopping off on their way to work.

that the Byzantine Empress Irene founded it between 797 and 802. It's more likely that Kapnikarea got its strange name from the Byzantine hearth-tax collectors *(kapnikarious)* who funded the church in the 11th century. (Kapnikarious assessed residents by how much smoke came out of their chimneys; lots of smoke meant lots of wealth.)

The church is made up of two adjoining chapels, one from the 11th century and the other a 12th-century building of Byzantine brickwork. Like other early Christian churches, it was likely built over an ancient Greek pagan temple. King Otto I, the first king of modern Greece, saved the church from destruction during the city's 19th-century modernization efforts. The church was restored in the 1950s and has both original Byzantine frescoes and modern frescoes by icon and fresco painter, Fotis Kontoglou.

War Museum
- ✉ Rizari 2, Vasilissis Sofias, Kolonaki
- ☎ (210) 724 4464
- 🕐 Closed Mon.
- Ⓜ Evangelismos

www.warmuseum.gr

Church of Panagia Kapnikarea
- ✉ Kapnikareas, Ermou, Monastiraki
- ☎ (210) 322 4462
- 🕐 Closed Sun. p.m. & Mon. p.m.
- Ⓜ Syntagma or Monastiraki

Numismatic Museum

🏛 55

✉ Panepistimio 12, Syntagma

☎ (210) 364 3774

🕐 Closed Mon.

💲 $$

🚇 Syntagma

www.nma.gr

Museum of the City of Athens

🏛 55

✉ Paparigopoulo 5-7, Syntagma

☎ (210) 324 6164

🕐 Closed Tues.

💲 $

🚇 Panepistimio

www.athenscity museum.gr

Toward Omonoia

From the northern side of Syntagma Square, two main roads (Stadiou and Panepistimio Streets) run roughly parallel all the way to Omonoia Square (see p. 92). The grand neoclassical buildings along these streets were once the mansions of wealthy Athenians, but have mostly now been converted into offices, apartments, and cultural institutions. The Panepistimio Metro station is located on the Korai, a small public park that connects the two streets. The area around the station is dominated by the neoclassical buildings of the university campus (see p. 93).

One of the grand mansions on Panepistimio Street now houses the **Numismatic Museum.** While the exhibits are unlikely to excite anyone not already interested in the subject, the museum itself is a fascinating place to visit. Before it was the Numismatic Museum, this building was the home of Heinrich Schliemann (1822–1890), an extremely wealthy philhellene and enthusiastic (if not particularly rigorous) archaeologist, best known for discovering the ruins of Troy. The rooms of the museum reflect Schliemann's lavish—if somewhat eccentric—tastes, while the hoards of gold and silver coins include many artifacts he unearthed on his archaeological expeditions.

Over on Stadiou Street, the **Museum of the City of Athens** traces the development of the city and its society during the first few decades of the modern Greek state. It is housed in king Otto's first Athenian residence,

---

EXPERIENCE: See the Changing of the Guard

Two honor guards watch over the Memorial of the Unknown Soldier, which features a modern relief showing a dying Greek that's based on a sculpture, thought to date from the fifth-century B.C., found on the island of Egina. The monument also has an inscription with an extract from Pericles's funeral oration memorializing the dead during the first year of the Peloponnesian War.

The honor guard, known as *evzones*, perform a changing-of-the-guard ritual at the tomb every hour. Two evzones march in step from behind parliament to the tomb, where they relieve the evzones on sentry duty. The evzones are dressed traditionally in short white *foustanellas* (a garment similar to a Scottish kilt) with 400 pleats that memorialize each year of the Ottoman occupation; white stockings; and red shoes with black pompoms. And though this outfit may sound ridiculous, it actually looks quite dignified on the men who wear it. The military handpicks a select group of young, tall, muscular, and disciplined men to be evzones. The honor guard is not allowed to talk to anyone while on sentry duty, especially the thousands of tourists who try to distract them with photographs, catcalls, or suggestive winks.

Every Sunday, scores of evzones do a special changing of the guard ceremony that also features a full military band. The evzones and musicians usually arrive in front of the Monument of the Unknown Soldier around 11:15 a.m. It's a popular event for tourists in the summer, so expect a big crowd.

Visit www.athensinfoguide.com/ wtsevzones.htm for more information.

Facade of the Grande Bretagne Hotel, one of the landmarks of Syntagma Square

where he and his wife lived while the royal palace was constructed. In addition to a large collection of 19th-century paintings and sculptures, several rooms have been restored to how they would have looked when the building was first inhabited, complete with period furnishings and items of interest.

The **Historical Museum of Greece** is nearby, in the building that housed the Greek parliament from 1875 to 1935. Especially notable are artifacts pertaining to the 1821 revolution against the Ottomans. There's a range of artifacts from the period, including the personal belongings of Lord Byron (who fought for the Greeks in the war) and the embalmed heart of war hero and Greek prime minister Konstantinos Kanaris.

Of the area's many neoclassical mansions, none was grander than the home of Antonis Dimitrios, which stood on the corner where Panepistimio Street joins the square. While many of its neighbors were converted into offices or museums, this building maintained its decadent air when it was converted into Athens's most luxurious hotel, the **Grande Bretagne** *(Plateia Syntagmos, Syntagma, tel 210/333 000, $$$$$, www .grandebretagne.gr).* This opulent hideaway has hosted world leaders, movie stars, and the international jet-set. Its long and varied history includes serving as the offices of the 1896 Olympics, a school, and a stint as a military headquarters during the Second World War (first British, later German). ■

Historical Museum of Greece

🅰 55

✉ Stadiou 13, Plateia Kolokotrani, Syntagma

☎ (210) 322 6370

🕐 Closed Mon.

💲 $; free on Sun.

🚇 Syntagma

Around Omonoia

In the 19th century, the area around Omonoia Square was the cultural and social heart of Athens. Over the years the character of the neighborhood has changed considerably. It is now primarily a low-income residential area inhabited by students and immigrant groups, but many of Athens's great cultural institutions remain in the area, even if they now seem a little out of place.

A bread-rings vendor in busy Omonoia Square

Omonoia Square
 55

Omonoia

Omonoia Square was once the centerpiece of Athens—a verdant public space surrounded by cafés and high-class hotels. Today, however, the square is still reeling from its long battle with Athenian traffic. It has been remodeled dozens of times over the years, usually in an attempt to solve the traffic problem. The current incarnation of the square—essentially a flat expanse of bare concrete—is almost universally loathed by Athenians, who want to see the return of the trees and fountains that previously graced it.

During the day, the area around Omonoia is a vibrant and busy commercial district: the square is filled with shoppers heading south to the city's central food market (see p. 96), tourists making their way up to the National Archaeological Museum, and teenagers skulking off to the music stores, cafés, and guitar shops in Exarcheia. By night, however, the area can be quite threatening. It has a significant drug problem, a large homeless population, and in Exarcheia and around the Polytechnio, an almost nonexistent police presence.

The Polytechnio

One landmark near Omonoia is the **National Technical University of Athens**—known locally as the Polytechnio—which marks the beginning of the Exarcheia neighborhood. Two worn neoclassical buildings house the university, which trains Greece's finest engineers. The Polytechnio was designed by the 19th-century Greek architect Lysandros Kaftandzoglou (1812–1885).

But its symbolism goes far beyond science and neoclassical architecture. For decades, it's been the capital's hotbed of leftist political activism. The "Polytechnio Leftists" rose to prominence between 1967 and 1974, when Greece was run by a military dictatorship. These students harshly criticized the junta and demanded freedom for the country. They planned strategy meetings to overthrow the government and broadcast calls for revolution on a secret radio station. Today, Polytechnio looks like a typically unkempt Athenian building; the only memorial to November 17th, 1973, when 24 were killed (see sidebar this page), is Memos Makris's sculpture "Head in Honor of the Dead."

Another consequence of the uprising is the law that prevents the police from entering the grounds of any educational institution without a warrant. This provides a safeguard against government oppression but also makes the area around the campus into something of a legal gray area that some argue encourages criminal activity.

National Technical University of Athens (Polytechnio)

⬛ 55

✉ 28 Oktovriou (Patision) 44, Exarcheia

☎ (201) 772 2017

Ⓜ Viktoria

www.ntua.gr

Rebellious Exarcheia

In the 1960s, the Exarcheia neighborhood of artists, anarchists, and left-leaning intellectuals produced a wave of activists that heavily influenced Greek society. When military dictators took over Greece in 1967, the activists bonded with students at the Polytechnio. In November 1973, they staged a historic sit-in against the junta on the university's grounds. Led by the famed Cretan singer, lyra player, and activist Nikos Xylouris, they sang an old Cretan rebel song called "When Will the Sky Be Clear Again." But troops rolled into the university on November 17, killed at least 24 people, and wounded hundreds more. The following year, the despised junta fell.

The neighborhood is still spirited, rebellious, and artistic, though it has struggled in recent years with an increasing number of heroin addicts and street fights between police and angry, amped-up teenagers. Police have increased their presence in Exarcheia since the December 2008 riots, sparked after a police officer shot a teenager there.

As of this writing, neighborhood residents had banded together to kick out drug dealers and create creative, communal spaces in the area. At the lively, café-lined main square, anarchists host outdoor movie screenings, talks, and concerts. At nearby Parko Navarinou, a former parking lot–turned–urban park, summer nights mean DJs playing a mix of rebel songs by Xylouris and carnal love songs by Algerian singer-songwriter Cheika Rimitti. Street artists show their latest works while people debate the collectivist anarchist philosophy of Mikhail Bakunin nearby. In Athens, there's no neighborhood quite like it.

National Archaeological Museum

National Archaeological Museum

🅰 55

✉ 28 Oktovriou (Patission) 44, Exarcheia

☎ (210) 821 7724

💲 $$

🚇 Omonoia

www.namuseum.gr

Pottery

Minor Objects

Prehistoric collection

Egyptian collection

Bronze collection

Temporary exhibitions

Sculpture

National Archaeological Museum

This museum, which is consistently rated as one of the best in the world, is Omonoia's main draw. It is located about a 10 minutes' walk northeast of Omonoia Square, next to the Polytechnio campus on Patission Street. To reach the museum from Omonoia Square, head west out of the square (toward the old university campus), and then turn left onto Patission Street and head north. The southern section of Patission Street was renamed Eikostis Ogdois Oktovriou (October 28th Street) in the 1990s, but some Athenians still use the old name.

The museum was founded in 1866 and is a protected monument in itself. Its broad neoclassical facade is the work of Ernst Ziller (see p. 85), who worked in Athens for many years as Theophilus Hansen's assistant, playing a key role in the design of the National Library. The museum has been expanded and renovated many times over the years. In peak season the museum is always bustling with visitors, sometimes

Room 38: The Antikythera Mechanism, thought to be a kind of simple mechanical computer.

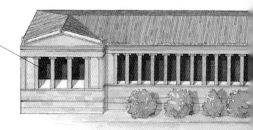

The Museum's grand neoclassical facade was designed by the German architect Ernst Ziller.

National Archaeological Museum

Room 21: The famous "Jockey Boy" statue, a life-size statue of a boy riding a galloping horse.

Room 48: Minoan frescoes recovered from the ancient settlement of Akrotiri on the island of Santorini.

Room 28: The Antikythera Ephebe, recovered from the sea in 1900.

Room 4: The "Mask of Agamemnon" and other artifacts from Heinrich Schliemann's excavations of Mycenae.

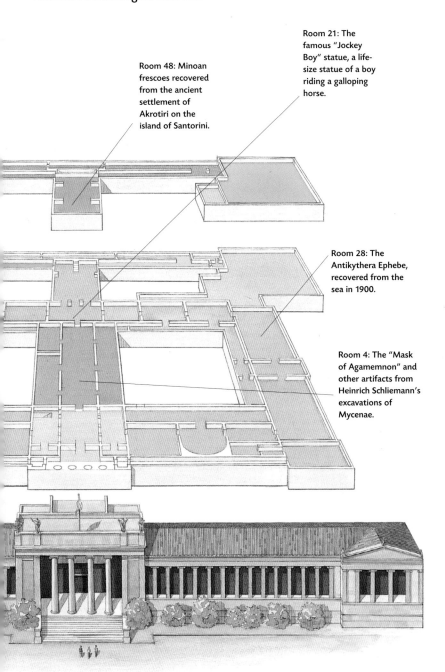

EXPERIENCE: Exploring Athinas Street's Markets

About a 10 minutes' walk south from Omonoia Square stands the vast 19th-century Central Market complex. This large covered market sells just about every kind of food imaginable, from freshly slaughtered pigs hanging on hooks to heaps of shellfish in ice-filled tubs. In the streets around the covered market there is a lively and informal network of street markets and outdoor stalls that stretch south close to Athinas Street all the way to Monastiraki.

The Central Market isn't all about fruits and vegetables.

Built in 1870 in the heart of Athens, the Central Market (or the Varvakios Market, as it's known by locals) is still where Athenian gourmands, food-savvy grandmothers, and downtown residents shop for the freshest meat, fish, and produce in the city. Though the stacks of fragrant fruits and vegetables are alluring, the market's heart is its phantasmagoric spreads of meat and fish. But beware if you are a member of the sheltered supermarket set because the imagery is not for the squeamish: Imagine hulks of lamb carcasses, just-plucked chickens, pig feet, and goat heads, all advertised by rough-talking butchers in blood-spattered smocks. In the seafood aisles, the stands offer a bouillabaisse of fish: Think octopus, deep-sea squid, shark, red snapper, tuna, and shellfish, for starters. The market opens at 3 a.m. for shoppers and strollers. It's also a popular after-party stop for clubbers who believe a bowl of tripe soup (patsas; see pp. 22–23) is the ultimate hangover cure.

Near Central Market, the scents of cinnamon, cardamom, oregano, chilies, and clove waft through Evripidou Street. This spice-laden stretch runs from Athinas to Aristofanous streets. Many doorways are decorated with braids of dried chilies and mushrooms and some of the mom-and-pop stores like **Elixirion** (at Evripidou 41) have been here for generations. The street is not a dainty European corridor but rather a gritty, raucous, and warm tribute to an Eastern market. Chinese immigrants have also opened food and clothing shops here in recent years.

making it hard to fully appreciate the exhibits. The best times to go are early in the morning and late in the evening. For those with a strong interest in ancient Greece, it is worth making several visits on different days rather than trying to see everything all at once.

Visitors pass through the museum's attractive formal gardens before going up the steps to the main entrance hall. Inside, the sheer scale of the museum's collection can be a little daunting. It is far too large to seen in one day—the museum has more than three square miles of exhibition space. Although every room contains some priceless treasure or beautiful work of ancient art, you will have to be very selective about what you go and see.

Main Collections: The museum's main collection is sorted into the following groups: prehistoric antiquities, sculpture, metalwork, vases and minor arts, and the Egyptian and Near-Eastern antiquities collection. In addition to these sections there are galleries devoted to specific types of artifacts, such as funerary stelae (grave markers), votive reliefs, and Hellenistic statues.

Although almost any exhibit here would be a prize possession in any other museum collection, there are a few clear highlights. The best known are probably the Mycenaean finds of the 19th-century archaeologist Heinrich Schliemann. These include lavish grave goods and solid gold death masks taken from the tombs of Mycenaean kings. Schliemann

asserted that one of these masks, depicting an elderly man with a thin mustache, was the mythical king Agamemnon. While this is almost certainly incorrect, the finds are still fascinating.

Antikythera Wreck: A less well known, but arguably more important set of exhibits are the artifacts recovered from the wreck of an ancient Greek ship near the small island of Antikythera, off the coast of Crete. These include the perfectly preserved **Antikythera Ephebe,** a bronze statue of a young man, and numerous other pieces of sculpture. The most significant exhibit, however, is the so-called **Antikythera Mechanism.** This enigmatic object—a metal plate covered in gears—is thought to be the remains of a complex mechanical computer. It is displayed next to a modern reconstruction, showing how it would have originally been used to calculate the the movements of the moon, planets, and other heavenly bodies. ■

Epigraphical Museum

The world's largest collection of Greek inscriptions is housed in the Epigraphical Museum (Tositsa 1, Exarcheia, tel 210/823 2950 or 210/821 7637, closed Mon., $), next to the National Archaeological Museum. The galleries feature stone inscriptions featuring some of the earliest Greek writing. Examples include public war memorials to Athenians killed in battle, ancient assembly minutes and decrees, and the Athenian Tribute Lists, which list a year-by-year account of the cities that paid taxes to Athens.

Modern boutiques, concert venues, a buzzing nightlife, and beach clubs—all part of 21st-century Athens

Modern Athens & the Suburbs

Lykavittos Hill looms over the new city.

Modern Athens & the Suburbs

The city's soul may well be defined by the legacy of the great civilizations of the ancient past, but Athens's beating heart is one of culture, commerce, and innovation. Around four million Greeks call Athens home, and they have pulled it very much into the 21st century. From trend-setting fashion designers to state-of-the-art sports stadia, Athens is very much a modern city.

A shaded shopping avenue in upscale Kifissia

Those who visited Athens two centuries ago saw a gloomy, worn-out town that had been devastated by years of war and occupation. The ancient city was in ruins, buildings were cracked and roofless, and churches were falling apart. Only about 6,000 people lived there.

After the modern Greek state was founded in 1830, the romantic appeal of the city's glorious ancient past helped establish Athens as the capital. It soon became a bustling center of commerce, industry, education, and government. Rural Greeks left the countryside, where job prospects were poor, and moved to the big city for work. Refugees from Asia Minor also resettled here and, more recently, so have immigrants from Eastern Europe and Africa. Today, around half of Greece's population live in Athens.

As a result, the central neighborhoods like Kolonaki have grown more densely populated, and farmland and scrubby forest around the city have sprouted suburbs in all directions. The greater Athens metropolitan area now consists of more than 73 crowded municipalities. The Athens suburbs are generally divided into the northern suburbs, which include Maroussi, Kifissia, Halandri, Psychiko, and Agia Paraskevi; the southern suburbs, including Palaio Faliro, Elliniko, Glyfada, Alimos, and Voula; the eastern suburbs of Zografou, Kaisariani, and Holargos; and Peristeri, Egaleo, Chaidari, and Pireas to the west. ■

NOT TO BE MISSED:

A hike or teleferik to the top of Lykavittos Hill 104–105

A concert at Megaron Mousikis, the Athens Concert hall 110

The Goulandris Natural History Museum's rich flora and fauna 110

Enjoying a fresh fish lunch at Mikrolimano harbor 119

Taking a relaxing soak in Limni Vouliagmeni on the Athens Riviera 121

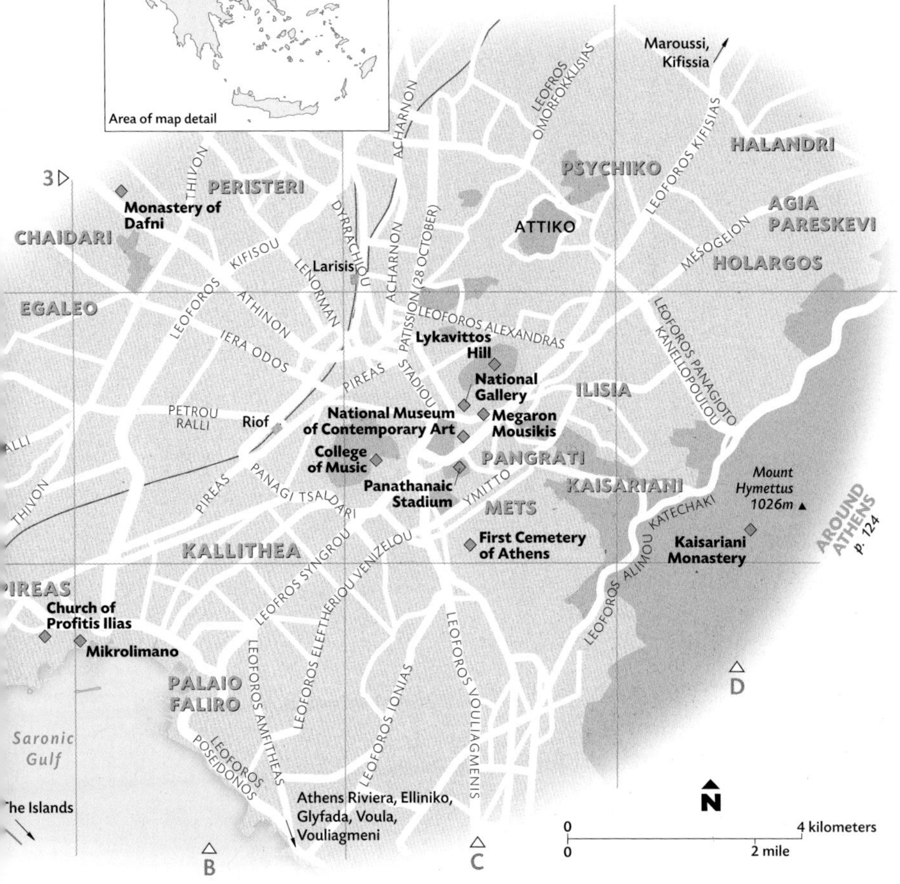

Area of map detail

3 ▷

Maroussi, Kifissia

HALANDRI

PSYCHIKO

AGIA PARESKEVI

ATTIKO

HOLARGOS

PERISTERI

Monastery of Dafni

CHAIDARI

Larisis

EGALEO

Lykavittos Hill

National Gallery

ILISIA

National Museum of Contemporary Art

Megaron Mousikis

PETROU RALLI

Riof

College of Music

PANGRATI

Panathanaic Stadium

KAISARIANI

Mount Hymettus 1026m ▲

METS

KALLITHEA

First Cemetery of Athens

Kaisariani Monastery

AROUND ATHENS p. 124

PIREAS

Church of Profitis Ilias

Mikrolimano

PALAIO FALIRO

Saronic Gulf

The Islands

Athens Riviera, Elliniko, Glyfada, Voula, Vouliagmeni

△ D

N

| 0 | | | | 4 kilometers |
| 0 | | 2 mile | | |

△ B

△ C

The Inner Suburbs

Stretching from the slopes of Lykavittos Hill to the lower reaches of Mount Hymettus, Athens's inner suburbs comprise a series of exclusive neighborhoods where haute couture and fine dining flourish. They are also home to cultural centers including the Megaron Mousikis concert hall, the National Gallery, and the National Museum of Contemporary Art.

Kolonaki is full of trendy boutiques.

Mets

To the east of the National Gardens (see pp. 83, 86), is the neighborhood of Mets. Mets is named for Athens's first *beeraria,* or beer-house, which itself was named by its German owner for Metz, the location of a decisive battle in the Franco-Prussian War. The neighborhood is known for its low-key, elegant restaurants and bars and well-preserved neoclassical architecture.

The **First Cemetery of Athens** is located in the south of Mets. Greece's most prominent leaders are buried here, including the War of Independence general Theodoros Kolokotronis (1770–1843), statesman and historian Charilaos Trikoupis (1833–1896), the actress and political activist Melina Mercouri (1920–1994), and the mercurial socialist prime minister and economist Andreas Papandreou (1919–1996). Notable foreigners are also buried here, including the German archaeologist Heinrich Schliemann (1822–1890), who discovered the city of Troy. He is interred in an unusual mausoleum that is shaped like a miniature Doric temple and decorated with friezes depicting him at work.

In the east of Mets, near the neighboring district of Pangrati, the impressive Roman stadium, now refurbished as the **Panathanaic Stadium** (or Kallimarmaro, which means "beautiful marble"), still stands in the natural valley between two low, forested hills. The architect Anastasios Metaxas restored the ancient stadium between 1870 and 1895, with funding coming from two noted Greek philanthropists. The first stages of restoration were funded by Evangelis Zappas and the last phase by George Averof, whose statue stands in the square near the stadium.

Kolonaki

Located on the southwestern slopes of **Lykavittos Hill** (see pp. 104–105, 107), the central Athens neighborhood of Kolonaki is one of the most exclusive locales in the capital city. It's the home of politicians, actors, and literary stars, as well as haute couture (some Athenians call it the Rodeo Drive or Fifth Avenue of their city) and fine jewelry on **Voukourestiou Street.** Kolonaki also has some of the top restaurants and cafés, including the well-known **Da Capo** (*Tsakalof 1, Kolonaki Square, tel 210/362 497, closed Sun.*), which specializes in excellent Italian espressos and local celebrity sightings.

The neighborhood is centered on Kolonaki Square, a quiet little plaza lined with cafés and restaurants. In the middle of the square there is a small ancient column—the *kolonaki* ("little column") for which the area is named. Kolonaki Square is also known as Filikis Etairias Square for a secret rebel group established in 1814 by three Greek businessmen (continued on p. 106)

Mets
- 101 C2

First Cemetery of Athens
- 101 C2
- Anapafseos Street, Mets
- Agios Ioannis

Panathanaic Stadium
- 101 C2
- Anapafseos
- Syntagma

Kolonaki
- 101 C2

Greek Fashion

The flowing robes and simple designs of ancient Greek fashion have inspired international designers for decades. A few modern Greek designers have also made a name for themselves internationally.

One of the brightest stars is Sophia Kokosalaki, a Greek-born designer now based in London. Kokosalaki's designs feature ancient Greek draping with modern twists. Another rising Greek star is Ioannis Guia, who is based in Paris. His designs borrow from ancient tradition but are also edgy and sleek.

There are also notable Greek designers at home. **Loukia** (*Kanari St. 24, tel 210/362 7334*), based in the Kolonaki neighborhood, specializes in embroidered lace shirts, wedding dresses and flowing skirts. Another Kolonaki-based designer is Orsalia Parthenis, who favors chic evening dresses, linen shifts and drawstring trousers. Finally, Dimitris Alexakis and Grigoris Triantafyllou of **Deux Hommes** (*Kanari St. 18, 210/361 4155, www.deuxhommes.gr*) in Kolonaki design sleek coats, elaborate evening dresses, and tailored trousers in fine fabrics.

In 2005, Greece also started a fashion week, called Athens Collections, to showcase Greek designers. Every March and October, journalists and buyers from around the world gather in Athens to seek out the latest in Greek fashion. It's a way to spread the word on an art form that has its roots in the ancient past but is adapting to modern tastes.

A Walk up Lykavittos Hill

The climb to the top of Lykavittos Hill offers sweeping views over the city of Athens and beyond to Pireas and the Saronic Gulf. The nighttime view from the summit is unparalleled. It's probably best not to attempt this walk, which is very steep in places, in the heat of the afternoon.

View from the Lykavittos Hill over the Orizontes restaurant to nighttime Athens

Leave **Evangelismos Metro station** ❶ by the northern entrance and walk west (toward the brown War Museum building), then take the first right onto Marasli Street. Follow this road as it works its way up the lower slopes of Lykavittos Hill. After about 350 yards (320 m), the road becomes so steep that it is replaced by a stone staircase.

By the time you've walked up to the junction with **Aristippou Street** ❷, it's worth asking yourself whether you really feel like climbing another few hundred feet up steps and steep paths. If you don't (and on a hot summer's day that's the wise choice), then turn left down Aristippou Street and walk the hundred yards or so (91 m) to the **funicular railway** ❸, known as the *teleferik*, which runs every 30 minutes from 9 a.m. to 3 a.m. Those who are feeling fit and adventurous, however, should continue past this point and up the steps into the **park** ❹.

NOT TO BE MISSED:

The view from the summit at dawn or dusk • Taking a well-earned break at Orizontes • Watching a play at the Lykavittos Theater

Once you're on the wooded slopes of Lykavittos, it doesn't really matter what route you take: As long as you're heading upward you'll get there eventually. Following the tended gravel paths is the quickest route, however, and takes you up to the **service road** ❺ that leads to the summit. If you follow this road to the end, it will take you to the top of the hill and its stunning view.

The Summit

The summit of Lykavittos is dominated by

the pure white church of **Agios Georgios** ❻, which looks like it has been brought here from an island in the Cyclades. It's rarely open but very photogenic. On clear mornings, you can see all the way to the port of Pireas and the Saronic Gulf. In the evenings, the hill is a coveted spot to view the Athenian sunset, and at night it becomes a magnet for young lovers who want to smooch under the moonlight.

Aside from the panoramic views, Lykavittos also has a pricey but consistently good restaurant, **Orizontes** (*Lykavittos Hill, tel 210/722 7065, $$$*), which features haute cuisine dishes like oven-baked prawns with green lemon zest and ginger confit. There are also a couple of cafés, where you can sip expensive coffee while taking in the view.

The Descent

The best route back down the hill is to walk down the **zig-zag path** ❼ on the side of the hill that faces the Acropolis. This path provides some of the most amazing views of Athens, especially during sunset, but be careful not to get too absorbed by the view—the descent is very steep!

After crossing the end of the **access road** ❽, take the gravel path that heads off downhill to your right. When the path zig-zags, head south (with the Acropolis to your right) and go down to the end of **Loukianou Street** ❾. From here you can walk straight back down to Vasilissis Sofias Avenue and turn left back to the Evangelismos Metro station.

This is just one of many routes you can take to the summit of the hill. Another good option is to start from **Ambelokipi station** and enter the park from the northeast. This route is a rather gentler climb and also takes you past the modern **Lykavittos Theater,** where Greek plays are staged on summer evenings.

🅜 See area map p. 101
▶ Evangelismos Metro station
🕐 2.5 hours
↔ 1.25 miles (2 km)
▶ Evangelismos Metro station

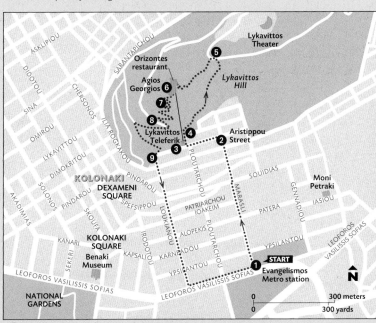

Agios Georgios: well worth the climb to the top of Lykavittos Hill

Moni Petraki

- ✉ Monis Petraki 17
- ☎ (210) 721 2402
- ⏰ Closed p.m.
- 🚇 Megaro Moussikis

www.monipetraki .gr

who hoped to start a revolution to free Greece from the Ottoman Empire. The square is a popular hangout for expatriates from the nearby **British School at Athens** and the **American School of Classical Studies.**

The British School opened in 1886 as a research center, hostel, library, and archaeological lab for British scholars. It conducts major excavations at Knossos (see pp. 188–189) and Mycenae (see p. 131). The American School, which opened in 1881, serves American scholars and has major excavations at Corinth (see p. 131) and the ancient Agora (see pp. 70–71). Both schools have beautiful private gardens. Not far from the schools is **Moni Petraki,** a 17th-century monastery that's now a seminary. The frescoes inside are by Georgios Markos of Argos, a prolific fresco painter who

worked in Attica during the first half of the 18th century.

Leafy and quiet **Dexameni Square** is the other main square in Kolonaki. It's located just above the neighborhood's main square on the walk up to Lykavittos Hill. Nobel Laureate Odysseas Elytis lived here, and a statue of the poet graces the square. There's also a café and open-air cinema nearby.

The square's name comes from the reservoir beneath it, which dates to Roman times. The philhellene Roman emperor Hadrian (see p. 32) began the project in A.D. 25. The reservoir held water brought in by aqueduct from the foothills of Mount Parnitha. It was reconstructed in 1849, then updated in 1869 and 1929, along with the aqueduct. Its water is used in the Blessing of the Waters ceremony during

Epiphany, celebrated by Ortho-dox Christians on January 6 (see sidebar p. 118).

Lykavittos Hill

Lykavittos is the tallest hill in Athens, at 968 feet (295 m) above sea level. It is named for the wolves that roamed here in ancient times (*lykos* means wolf in Greek). The wolves are now long gone, however, and today the hill is much visited (see pp. 104–105). Lykavittos is crowned by **Agios Georgios** (Chapel of St. George) a pure white church that looks like it has been transported from an island in the Cyclades. The church is rarely open, but its exterior is worth a photograph. There are a few informal cafés at the top, and the observation area offers some of the finest views in Athens.

Ilisia

To the southeast of Lykavittos Hill, the 19th-century houses of Kolonaki give way to the modern buildings of Ilisia. The neighborhood takes its name from the Ilissos River, which once ran down from Mount Hymettus and through the area now occupied by Ilisia, Pangrati, and Mets. Today, the river is buried beneath the streets of Athens, and only a small section of it is still visible south of the Temple of Olympian Zeus (see pp. 86–87).

Ilisia is characterized by its modern architecture, large hotels, and impressive public buildings. Coming from central Athens its most recognizable landmark is the tall white tower of the **Athens Hilton** *(see Travelwise, p. 243)* one of the largest hotels in Athens.

The neighborhood's main attraction, however, is the **National Gallery & Alexander Soutzos Museum**—Greece's most prestigious art gallery. The museum owes its existence (and its long name) to Alexandros Soutzos, a lawyer and philanthro-pist who bequeathed his estate and vast art collection to the Greek state in 1896. He hoped that the endowment would one

INSIDER TIP:

Lykavittos, or Wolves Hill, affords spectacu-lar views thanks to the goddess Athena, who unexpectedly dropped an enormous rock that forever remains the city's highest point.

—KATHLEEN CROMWELL
Travel writer and author

day finance an art museum. The original National Gallery, estab-lished in 1900, was consolidated with the Soutzos legacy in 1954, but the new Ethniki Pinakothiki, or National Gallery, didn't open until 1976.

The National Gallery contains a wide collection of art from the 14th to 20th centuries. Greek artists in the collection include El Greco, the Crete-born Domenikos Theotokopoulos (1541–1614)

(continued on p. 110)

Lykavittos Hill
🄰 101 C2

Ilisia
🄰 101 C2, D2

National Gallery & Alexander Soutzos Museum
🄰 101 C2
✉ Leoforos Vasileos Konstantinou 50
☎ (210) 723 5937
💲 $$$
🚇 Evangelismos
www.culture.gr

Rembetika: Songs of Love, Joy, & Sorrow

For many Athenians, the lilting, mournful tones of *rembetika* are an essential part of everyday life. You'll hear these songs playing in bars and on radios, and if you go to the right places, you'll get to experience it performed live.

Rembetika star Giannis Lempesis (center) and his band perform at Karabani.

The famous Greek composer Manos Hadjidakis (1925–1994) distilled the essence of rembetika, songs that sound like a kind of Near Eastern blues, to three words: *meraki, kefi,* and *kaimos,* or "love, joy, and sorrow." Sung in a quiet, hoarse and often mournful voice and backed by the long-necked lute called the bouzouki, the musical style of rembetika is rooted in traditional Ottoman music fused with Byzantine chants and the traditional songs of rural Greece and the islands. The lyrics are often dark and gritty, reflecting the lives of people who have lived on society's margins. Like traditional blues in the U.S., the lyrical themes are

not for the fainthearted, with songs that touch on crime, drugs, death, sex, disease, poverty, and prostitution. The so-called *hasiklidika* (hashish songs) are among the most notorious rembetika.

The first rembetika were recorded in the 1920s using Ottoman instruments such as the oud, santouri, vioncello, tsimbalo, and konaki. This strand of rembetika came from the Greeks of Asia Minor and was known as Smyrnaika. The songs were often called *amanadhes,* which derived their name from the improvised lament of *"aman, aman,"* a common expression of grief in Ottoman times. The songs were inspired by the everyday hardships and homesickness of a community that had been uprooted from its homeland and now found itself in a crowded city and culture with whom it had few cultural links.

In Pireas in the 1930s, rembetika singer-songwriters added the bouzouki as the primary instrument, thus splitting rembetika into the Smyrnaika and Pireas styles. Elias Petropoulos, an urban anthropologist and iconoclast scholar who did extensive research on rembetika, wrote that the song form really developed in jails and hash dens in working-class cities such as Pireas, where subversive lyrics and marginalized themes found voice in artistic prisoners. (Baglamas, lutes which are essentially smaller versions of the bouzouki, were more portable instruments, originally designed for use by prisoners.)

An early giant in rembetika songwriting was Vassilis Tsitsanis (1915–1984), who was also among the finest bouzouki players of his time. Tsitsanis, who was born in the central Greek city of Trikala, penned more than 500 rembetika songs. One singer who took to those songs was Sotiria Bellou (1921–1997), who had been singing and picking at homemade guitars in her village near Halkida, on the island of Evia, since she was three years old. She became one of the most prominent female singers of rembetika and enjoyed a resurgence in popularity later in life, when younger generations of Greeks rediscovered rembetika.

Government Censorship

In 1936, after King George II appointed conservative General Ioannis Metaxas as prime minister of Greece, the government considered rembetika of low repute and decided to ban the songs. State-run radio stations refused to play rembetika because of the references to crime, drugs, sex, violence, or marginalization—in other words, most of the genre's repertoire. Because Metaxas was also trying to make Greek music sound less Turkish and more European, some radio stations also banned amanadhes, whose laments of "*aman, aman*" recalled the strong

cultural influence that Ottoman traditions still had on many Greeks.

Popular singers such as Stelios Kazantzidis (1931–2001), who specialized in the early pop songs called *laika*, did some of their best recordings using rembetika songs. Kazantzidis teamed up with the composer Tsitanis and recorded hits such as "Synefiasmeni Kyriaki" (Overcast Sunday). By 1960, rembetika was enjoying a full-blown resurgence, thanks also to interest by the composers Hadjidakis and Mikis Theodorakis.

Rembetika Today

Rembetika still has a devoted following today, though many young Greeks listen to Greek and foreign pop music. You can catch live shows at reliable venues like **Karabani** *(Zakynthou 1, Kypseli, tel 210/825 1896, evening performances Fri.–Sat.)* in Kypseli, **Aptaliko** *(Ironda Street 6, tel 210/724 5385, evening performances Thurs.–Sat; afternoon performance Sun.)* in Pangrati, and **Magiopoula** *(Odemisiou Street 9, tel 210/721 4934, evening performances Thurs. & Sat; afternoon performance Sun.)* in nearby Kaisariani. The best venue, however, is the lovely family-run café **Kapnikarea** *(Hristopoulou Street 2, Plaka, tel 210/322 7394)* that holds small, live rembetika nights. It has only about 20 tables, so it's never a big crowd, but the music is infectious and everyone sings along. The songs may be about loss and pain and living on the edge, but the vibe is always joyful.

Megaron Mousikis

🅼 101 C2

✉ Leoforos Vasilissis Sofias, Ambelokipi

☎ (210) 728 2333

Ⓜ Megaro Mousikis

www.megaron.gr

Pangrati

🅼 101 C2, D2

National Museum of Contemporary Art (EMST)

🅼 101 C2

✉ Vasilissis Georgiou B 17–19, Pangrati

☎ (210) 924 2111

🕐 Closed Mon.

💲 $$

Ⓜ Megaro Mousikis

www.emst.gr

who made his name in Spain with his dramatic paintings, as well as the 19th-century painters Nikiforos Litras (1832–1904) and Nikolaos Ghizis (1842–1901). Foreign artists include Auguste Rodin, Rembrandt, Pablo Picasso, and Eugene Delacroix—including his notable "Greek Warrior" (1856).

What the National Gallery is to visual arts in Athens, the nearby **Megaron Mousikis,** or Athens Concert Hall, is to music. The first two halls—the Christos Lambrakis Hall, where concerts and recitals are performed, and the Dimitris Mitropoulos Hall, which features chamber music performances—opened in 1991. The Christos Lambrakis Hall has the largest pipe organ in Greece. Two more spaces, the Alexandra Trianti Hall (for operas and ballets) and Nikos Skalkoltas Hall, were added later.

The Megaron Mousikis features performances by big-name international artists as well as local Greek stars of opera, ballet, classical, and popular music. It also features lectures by intellectual and literary luminaries in Greece and beyond, and has a beautiful garden that offers a bit of natural respite from the concretized capital city.

Pangrati

Pangrati lies along Vasileos Konstantinou Road, just beyond the stadium, and is centered on the cafés and restaurants of **Plastira Square.** Nearby **Varnava Square** also has one of the most notable restaurants in Athens, **Spondi** (*Pyrronos 5, Plateia Varnava, Pangrati, tel 210/756 4021),* which serves French cuisine and has two Michelin stars. The neighborhood gets its name from the *pankration,* a type of martial art that dates to the ancient Olympic Games in 648 B.C. and combined boxing and wrestling.

Another famous site is the **statue of U.S. president Harry Truman,** whose Truman doctrine promised military and economic support for Greece and Turkey to prevent Soviet influence. The 6.5-foot (2 m) bronze statue of Truman has been toppled by anti-American demonstrators several times since 1963, when it was erected.

Pangrati is also the home of the **National Museum of Contemporary Art (EMST),** an exciting and innovative art gallery that has an extensive collection of

---

Natural History Museum

When Angelos and Niki Goulandris opened the **Goulandris Natural History Museum** (*Levidou Street 13, Kifissia, tel 210/801 5870, www.gnhm.gr, $$*) in 1964, they were already devoted environmentalists who wanted to catalogue Greece's rich collection of flora and fauna and its layers of geophysical history. Angelos Goulandris, who hailed from a successful shipping family from the island of Andros, hoped the museum would help Greeks understand their country's ecological and geological history. His wife, Niki, who later became known for her vivid and detailed botanical paintings, joined him in his quest. Angelos served as president of the museum until his death in 1996; Niki Goulandris now runs it. It's located in a stately old mansion off Levidou Street in upscale Kifissia (see p. 114).

visual art by contemporary Greek and international artists. It also hosts exhibitions of new painting, photography, video, and industrial design. Since its founding in 2000, the museum was housed in several different buildings, before moving to its current site in 2003. It is hoped that the museum will move to its permanent home, the former **Fix Brewery** *(Syngrou Avenue 106)*, when the renovation is completed in late 2011.

land smelled of thyme, gorse, and wild mint," he wrote in *The Miracle of Kaisariani.* "A crowd of people, a bunch of women, many men and a swarm of children, some standing, others seated, some ill of different sicknesses, misshapen and crippled, were there, praying."

After 1922, the wild, craggy space became a refugee camp for thousands of Greeks forced out of Asia Minor. The shoddily built

Kaisariani
101 D2

Mount Hymettus
101 D2

The olive tree–shaded facade of Megaron Mousikis

Kaisariani & Mount Hymettus

The eastern Athens suburb of Kaisariani was once a rocky, coarse outpost that, in the 1920s census, counted only a Macedonian warlord named Exarchos as its sole permanent resident. In a 1901 short story, the Greek writer Alexandros Papadiamantis remembered the area for its healing springs, which had been praised since ancient times. "The

houses, poor infrastructure, and lack of safe drinking water strained the settlement for years. Many refugees who relocated to Kaisariani defended Greece during World War II and several paid with their lives. The Nazis used a notorious rifle range in Kaisariani to execute Greeks who resisted them. On May 1, 1944, the Nazis murdered 200 Greek political activists as revenge for the killing of a German general in southern Greece.

Detail of a church fresco inside Kaisariani Monastery

Kaisariani Monastery

▲ 101 D3

✉ Kaisariani

☎ (210) 723 6619

🕐 Closed Mon. & afternoons; grounds open sunrise to sunset

💲 $

🚇 Ethniki Amyna

Olympic Complex

✉ Maroussi, Athens

☎ (210) 683 4777

🕐 Open only to organized tour groups (email oakaprel@ otenet.gr to book)

💲 $$

🚇 Irini

www.oaka.com.gr

Today, this part of the city is known for its home-style fish tavernas and *mezedopoleia*, as well as for neighboring Mount Hymettus, which the ancients believed was the source of honey. The forested Mount Hymettus covers 81,230 acres (32,900 ha), has more than 600 plant species and many animals and birds. It's a popular picnic area in the spring, when the hill blooms with thyme and lavender. Hymettus is also home to the 11th-century **Kaisariani Monastery,** which is dedicated to the presentation of the Virgin Mary and has frescoes dating to the 16th and 17th centuries. There are also remains of an early Christian basilica and two other churches there.

Along the Sacred Way

To the west of Athens, on the opposite side of town to the trendy communities of Kolonaki and Pangrati, lie the suburbs of Egaleo and Chaidari. They are located on what was once the Iera Odos, or Sacred Way, an ancient road that led from the Acropolis to the town of Eleusis (12 miles/19.3 km northwest of Athens).

To the ancient Greeks, Eleusis was a place of pilgrimage and the second holiest site after Delphi. It is best known as the home of a secret religious ritual known as the Eleusinian Mysteries. Every year, hundreds of Athenians traveled along the Sacred Way to take part in the mysteries. What happened at this festival is not known, as the punishment for talking about it was death. Sadly, there is little left of ancient Eleusis that could give modern historians any clues about the mysteries, as the sanctuary has largely vanished beneath the industrial port city that stands there today.

Present-day Iera Odos Street, which generally follows the route of the ancient road, cuts through the western suburbs of Athens. This area is quiet and residential and doesn't have much to attract visitors. There are some places of interest, however. At the western end of the neighborhood of **Egaleo,** the forested slopes of **Mount Egaleos** are a popular spot with hikers and cyclists. The 800-foot-high (243 m) summit offers sweeping views over Athens and Pireas.

The suburb of **Chaidari,** to the northwest of Egaleo, is home to the **Monastery of Dafni,** a UNESCO World Heritage site. The monastery, which dates from the fifth or sixth century, was built with materials from a sanctuary that was dedicated to Apollo. The monastery gets its name from the bay trees, called *daphnai* in Greek, which are sacred to Apollo and which once flourished here. The monastery showcases Byzantine architecture from the 11th century and has mosaics that are both intricate and well preserved.

The church houses what is arguably the best-preserved set of mosaics from the early Comnenian period, which refers to the time between 1081 and 1185, when the prominent Comnenoi dynasty ruled the Byzantine empire. The church was sacked and rebuilt a few times over the centuries and was badly damaged in the 1999 earthquake. Its interior is still closed for restoration.

The Northern Suburbs

Mention "northern suburbs" to most Athenians, and they will talk, perhaps longingly, about places synonymous with wealth and glamor. The northern suburbs are indeed coveted, for many reasons. They have the city's best homes and most lush green spaces. And the rich and famous do live there; a few years ago, there was even a popular soap opera, *Ta Voreia Proastia* (The Northern Suburbs), made about the beautiful, star-crossed couples who lived in luxurious homes complete with

Egaleo
101 A2, B2

Chaidari
101 A3, B3

Monastery of Dafni
101 B3
Leoforos Athinon, Chaidari
(210) 581 1558

OAKA Olympic Complex

OAKA stands for Olympiako Athletiko Kentro Athinon, which means Olympic Athletic Center of Athens, though most of the complex was built long before the 2004 Olympics in Athens.

The complex is named for Spiridon Louis, the Greek who won the first modern-day Olympic marathon at the 1896 Summer Olympics in Athens. Louis, who delivered the mineral water his father sold, was born in Maroussi, a suburban area northeast of Athens where the Olympic Complex now stands.

The complex consists of the Olympic Stadium, an Olympic Indoor Hall, the Athens Aquatic Center, the Athens Olympic Velodrome, and the Athens Olympic Tennis Center. The stadium was originally designed in 1972 and built in 1980–1982. Spanish architect Santiago Calatrava gave it a major makeover, with a breathtaking roof, between 2002 and 2004 for the 2004 Summer Games.

The stadium hosted the soccer final and athletics events of the Games, as well as the opening and closing ceremonies. It has also been a venue for the three major soccer clubs in the Athens area: Olympiakos Pireas, Panathinaikos, and AEK Athens. The stadium's record for attendance was set on November 3, 1983, when more than 75,000 people watched a match between Olympiakos and Hamburg. The Olympic Indoor Halls was built in 1995 and is home for two basketball teams: the Greek National Team and Panathinaikos. It also hosts gymnastic events. The aquatics and tennis centers have hosted regional events and tournaments.

Psychiko
◭ 101 C3, D3

Maroussi
◭ 101 D3

Kifissia
◭ 101 D3

fountains and swimming pools.

Visiting this part of the Athens metro area is easy enough via train, Metro, or bus. The most visitor-friendly northern suburbs are the ones closest to the city.

INSIDER TIP:

Only organized groups may visit the Olympic complex, so to make sure you don't miss out, you should book on a tour party beforehand: email oakaprel@otenet.gr.

—CLIVE CARPENTER
National Geographic contributor

Psychiko: Located just south of the new Olympic complex (see sidebar p. 112), the genteel neighborhood of Psychiko was once home to the most aristocratic Athenians. From the early to mid-20th century, members of the Greek royal family, including Queen Frederika, as well as notable artists, writers, scholars, and playwrights lived here. Many still do, though the beautiful neighborhood of stately neoclassical homes has been engulfed by the growing Athens metropolitan area. Psychiko is also home to several embassies and consulates and is still primarily a residential area. For shops and cafés, cross the major Kifissias thoroughfare to Neo Psychiko.

Maroussi: Closer to the Olympic complex is Maroussi, a pretty, lush suburb that's also a hub for finance, transportation and café culture. In 1941, when Henry Miller published *The Colossus of Maroussi,* his exuberant travelogue about Greece, Maroussi was a small town on the outskirts of Athens. Today, almost 70,000 people live here. Maroussi has two suburban railway stations and is also home to Greece's largest shopping center, which is simply called The Mall.

Kifissia: At the end of the ISAP train line is Kifissia, a wealthy suburb where the rich of Athens and Attica retreated. The city has its roots in the ancient town of Epicephesia. The philhellene emperor Hadrian hosted philosophers at his home here, and the sophist and rhetorician Herodus Atticus (A.D. 101–177) built an elaborate villa here. Remains of his family's funeral monuments remain in the center of town. In the 20th century, it became a summer resort for rich Athenians.

Today, Kifissia is one of the few neighborhoods in Athens where you will see homes with lawns and gardens, along with well-kept streets and sidewalks. The well-to-do live in mansions, modernist homes, or roomy apartments here. Along with the Goulandris Natural History Museum (see sidebar p. 110), the suburb is also known for its clothing boutiques, high-end restaurants, excellent bakeries, and leafy squares where privileged young Athenians hang out at cafés. ■

EXPERIENCE: Drinking in the Athens Nightlife

As in many Mediterranean cities, Athens's baking summer heat seems to encourage people to become nocturnal. Get up early on a summer morning and you'll likely have only fellow visitors for company; head to a bar or taverna before 10 p.m. and you'll find that, for Athenians, the night has not yet begun. Once it gets going, however, few cities can rival Athens for the variety and quality of its nightlife.

Enjoying a night out in the city really begins with a feeling the Greeks call *kefi*, which originates in the Turkish word for delight. When you have kefi, you are bursting with energy and joy and ready to dance on the tables.

In the city center, there are several neighborhoods known for their clubs and bars. The most popular is **Gazi** (see p. 81), the site of the former gasworks, which has morphed in recent years from a crumbling post-industrial neighborhood into the hottest and sometimes loudest place in Athens.

Young people at an exclusive nightclub in Kolonaki

Gay clubs started the trend here, creating a vibrant trance and techno scene that attracts tourists and locals alike—**Blue Train** (Konstantinoupoleos, tel 210/346 0677) is a standout. But in the last couple of years, the scene here has broadened to include everyone from the teenagers in black who hang out in the big square around the Kerameikos Metro station to twentysomethings jamming to noveau jazz at **GazArte** (Voutadon 32–34, tel 021/346 0347, www .gazarte.gr). Other hot clubs include **Bios** (Pireas 84, tel 210/342 5335, www.bios .gr) and **Hoxton** (Voutadon St. 42, tel 210/341 3395).

Near Gazi, the clubs around Iera Odos Street cater to Greeks who love their bouzouki, the long-necked lute that resembles a mandolin and is a mainstay of Greek music. The **bouzouki clubs** (see pp. 108–109) feature live music, garish stage shows, and patrons sipping expensive whiskey.

The high-end clubs feature the biggest names in Greek music—Michalis Hadziyiannis, Peggy Zina, Anna Vissi—and the more humble places feature crooners who are sometimes less melodic. These places are called *skyladika*, "the place of the dogs," an inelegant reference to the quality of

the music. Nevertheless, sky-ladika are often more fun to visit than the fancy bouzouki clubs. They give an honest, if unpolished, look into the Greek spirit for releasing the day's worries by singing, dancing, and just letting go.

Other nightlife districts include the grungy post-industrial neighborhood of **Psirri** (see p. 80) and the anarchist neighborhood of **Exarcheia** (see p. 93). Psirri's nightlife has taken a nosedive in recent years as a growing number of drug addicts and gangs have plunged that part of Athens into chaos. Many Psirri clubs and restaurants have closed or moved their operations elsewhere.

Pireas

Most visitors to Greece only see the small stretch of Pireas that stands between the Metro station and the ferry terminals. Based on this experience alone, Pireas does not seem like the sort of place you'd want to explore, but away from the shipping agents and dockside industries this harbor town has a surprising amount to offer visitors.

Almost all of Athens's seafood is landed at Pireas, and local restaurants get the pick of the catch.

Pireas

 101 A1

🚇 Pireas Metro
station is on
Line 1, which
has stations
at Thissio,
Monastiraki,
and Omonoia in
central Athens.

Pireas—the name means "place of the passage"—has a storied past. Archaeologists have found evidence of settlement here dating to the third millennium B.C. In prehistoric times, the town connected to the mainland via a shallow piece of land, which was flooded with seawater most of the time. Residents at the time apparently used the connecting isthmus as a salt field.

The city became the chief harbor of ancient Greece. The Athenian politician and general Themistocles (524–459 B.C.) pushed to fortify the city and told Athenian leaders to use its natural harbor. The Athenians listened, and by 483 B.C. they had transferred their existing fleet to Pireas and also opened a shipyard there. The Athenian fleet defeated the Persians in the Battle of Salamis, named for the small island in the Saronic Gulf next to where the battle took place. After the victory, Pireas became ancient Greece's permanent naval base.

INSIDER TIP:

Ignore the restaurants and cafés near the main harbor in Pireas in favor of the tavernas and fish restaurants alongside Mikrolimano harbor.

—CLIVE CARPENTER
National Geographic contributor

Themistocles refurbished the three harbors of Pireas after the second Persian invasion. He also built *neosoikoi,* or stone docking ramps. Themistocles ordered the building of the so-called Long Walls, or Themistoclean Walls, which were completed in 471 B.C., around Athens and Pireas. Parts of the wall are still visible today in Pireas. After the Spartans defeated Athens in the Peloponnesian Wars, they tore down the walls and destroyed much of what was in the shipyards, including many triremes, Hellenic warships.

Later, when the Venetians took over the port, they renamed it Porto Leone, or Lion's Port, after a statue of a lion erected there. Pireas was largely ignored during the Byzantine Empire as Constantinople became the empire's primary port city. By Ottoman times, the port was virtually deserted until fishermen began migrating there in the early 19th century.

The Ferry Port

The main harbor at Pireas is one of the busiest passenger ports in the Mediterranean. From dawn till dusk, it's usually a chaotic river of travelers and sailors getting on or off the ships. For many years it boasted the most chaotic pedestrian crossing in Athens (which was quite an achievement at the time), where the river of pedestrians coming from the Metro station had to cross a busy eight-lane road to reach the waterfront. The bridge across the road, along with various other developments has improved downtown Pireas but falls short of making it somewhere you'd like to spent any time.

Zea Marina

Pireas is not all passenger ferries and container ships, however. About a 20-minute walk (or short taxi ride) to the southeast of the municipal port is the

Zea Marina

🅼 100 A1

Ferry Travel from Pireas

Ferries from the port of Pireas are the most popular way of getting to the Greek islands. As recently as a decade ago, many of the ships still took 12 or more hours to get to the far-flung Aegean islands. In recent years, however, faster ships have cut down travel time considerably, reducing it by half in some cases.

You can find a comprehensive list of ferry departure and arrival times at www .greekferries.gr. Top carriers include ANEK Lines (*www.anek.gr*), Hellenic Seaways (*www.hellenicseaways.gr*), and Minoan Lines (*www.minoan.gr*). The new Superfast Ferries (*www.superfast.com*) is also a popular choice for travelers who want to enjoy the quintessentially Greek journey by sea but in less time.

Hellenic Maritime Museum

 Akti Hermistokleous, Plateia Freatidas, Zea Marina, Pireas

☎ (210) 451 6264

🕐 Closed Sun., Mon., & afternoons

💲 $$

Archaeological Museum of Pireas

 Harilaou Trikoupi 31, Zea Marina, Pireas

☎ (210) 452 1598

🕐 Closed Mon.

💲 $$

beautiful little harbor of Zea Marina (also known as Pasalimani). Here the sleek lines of the harbor's gigantic catamarans give way to a joyously chaotic jumble of masts, sails, and rigging. Hundreds of small (and not so small) sailing vessels are moored here, from century-old wooden yawls to gleaming modern glass-fiber sloops. On quiet evenings the wake churned up by a departing outboard engine can trigger a chorus of clattering shackles and seagull cries that carries on long after the boat has left the marina.

If you walk around the northern side of the harbor you'll find yourself in **Alexandras Square,** a neat little waterfront park dominated by a treelike abstract sculpture. From here you can see the jetties of the outer harbor, where the double-masted sailing ships and enormous motor-yachts of Athens's rich and famous are moored.

Directly across the mouth of the harbor from Alexandras Square, on Bouga Taki Street, is the **Hellenic Maritime Museum.** This museum's innovative sunken design makes it almost invisible from a distance (something that can make finding it difficult). The museum consists of a long curved gallery that runs around a neatly landscaped square. Here you can chart Greece's long love affair with the sea, from Odysseus to Aristotle Onassis. The exhibits include models of prehistoric ships as well as ancient navigation tools, paintings, maps, and flags. Out in the square there are some larger exhibits, such as ship guns, statues of naval heroes, and the conning tower of the famous Second World War submarine *Papanikolis,* which kept the resistance movement in the islands supplied throughout the war.

Just off the western side of the inner harbor, on Harilaou Trikoupi Street, stands a small but

---

EXPERIENCE: The Blessing of the Waters

Every year on January 6, the harbor at Pireas plays host to the most quintessential of Greek customs, the Blessing of the Waters. This is one of the traditional celebrations held to mark the Theofania, or Feast of the Epiphany.

After the morning ceremony at the Church of the Holy Trinity on the east side of the harbor, the Archbishop of Athens walks down to the waterfront to deliver a short sermon. He then blesses the water and finishes by casting a large crucifix into the harbor. At this moment the ceremony breaks out into a lively celebration: Everyone cheers and the cold winter air

fills with a cacophony of ships' horns while dozens of people dive into the chilly sea to retrieve the cross. The person who manages to bring it ashore traditionally receives a special blessing, one that grants luck in the coming year.

Although the event at Pireas is the most prestigious, the ceremony takes place in rivers and harbors all over Greece. You could visit the smaller events at Glyfada (see p. 121) or Perama to witness the ceremony as it has been for thousands of years—a celebration of the sea's bounty and, for the swimmers, a test of devotion and strength.

fascinating museum, the **Archaeological Museum of Pireas.** The unassuming modern building is constructed around the excavated ruins of an ancient theater, and many of the museum's larger stone exhibits are displayed under awnings around its edges. Inside, the museum features rare bronze sculptures of Athena, Artemis, and Apollo that graced the port during the days of Athenian leader and general Themistocles. Most bronze art from classical times was melted down and reused as weapons or tools by later generations, but these statues were discovered by archaeologists in relatively good condition during an undersea excavation in 1959. There are also artifacts that testify to Pireas's long maritime heritage, including the tip of a trireme's bronze ram and a marble eye that once adorned its bow.

Mikrolimano

The prettiest of Pireas's three harbors is Mikrolimano, which means "little harbor" and is also called Tourkolimano. The scenic port has fish taverns, cafés, and a pretty seaside view lined with yachts and fishing boats. The best fish tavernas include **Plous Podilatou** *(Akti Koumoundourou 42, tel 210/413 7790, www.plous-podilatou.gr, $$$$),* the ever-popular **Jimmy & the Fish** *(Akti Koumoundourou 46, 210/412 4417, www.jimmy andthefish.gr, $$$$$),* and, up in the hills above the harbor, **Panorama** *(Irakliou Street 18–20, Kastella, tel 210/417 3475, www .panorama-seafood.gr, $$$$).*

Enjoying a seafood lunch at the harborside in Pireas

Behind Mikrolimano is the attractive hillside neighborhood of **Kastella,** which rises sharply up from the waterfront. This is a genteel and wealthy part of town, with lovely neoclassical mansions perched on the steep slopes, winding streets, and several lovely small churches.

At the summit of the hill is the large and attractive **Church of Profitis Ilias,** which stands in a small public park. The views from this area are stunning, particularly at night, when you can watch the twinkling lights of the ferries until they disappear over the horizon. An ideal place to enjoy the view— and rest your feet after the long climb—is the curiously named **Bowling Center Café** *(Profitis Ilias, Kastella tel 210/412 0271),* which stands on the hilltop next to the church. There's nothing particularly remarkable about the café itself, but it stays open until 3 a.m. and the view is stunning. ∎

Mikrolimano
🅜 101 B1

Church of Profitis Ilias
🅜 101 A1
✉ Kastella, Pireas

The Athens Riviera

The Athens Riviera is the name given to the 10-mile (16 km) stretch of coast southeast of Pireas, where the suburbs of Athens meet the sea. This is where Athenians come on summer weekends to cool off in the sea and work on their suntans. A variety of private and public beaches give visitors many options within about an hour's travel of the city center.

Popular Edem beach, near Glyfada

Athens Riviera
 101 D1

Riviera is probably rather too strong a term to describe the stretch of urbanized shoreline from Glyfada to Cape Sounion (see p. 132), but there are sections that live up to the name. Since the 2004 Olympics, the shoreline has indeed become an attractive and enticing stretch of coast, with excellent hotels, restaurants, and cafés.

One of the key factors in the Riviera's renaissance has been the decision to move Athens's main international airport from Ellinikon (just north of Glyfada) to its current site, farther east near Paiania. Until its closure in 2001, the two

runways at Ellinikon operated at full capacity throughout the summer, sending hundreds of planes roaring over the beaches along the coast.

The northern end of the now largely abandoned site is occupied by a number of sporting venues from the 2004 Olympics, including a state-of-the-art white-water kayaking course and a baseball stadium, now rarely used. In the immediate aftermath of the Olympics, ambitious plans were drawn up to redevelop the site as a huge public park, but this project is not due to be completed until 2013 at the earliest.

Glyfada

The suburb of Glyfada, located just to the south of Ellinikon, is the anchor of the Athens Riviera. Many of Greece's ship-owners, politicians, movie stars, singers, and other celebrities have their homes here. The suburb begins at the foot of Mount Hymettus and stretches to the Saronic Gulf. It's connected to Athens via Leoforos Poseidonos and Leoforos Vouliagmenis and by the new tram line that begins at Syntagma Square.

In ancient times, the area was known as Aixone, one of the *demes* (adminstrative divisions) of Athenian Attica. A quiet coastal village for much of its history, it began to develop rapidly with the expansion of Pireas and Athens following Greek independence. Throughout the Cold War, Glyfada's proximity to the large U.S. airbase at Ellinikon gave the neighborhood a unique Greek-American atmosphere. Although the airbase closed in 1993, the U.S. influence can still be seen in the area's unusual number of bars, steakhouses, and rock clubs. The shopping district of Glyfada runs across Metaxa Avenue, and Grigoriou Lambraki Street is the haunt of young millionaires and rich expatriates.

The coast isn't known for its cultural offerings, but one place worth a visit is the new **Eugenides Planetarium,** also called the Evgenidio Planetarium. Glyfada also has **Glyfada Golf Club** *(Terma Pronois, Glyfada, tel 210/894 6459, www.ggca.gr),* the only golf course in or around Athens.

Athens's Beaches

For those looking to enjoy the sunshine, however, there is only one place to be, the beach. The Athens coast has both public and private beaches, and it's a nearby swimming stop in the summer after a long, hot day at the Acropolis. The public beaches are open year-round, but most of the private beaches are only open from mid-May to mid-September. All the private

Euginides Planetarium

- ✉ Syngrou 387, Palio Faliro, Glyfada
- ☎ (210) 946 9600
- 🕐 Closed Mon.–Tues.
- 💲 $$$

Limni Vouliagmeni

Just to the south of Vouliagmeni (4 miles/ 6 km south of Glyfada), in a quiet spot sheltered by high coastal cliffs, is a small, picturesque lake. **Limni Vouliagmeni** *(Limni Vouliagmeni, Vouliagmeni, tel 210/896 2237, www.limnivouliagmenis.gr, $$)* is a natural wonder, filled with warm brackish water (which remains at about 75°F/24°C year-round) that gushes up from hot springs about 300 feet (91 m) below the surface.

The lake is surrounded by high, jagged cliffs and lush vegetation. It is located on the island side of the main coast road and can be easily reached by taking the E22 bus from Syntagma Square.

Limni Vouliagmeni is the centerpiece of a small outdoor spa that includes restrooms, changing rooms, and a good (if rather expensive) café. The warm, mineral-infused waters are home to thousands of tiny, inquisitive black fish, which carefully examine each new bather before darting out of sight. Swimmers are not allowed to wear sunscreen as it tends to disturb the chemical balance of the water.

EXPERIENCE: Nights on the Beach

In the summer, many Athenians like their nightlife on the beach. These clubs have a unique atmosphere and the cool sea breeze makes a night on the sand much more enjoyable than a night in the sweaty heat of a city-center club. The coastal suburbs have big, glamorous clubs where people dance until dawn to disco, techno, trance, eighties rock, and Greek pop and bouzouki music.

From May to September, young Greeks flock to the Athens Riviera, as well as to suburbs like Palaio Faliro and Elliniko, for long evenings of dancing in the salty sea air. These open-air clubs are an ideally Mediterranean way to spend a night out, although they are often quite expensive. If you take public transportation instead of a taxi, it can also take about an hour to get to the clubs if you travel from the city center. It is typically cheaper than many of the city center's more exclusive clubs, however, and much more exciting.

Two of the best beach clubs in Athens are also two of the oldest. **Akrotiri** (*Leoforos Vas, Georgiou B5, Agios Kosmas, tel 210/985 9147, www.akrotirilounge. gr, $$ Mon–Thurs & Sun; $$$ Fri.–Sat.*) is open from 11 p.m. to 5 a.m. and attracts the glitterati of Athens. It has dance floors, a huge pool, deck seating by the beach, excellent views of the sea, and a restaurant that serves expensive but excellent Mediterranean-fusion cuisine. On Fridays and Saturdays the entry fee rises, although that does include a drink.

Another favorite club is **Bos** (*Karamanli 14, Voula, 210/895 9645*), which has a small private beach lined with palm trees. The club, which is open from 11 a.m. to 4 a.m., turns into a bar during the day.

Beach clubs offer sun, sea, entertainment, food, and drink.

INSIDER TIP:

You will find many of Athens's beaches to be comfortably empty if you visit them on a weekday morning outside of the local school summer holiday (mid-June to mid-September).

—SALLY MCFALL
National Geographic contributor

beaches have umbrellas, sun chairs, changing cabins, showers, canteens, and clean bathrooms, and the upscale ones also have cafés, restaurants, tennis courts, water sports facilities, and even rental bungalows.

Be warned, however, that the entry fees on the ritziest beaches are steep (*$$$*). Also, the Athens Riviera gets very crowded in the summer. The main drag, Leoforos Poseidonos, is full of cars all day nearly every weekend in the summer and parking is scarce. It's best to take the tram if you want to swim here.

The closest decent beach to the city center is **Edem beach** in Faliro. It's pleasant enough, but because of its location and the fact that it's one of the few public beaches in the area, it tends to get very crowded, especially on weekends.

A short distance farther south is the beach at **Agios Kosmas,** another popular spot. This stretch of coast was privately owned until the municipality's mayor took the unusual step of going on a hunger strike in 2007 to force it to go public, arguing that Greek law gives free access to the sea. The water here is filtered, so it's relatively clear despite its proximity to the city. The beach also has a good bathroom, outdoor showers, and a small garden.

Although Glyfada boasts the best beaches within the city limits, you'll have to pay to get access to them. Of these private beaches, **Asteria beach** is probably the best. It has an entry fee (*$$*) on weekends, but it also has great bathrooms, lots of dressing rooms, lush gardens, a volleyball court, a pool, and a playground, among other amenities.

Beyond the City Limits: The beaches south of Glyfada are outside the Athens prefecture and only the northernmost one, Voula, can be reached by the Athens coastal tram.

In the quiet suburb of **Voula,** the beaches divided into **Beach A** (with a trendy café) and **Beach B** (with tennis courts and a seaside rental bungalow) have an entry fee (*$*). **Astir beach** in Vouliagmeni is the fanciest private beach on the stretch. It's on a secluded bay and is near both an exclusive resort (Astir Palace) and an ancient temple dedicated to Apollo. In **Varkiza,** the beach is clean and relaxed, surrounded by plenty of cafés and fish tavernas. Part is private and has an entry fee (*$$*) on weekends; the public portion is also pleasant, despite the lack of amenities, and has a more diverse crowd. ∎

Dozens of top-tier attractions just a few hours out of Athens—
from the "navel of the world" at Delphi to historic Nafplio

Around Athens

A traditional village on the Attica Peninsula

Around Athens

Visitors who manage to draw themselves away from Athens will discover that the surrounding region—which includes the Peloponnese, the Attica Peninsula, and Delphi—is packed with cultural and historical sites, dramatic scenery, and friendly, hospitable people.

In the works of ancient writers such as Homer and Herodotus, places like Delphi, Mycenae, and Cape Sounion (Akra Sounion) are portrayed as distant and mysterious locations, many days' travel from Athens. It can be a little surprising, therefore, when you look at a map and see that these "far-flung" places are, to modern visitors, never more than two or three hours' travel from the city. The Attica Peninsula, as well as the historic sites at Delphi and Corinth (Korinthos), are all easily accessible as day trips from the city, and even slightly more distant destinations such as Nafplio and Mycenae (Mykinai) can be visited in a day if you leave early enough.

The Peloponnese

West of Athens and west of the Corinth Canal, a relatively modern engineering project that makes it an island, the Peloponnese has a very different atmosphere from Attica to the east. The quiet towns and coastal villages of the rural Peloponnese attract fewer visitors than Attica or the Greek islands.

While the Peloponnese is something of a backwater today, it has not always been so. In ancient times this region was home to the mighty city-states of Mycenae, Corinth, and Sparta (Sparti), as well as numerous other, smaller kingdoms. In the time of Homer, this area was the center of civilization in the Aegean. This proud history is an important part of the local identity; Peloponnesians often describe themselves as the true Greeks—the people with the strongest claim to Greece's glorious history.

This claim is backed up by the presence of some of Greece's most important historic and cultural sites—including the Homeric city of Mycenae, the famous ancient theater at Epidavros, and the modern Greek state's first capital city, Nafplio. Visitors to this part of Greece will find an area that, despite its proximity to Athens, offers a tranquil atmosphere to rival that of even the smallest islands.

Attica Peninsula

In ancient times, the area now covered by the Attica prefecture was the heartland of the Athenian state. The numerous municipalities and communities of the region provided Athens with its food, soldiers, and, in the case of Lavrion, its riches. The Athenian aristocracy had their grand country villas in the hills around the city, each served by a farming community of slaves and peasants.

United under the rule of the tyrants of Athens in the sixth century B.C. (see p. 27) the area entered a golden age, during which fantastic monuments and temples were built as a symbol of Athenian prosperity. Remnants of that period can still be found throughout the region, including the imposing cliff-top pillars

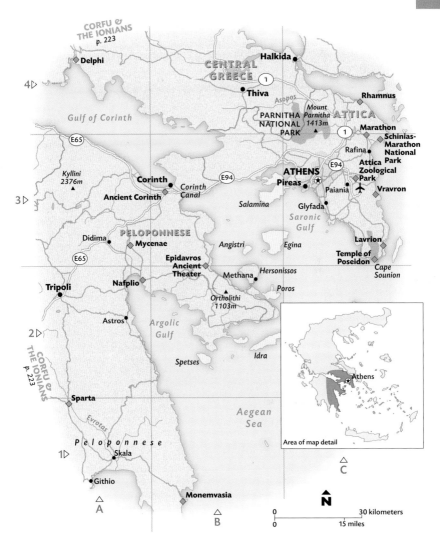

CORFU &
THE IONIANS
p. 223

Delphi

CENTRAL
GREECE

Halkida

Thiva

4▷

Gulf of Corinth

Asopos

PARNITHA
NATIONAL
PARK

Mount
Parnitha
1413m

ATTICA

Rhamnus

Marathon

Schinias-
Marathon
National
Park

E65

Rafina

E94

ATHENS

Pireas

Attica
Zoological
Park

Kyllini
2376m

Corinth

Corinth
Canal

E94

Paiania

Vravron

Ancient Corinth

3▷

PELOPONNESE

Salamina

Saronic
Gulf

Glyfada

Lavrion

Didima

Mycenae

Angistri

Egina

Temple of
Poseidon

Cape
Sounion

E65

Epidavros
Ancient
Theater

Methana

Hersonissos

Tripoli

Nafplio

Ortholithi
1103m

Poros

Astros

Argolic
Gulf

2▷

CORFU &
THE IONIANS
p. 223

Spetses

Idra

Sparta

Aegean
Sea

Evrotas

Peloponnese

Athens

1▷

Skala

Githio

Area of map detail

△
A

Monemvasia

△
B

△
C

N

0   30 kilometers
0   15 miles

of the Temple of Poseidon and the vast temple complex at Delphi. In the north of Attica lies the plain of Marathon, the site of one of the most significant battles in Western history, in which the Greeks defeated the Persians (see pp. 28–29), demonstrating that the citizen soldiers of a free state could resist the conscript army of a tyrant.

The prefecture of Attica has grown quickly in the last ten years, especially with the construction of a new international airport and highways called the Attiki Odos and

the Hymettus Ring. Villages and settlements have exploded into suburbs, and a wave of government investment has seen the revival of long-forgotten sites such as the Temple of Artemis at Vravron, the Sanctuary of Nemesis at Rhamnus, and the Lavrion Mines. In other ways, however, the area is similar to the Attica of ancient times. While they may not be aristocrats, the rich and the powerful of Athens still reside among the hills of the southern peninsula, sheltering from Athens's oppressive summer heat. ■

West of Athens

For those who have a little time to explore, the region to the north and west of Athens—once home to the rival city-states of ancient Greece—has several renowned historic sites, most within two or three hours' drive of the city, ideal for a day trip or one-night stay.

A cruise ship being steered through the Corinth Canal

Corinth Canal
🗺 127 B3

Ancient Corinth & Archaeological Museum
🗺 127 B3
✉ Ancient Corinth
☎ (274) 103 1207
💲 $$

www.ancientcorinth
.net

Corinth & Mycenae

About 51 miles (82 km) west of Athens lies the town of Corinth, where a strip of land only 4 miles wide (6 km) connects mainland Greece with the Peloponnese—a rural peninsula about the size of New Jersey.

Today the Peloponnese is technically an island, separated from the rest of Greece by the **Corinth Canal** (first opened in 1893)—a 79-foot-wide (24 m) channel that was blasted through 4 miles (6 km) of solid rock to connect the Saronic Gulf and the Gulf of Corinth. Although it is no longer a major trade route, you may catch sight of a ship

passing through the narrow canal with a chugging tugboat skillfully keeping it away from the sheer stone walls.

The ruins of **ancient Corinth** (see p. 131) are located around 5.5 miles (9 km) west of the modern town of Corinth, and the ruins of **Mycenae** (see p. 131) lie 21 miles (34 km) farther to the southwest.

Nafplio & Monemvasia

Located two or three hours by car or bus from the heart of Athens, the beautiful medieval town of Nafplio offers something different for those who have grown tired of ancient ruins and would prefer something a little more recent. The town has long been an important defensive stronghold, with marshes protecting its landward side. It is dominated by three huge fortresses: the Palamidi, Acronauplia, and Bourtzi.

The **Palamidi** fortress is by far the most impressive of the three, located at the summit of an enormous rocky outcrop above the town. It is reached by climbing a thousand stone steps that wind up the cliffs to the gatehouse. The **Acronauplia** is an Ottoman fortress built on the site of what was once the town's acropolis. It is not as well maintained as the Palamidi, with a large area of the old fortress now occupied by a 1970s hotel, but is still worth a visit for its views over the town and harbor. The **Bourtzi** is a small island fortress that looks like a stone battleship. It is located about 300 yards (274 m) from the seafront at the mouth of the harbor. One of the local boatmen will row you over to the island and pick you up when you're done (*$*).

In addition to these castles, the town boasts a number of excellent museums. The **Nafplio Archaeological Museum** collection includes ancient artifacts from nearby Mycenaean towns. There's also the **Peloponnese Folklore Foundation Museum,** which houses a collection of craft goods, traditional costumes, and artworks illustrating the vibrant local culture. Its shop is a good place to get locally made crafts.

Those who want to experience something genuinely unspoiled should visit the town of **Monemvasia** in the far south of the Peloponnese. This town is hidden on the seaward side of a gigantic volcanic outcrop. Monemvasia has only one entrance from the mainland, a narrow stone gatehouse, and has changed little since the time of the Byzantines. If you take time to visit and explore the town's cobbled streets, make sure to ascend the steep and twisting path to the old citadel, which offers bird's-eye views of the town. ∎

Nafplio
🅰 127 A2

Visitor Information
✉ Municipal Tourist Office, Martioy 25
☎ (27520) 24444

www.greeka.com/peloponnese/nafplion

Nafplio Archaeological Museum
✉ Plateia Syntagmatos, Nafplio
☎ (27520) 27502
🕒 Closed Mon.

Peloponnese Folklore Foundation Museum
✉ Vasileos Alexandros 1, Nafplio
☎ (27520) 28947
🕒 Closed Tues. & Feb.
💲 $$

Monemvasia
🅰 127 B1

EXPERIENCE: A Performance at Epidavros

About 20 miles (32 km) east of Nafplio stands the **Epidavros Ancient Theater** (*Sanctuary of Asklepios, Epidavros, tel 27530/22009, $$*), a massive, 14,000-seat amphitheater. Although you can visit at any time, the best way to experience the site and its extraordinary acoustics is to see a performance there.

Between June and September the ancient theater is one of the principal venues for the **Athens & Epidavros Festival** (*www.greekfestival.gr*). During the festival the theater hosts events ranging from modern dance productions to performances of ancient Greek classics. It hosts performances by theater companies from around the world, each performing in their own language, so there are usually a few English-language productions. Tickets (*$$$–$$$$$*) are priced according to the location of the seats and don't usually go on sale until a few weeks before performances—so you don't have to plan your visit months in advance.

Classical Sites near Athens

Two millennia of Greek history may be explored just a short distance from Athens. The ancient city of Mycenae reached its peak centuries before the rise of Sparta and Athens. The ancient city of Corinth and the sanctuary at Delphi, on the other hand, endured well into the Roman era.

The ruined tholos in the Sanctuary of Athena Pronaia at Delphi

Delphi

Located about 105 miles (170 km) to the northwest of Athens, the ancient religious center at Delphi is a popular day trip destination for visitors to Athens. Delphi was once the holiest sanctuary in the ancient Greek religion. Poseidon and Gaia were first worshipped here on the slopes of the Parnassus Mountains before it became a sanctuary for Apollo. The famous oracle was inside the **Sanctuary of Apollo,** which still stands today and where the Pythia, or temple priestess, would deliver the oracle's pronouncements.

The steeply sloping site of Delphi's sanctuary is dominated by the huge pedestal that once held the **Temple of Apollo.** Some of the fourth-century B.C. columns of the temple are still standing. The road that leads to the temple is lined by the treasuries established by each of the ancient city-states. Some, like the **Treasury of the Athenians,** have been restored. At the base of Mount Parnassus, below the main site, is the **Sanctuary of Athena Pronaia,** known for its round *tholos,* or rotunda. Above the temple a large **theater** once held audiences of up to 5,500 and a **stadium** held a precursor to the Olympic games and had seating for 6,500 spectators. The stadium is fascinating because you can still see the athletes' starting blocks carved in stone. Close to the site is the **Archaeological**

Museum *(Delphi, tel 22650/82313, $$ for ruins and museum, http://odysseus.culture.gr)*, which holds many of the statues unearthed on the site, including one of a charioteer that still has its original decoration.

Ancient Corinth

Just 4 miles (7 km) southwest of the modern city of Corinth are the ruins of ancient Corinth *(Corinth, tel 27410/31207, $ for ruins & museum, www.ancientcorinth.net)*. The site is dominated by the grand Doric columns of the **Temple of Apollo,** one of the few ancient Greek buildings to survive the Roman reconstruction of the town in 44 B.C. A few decades later, the city may have had as many as 800,000 inhabitants. Archaeologists working on this site have uncovered the remains of a large Roman market, as well as several impressive mansions, but a great deal of the city remains covered up.

Visitors to Corinth shouldn't miss the opportunity to visit **Akrokorinthos** (Upper Corinth), a fortified acropolis high above the rest of the site. It takes about 30 minutes to ascend the steep path up to the entrance, but those who reach the summit are rewarded with breathtaking views of the Isthmus of Corinth and the Peloponnese—and the ruins of the Greek **Temple of Aphrodite** and the Roman **Temple of Octavia.**

Near the ancient ruins, the **Archaeological Museum of Ancient Corinth** houses a collection of artifacts and statues from the site, as well as maps and models to explain what it would have looked like in its heyday. Travel south from Corinth and you can either head for Epidavros with its ancient theater (see sidebar p. 129) or to Mycenae.

Mycenae

Although it is hard to believe now, the city of Mycenae *(7 miles/11 km north of Argos)* was already ruined by the time the great temples of Athens and Delphi were built. During the classical period of Greek history, the Myceneans were no longer a powerful people, and were known mostly through ancient literary works like Homer's *Odyssey*.

The ruins of ancient Mycenae are a fascinating place to explore. With their dark, chunky stone walls and strange architecture, it is fairly obvious that they belong to a different age from Corinth or Athens. Enter the fortified town through a great stone **gateway** that has a mysterious carving of a pair of lions standing against a pillar over the lintel. The most impressive sights in the ancient city are the grand tombs, such as the **Tomb of Clytemnestra,** which consists of a large domed room built into an earthen mound with a stone entranceway

INSIDER TIP:

After Corinth and Mycenae, Sparta tends to be something of a disappointment. From Mycenae, visitors are better off heading east to Epidavros.

—SALLY MCFALL
National Geographic contributor

carved into it. The nearby **Archaeological Museum** *(Mycenae, 27510/76585, $, www.greeka.com/peloponnese/mycenae/mycenae-museums.htm)* houses many of the artifacts found on the site, but given how little is known about the Mycenaeans, it isn't able to provide much additional information.

Sparta

Though it is a site of great historic importance, the ancient city of Sparta doesn't have much to recommend it as an attraction. The Spartans had no patience with grand public projects and thought that city walls were for cowards, so there's not much to see other than a crumbling **theater** and a small **museum** *(Agiou Nikonos 71, Sparta, tel 27310/1516, closed Mon.)*.

The Attica Peninsula

The Attica Peninsula extends from Mount Parnitha and the city of Marathon down to Cape Sounion at its southernmost point. Within one or two hours' travel of Athens, there you will find ancient ruins, historic sites, a wealth of national parks, and a welcome respite from the noise of the city.

The towering pillars of the Temple of Poseidon dominate the rocky outcrop of Cape Sounion.

Temple of Poseidon

  127 C3
✉ Cape Sounion
☎ (22920) 39363
💲 $$

Cape Sounion

Standing on the high headland at Cape Sounion, with the wind blowing in from the sea and the waves crashing against the rocks below, it's easy to see why the ancient Greeks associated this spot with the god of the seas, Poseidon. As the southernmost point of the Attica Peninsula, Cape Sounion was the symbolic meeting point of land and sea, a sacred site for a maritime people like the Greeks.

The first shrines were built here in around the seventh century B.C., although the massive pillars that stand on the site today are the remains of a later construction, likely built around 440 B.C. Although not the best preserved of Greece's ancient religious centers, the ruins of the **Temple of Poseidon** are arguably the most atmospheric, especially at sunset. As the site is particularly exposed to the elements, most of the fragile statues and artifacts, including an impressive statue of Poseidon, have long since been taken to the National Archaeological Museum in Athens (see pp. 94–95, 97). Tour buses often stop here, so it can get crowded at times, but outside of peak season it is usually pretty empty. There is a restaurant and gift shop near the temple.

Lavrion

Located 24 miles (39 km) southeast of Athens and just north of Cape Sounion, the port of Lavrion thrived in ancient times thanks to its silver mines (see sidebar below). These mines provided Athens with the wealth it required to build its navy and its great monuments. Surprisingly, the town itself saw little of this wealth as its inhabitants were mostly slaves.

Today Lavrion serves as a major ferry port connecting Attica with the islands. During the day the town is often filled with travelers aimlessly passing the time in the delightful cafés and bars by the docks until their ferry arrives. Given the number of people who pass through the town, it's surprising to find that its large and impressive **ancient amphitheater,** a few minutes walk uphill from the docks, is usually largely deserted.

Vravron

The coastal town of Vravron is about 15 miles (24 km) north of Lavrion on the coast road.

The modern town stands on the site of the ancient settlement of Brauron, home of the ancient Athenian leader Peisistratus. Just outside the town lie the ruins of the ancient **Sanctuary of Artemis.** This sanctuary was constructed around 420 B.C. but abandoned about a century later because of regional conflicts. According to the playwright Euripides, Iphigenia, the daughter of king Agamemnon of Mycenae, lived here as a priestess having been spared death by Artemis.

Today this remarkable site consists of a many-columned temple building, complete with ceremonial dining areas, and a group of smaller shrines clustered around a sacred spring. Close to the ruins a modern **Archaeological Museum** houses a collection of votive statues and other artifacts that have been found during the excavations.

Rafina

A little farther up the east coast lies Rafina. Rafina was

Lavrion
🅰 127 C3

Vravron
🅰 127 C3

Sanctuary of Artemis & Archaeological Musum
✉ Near Vravron
☎ (22990) 27020
🕐 Closed Mon.
💲 $$

Rafina
🅰 127 C3

The Lavrion Mines

Little remains of Lavrion's mining industry today as the silver mines have long since fallen into disuse. They were already mostly abandoned when the travel writer Pausanias passed through the town in the second century A.D. and have been revived only sporadically since then.

The mines have left the town with a fascinating legacy, however, which can be seen if you walk down to the beaches around the port. Where the blue sea meets the yellow sand, it is common to find beautiful crystals and sea-polished exotic stones in the sand. These are remnants of the spoil dug out from the ancient mines. Large numbers of these rare stones and crystals are deposited on the beaches by winter storms every year, attracting collectors from across Europe. Those with an interest in the subject should pay a visit to the **Lavrion Mineraleralogical Museum** *(Heroon Polytechneiou Square, tel 02920/25295, Closed Mon., $)* in the town.

EXPERIENCE: Schinias-Marathon National Park

If you fancy a break from visiting archaeological sites on the Attica Peninsula, Schinias-Marathon National Park, on the coast just to the east of Marathon, offers peaceful and non-strenuous walking or cycling—or seriously energetic rowing and canoeing. And if you're into your birding, then this really is a top place to spend a few hours.

A black-headed wagtail surveys its territory in Schinias wetland.

Just a 90-minute drive from downtown Athens and directly north of Schinias beach, Schinias-Marathon National Park is one of the largest wetlands in southern Greece.

An artificial lake (for rowing events) was built on the edge of the park for the 2004 Olympic Games. The wetlands suffered during its construction and just a few years after the Olympics the whole area was badly neglected. Local naturalists mobilized a clean up group and formed a committee to revive the park and promote tourism. The park is now thriving again, and the rowing center is now open to the public during the summer months (Olympic Rowing & Canoeing Center, Schinias National Park, Marathon, tel 210/870 7000).

Walking & Cycling

The best time to visit Schinias-Marathon is in the fall and spring, when it's not so crowded, though the park is quietest in the winter. Hikers can trek through the Mediterranean pine forest and surrounding hills, while cyclists can investigate the labyrinthine paths in the marshland. If you fancy the latter form of transport, **Pame Volta** (tel 210/675 2885, www.pame volta.gr, email Vasilis Kampas at vkampas@pamevolta.gr) is recommended for bike rentals.

Schinias-Marathon has one of the Attica Peninsula's best beaches as well as a beautiful pine forest and, of course, its wetland. So, be sure to pack a picnic (or two), some good shoes, and some binoculars.

Birding

There are unusual breeding birds, such as great egrets, ferruginous ducks, glossy ibis, and many migratory species. **Spyros Skareas** (http://greekbirding.blogspot .com, s.skareas@gmail.com, tours from $$$), a longtime naturalist, takes visitors on tours of the park. Spyros recommends spring as the best time to visit, especially between mid-March and mid-May, when birds from Africa and Asia stop here on their way to northern Europe. You will see hundreds of sandpipers, plovers, herons, and ducks at this time. May and June are the best months for birdsong, and you will see warblers, wheatears, buntings, harriers, and eagles. Spyros usually meets visitors at the Katehaki or Pallini Metro stations in Athens, but he can also arrange to meet you at your hotel.

Rafina has a long beach, sheltered to the north and south, that seldom gets crowded, except on Sundays, when Athenian families descend.

—CLIVE CARPENTER
National Geographic contributor

established in the 1920s by Greek refugees who fled Asia Minor. In the 1940s, Greeks who had been spared execution by the Nazis built the **Chapel of Agios Nikolaos** here.

Like Lavrion to the south, the small town of Rafina is growing rapidly now that Greece's major airport has been moved out of Athens and closer to this area. Many island-bound tourists now head to east coast ferry ports rather than the docks at Pireas. Despite this growth, however, Rafina retains a relaxed small town atmosphere. Daily life here still revolves around the picturesque fishing port, where all manner of fish and seafood is landed every morning. As a result of this reliable daily catch, the restaurants around the harbor offer some of the finest fish and seafood dishes in the region.

Schinias Beach

Located near the town of Marathon, Schinias beach is sandy and good for camping. Though Schinias once had trouble with murky water and not-so-clean beach space, it has cleaned up in recent years. In fall and winter the area around Schinias beach is very popular with windsurfers and kitesurfers. If you're interested in learning to windsurf then the nearby **Karavi Schinias Beach Club** *(Poseidonos Ave. 198, tel 22940/55950, www.karavi .gr)*, with its trained instructors and equipment rental, is a good place to start. Athenians who want both authentic village coziness and stunning natural beauty go to nearby **Porto Rafti,** a seaside town about 24 miles (38 km) out of Athens.

Marathon

Though greatly outnumbered, the Greeks won a historic victory over the Persians here in September 490 b.c. (see pp. 28–29). The foot soldiers who fell in battle were cremated and buried together in the **Tumulus of Marathon,** a funeral mound that's still visible on the battlefield. When archaeologists excavated the site in the 19th century, they discovered ashes, bones, and even some armor. A few miles away, there's a relatively new **Archaeological Museum** devoted to the famous battle. It exhibits archaeological finds from the area dating from Neolithic to Roman times and including marble statues from the nearby Temple of Isis.

The Real Marathon: The Battle of Marathon is best known today for its association with the story of Pheidippides.

Schinias-Marathon National Park & Beach
127 C3

Marathon
127 C3

Tumulus of Marathon
✉ Marathon
☎ (22930) 55462
🕐 Closed Mon. & Nov.–May
💲 $$

Marathon Archaeological Museum
✉ Plataion St. 114, Vranas, Marathon
☎ (22940) 55155
🕐 Closed Mon.
💲 $

Athens's marathon is inspired by the famous run of **Pheidippides, the ancient Greek messenger.**

Rhamnus

⬛ 127 C4

**Sanctuary
of Nemesis
& Rhamnus
Ancient Port
Archaeological
Site**

✉ Near Kato Souli

☎ (22940) 63477

🕐 Closed winter
months

💲 $$

According to Herodotus, Pheidippides was a messenger runner who carried a plea for help 152 miles (246 km) from Athens to the city of Sparta. He is said to have covered the distance in a day and a half. After the Spartans decided they couldn't send troops for another week, he ran back to Athens, just as quickly, to relay the news. Contrary to legend, however, there is no mention of him dying of exhaustion when he returned.

In recent years it has been shown that Pheidippides's feat was indeed possible. Every year a group of ultra-marathon runners hold an event called the Spartathlon (*www.spartathlon.gr*), which covers the full distance from Athens to Sparta. The current record is held by Greek runner Yiannis Kouros, who completed the race in an astonishing 20 hours and 25 minutes!

Rhamnus

The ancient city of Rhamnus was once an important religious and commercial center. With its strategically important location overlooking the Euboean Strait, the town was heavily fortified and well defended. It was best known, however, for being the home of the **Sanctuary of Nemesis,** the goddess of retribution who pursued the wicked with a determined vengeance. There was also a small temple devoted to Themis, goddess of justice and humanity.

Today this site, around 5 miles (8 km) northwest of Marathon, is one of the most isolated and tranquil of Attica's ancient ruins. Archaeologists have been working at Rhamnus since the mid-1970s, and much of the ancient settlement is still being excavated. Visitors can tour most of the **archaeological site** and sometimes get to see the archaeologists at work in other, closed, areas.

Mount Parnitha & Back to Athens

Mount Parnitha, the highest of the peaks north of Athens, is in **Parnitha National Park,** a big area of beautiful pine forests (though much forest was destroyed in the fires of 2007), rugged peaks, and cool mountain streams. The park is popular with hikers and nature-lovers who want to enjoy peace and quiet on its hundreds of miles of tracks and trails.

Farther south, on the outskirts of **Paiania** is the spectacular **Koutouki Cave,** a vast chamber filled with stalactites and stalagmites. This natural curiosity was discovered by a goatherd in the 1920s. Paiania is only a few miles from the eastern suburbs of Athens and is also home to the **Vorres Museum,** dedicated to modern Greek art and architecture. The museum showcases art and sculpture made by Greek artists in the second half of the 20th century; artisanal furniture and rugs; pottery; and engravings. ∎

**Parnitha
National Park**
◪ 127 C4
www.parnitha-np.gr

Paiania
◪ 127 C3

Vorres Museum
✉ Parados
   Diadohou
   Konstantinou 4,
   Paiania
☎ (21066) 42520
🕐 Open Aug. a.m.
   only
💲 $$

The Athens Classic Marathon

Greece revived the ancient route from Marathon to Athens as a modern marathon course in 1982. The **Athens Classic Marathon** (www.athensclassic marathon.gr) now attracts thousands of participants and spectators every October. The course begins in the town of Marathon, passing the burial mound and the war memorial for the Marathon dead (see p. 135) before working its way through the districts of Pikermi, Pallini, Gerakas, and Agia Paraskevi. It meanders through the northern Athenian neighborhoods of Halandri and Holargos before leading into the center of Athens. Runners finish in the Kallimarmaro, the old Olympic Stadium, where they run 560 feet (170 m) around the track before crossing the finish line.

The Athens Classic Marathon also hosts 5-km and 10-km races as well as marathon power walking, but the runners' marathon remains the showcase. In the hot summer months before the marathon, many runners train in the city to try and adjust to the dry heat. In 2010, the marathon celebrated 2,500 years since Pheidippides's mythical run. More than 12,500 runners took part in the race despite one of the hottest summers on record.

Prospective entrants should bear in mind that this certainly isn't the easiest event. There are many punishing uphill sections and few spectators to encourage you, especially in the gloomy industrial areas in the middle of the course. However, crowds do gather at the beginning of the race in Marathon and at the end. The race finishes with a victory lap of the old Olympic stadium, an unforgettable finish that twins past and present.

For those who like to combine their endurance running with scrupulous historical accuracy, there is an alternative event, the **Spartathlon** (see p. 136) that follows the 152-mile (246 km) route taken by Pheidippides.

the islands

Fish tavernas, sandy beaches, pine-scented forests, and medieval monasteries on the islands located to the south and east of Athens

The Near Islands

Pages 138–139: A Mikonos church
Opposite: Off the coast of Evia at dawn

The Near Islands

The Greek islands evoke images of quintessentially Mediterranean wonder: white-washed stone cottages, old-fashioned windmills, and stark landscapes carved by volcanoes and eroded by waves and wind, all surrounded by a calm, blue sea.

Greece has more than 6,000 islands and islets, but only 227 of them are inhabited. The closest islands to the city of Athens are those scattered around the Saronic Gulf, the large island of Evia, and the smaller islands of the Sporades.

The Argo-Saronic Islands

Located just a short ferry ride from the port of Pireas, these islands provide visitors with a taste of the relaxed pace of island life without the need to spend hours traveling to distant specks on the horizon. Most of the islands are in the Saronic Gulf, though the island of Spetses is actually between the Saronic and Argolic Gulfs. Other easy-to-reach islands include Egina,

Angistri, Poros, and Idra. Just off the coast of Pireas is the largely residential island of Salamina.

Egina is the most visited of the islands, since it's just 30 minutes from Pireas by hydrofoil. Spetses is the most lush but also the farthest away—by high-speed ferry, it takes 90 minutes to get there from Pireas. Near Egina are the tiny islands of Angistri and Poros, notable for their natural beauty. Though one of the largest of the islands, Idra feels more like Angistri and Poros—a quiet place where horse-drawn carts

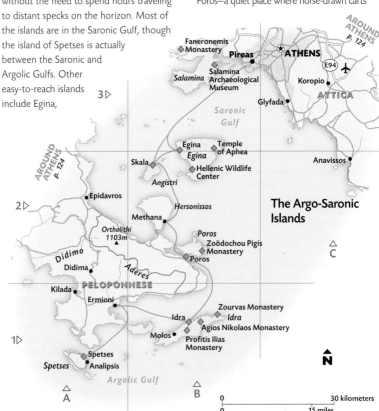

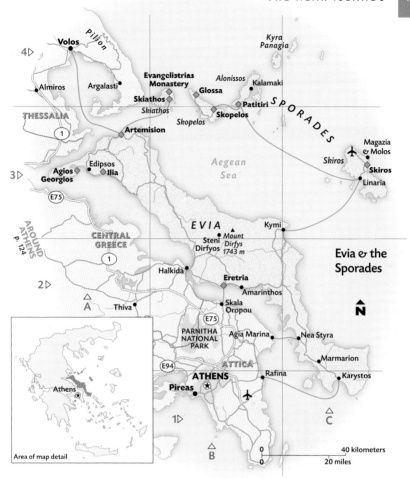

Evia & the Sporades

N

Area of map detail

0   40 kilometers
0   20 miles

are a common sight. Both Idra and Spetses are
known for their lively carnivals. The two islands
also have festivals celebrating the start of Lent
and Greek Independence day (March 25).

Evia & the Sporades

To the east of Athens is the island of Evia—
an island so large and so close to the mainland (it's connected by a bridge) that few
Athenians consider it an island at all. Evia is
a popular weekend getaway with Athenians,
and its beaches are usually packed in summer. Farther afield, to the northeast of Evia,
lie the Sporades—a group of small islands
(Skopelos, Skiathos, Alonissos, and Skiros)
that retain an authentic and unspoiled
atmosphere. ■

NOT TO BE MISSED:

The amazingly well-preserved
   Temple of Aphea on Egina   **145**

Greece's rare wildlife at the Hellenic
   Wildlife Rehabilitation Center   **145**

A visit to the Greek revolutionary
   Laskarina Bouboulina's house
   on Spetses   **148–149**

Island-hopping in the Saronic
   Gulf   **150–151**

Taking a dip in the healing waters of
   Edipsos on the island of Evia   **153**

Watching the traditional Goat Dance
   on Skiros   **159**

The Argo-Saronic Islands

On a clear day, the closest of these islands can be seen from the Acropolis in Athens. This proximity to the city makes them popular destinations for Athenians to relax on weekends. During the week the islands can be surprisingly quiet, even in summer.

Horse-drawn carts remain a popular mode of transport on the islands.

Salamina

📍 142 B3

Visitor Information

www.salamina.gr

NOTE: The ferry crossing from Perama (north of Pireas harbor) to Salamina ($$) takes about 15 minutes. Ferries run every 15 minutes from 5:30 a.m. to 10 p.m., then every 20–30 minutes from 10 p.m. to 5:30 a.m.

www.hellenic seaways.gr

Salamina

Salamina is equal parts crowded suburb and naval base, like a cross between Staten Island and Norfolk, Virginia. It's linked to Athens by frequent ferries that leave from Pireas and the dedicated ferry terminal at Perama. The island has some nice beaches, but the murky waters mean they're rarely visited by travelers. The 17th-century **Faneronemis Monastery** *(near Steno, tel 21046/81861)* in the northwest of the island is worth a visit, however, and the **Salamina Archaeological Museum** has some interesting exhibits.

Egina

From the broad harbor at Egina town this once powerful island state launched its fleet of privateers and trading vessels. They were all weapons in the island's long-running rivalry with neighboring Athens. Today the Athenian invaders are welcomed to the island, coming as they do with beach towels and cameras, rather than spears.

   Egina town is a pleasant place, dominated by grand 19th-century mansions and the solitary ruins of its **acropolis.** It gets extremely crowded on weekends, however, as Athenians flock here to escape the noise of the city. The island has several fascinating historical and cultural sites.

About 4 miles (6 km) east of Egina town is **Agios Nektarios Monastery** (*Aiginis Kontou St., $ donation recommended*), one of the largest monasteries in Greece. This impressive red-roofed and many-domed building houses the remains of St. Nektarios (1846–1920). On Novermber 9 every year, pilgrims gather from across Greece for a mass on the saint's holy day. Beyond the monastery a path winds about half a mile (0.8 km) northwest to the ruins of medieval **Palaiachora,** the island's ruined former capital. Those who make the steep climb up to the site get to explore an almost completely deserted ruined town, where there are a few surviving Byzantine churches.

The island's main attraction, however, is located on the opposite side of the island, around 1 mile (1.6 km) on the main road north from the coastal village of Agia Marina, 7 miles (11 km) east of Egina town. Here you will find the 2,500-year-old **Temple of Aphea** (*tel 22970/32398, $$*), one of the best preserved temples in Greece. Most of its columns are still standing, and significant portions of the pediment are largely intact. The entry fee includes the nearby museum that features artifacts from the site and from Egina's ancient glory days

Angistri

Angistri is a small island near Egina that's almost completely covered by a dense pine forest. Its people were allied with the Eginian kingdom during the Homeric age. With a population of fewer than 1,000 people, the island has always been something of a backwater—it was only hooked up to the national power grid in the 1970s—and

Salamina Archaeological Museum
- 142 B3
- 42 Polychroni Lempesi St.
- (21046) 40759
- Closed Mon.
- $$

Egina
- 142 B2, B3

Visitor Information
- City Hall, Egina
- (22970) 26967

www.greeka.com/saronic/aegina/aegina-tourism.htm

NOTE: The high-speed ferry from Pireas ($$) takes 1 hour.

Angistri
- 142 B2

Visitor Information
www.greeka.com/saronic/agistri/index.htm

NOTE: The high-speed ferry from Pireas ($$) takes 45 minutes.

EXPERIENCE: Volunteering at a Wildlife Rehabilitation Center

Egina is the headquarters of the **Hellenic Wildlife Rehabilitation Center** (*Panchia Rachi, Egina, tel 22970/28267, closed Sat.–Sun., www.ekpazp.gr*), a nonprofit organization dedicated to treating injured and ill wildlife and protecting endangered animals.

Staff and volunteers treat some 4,500 wild animals every year, with a special focus on pelicans, falcons, eagles, vultures, storks, and other rare birds. Volunteering here is an intimate way to learn about Greece's indigenous wildlife. It's a bit like volunteering at a humane society

back in the United States but with wild animals as the boarders. Volunteers help feed and clean the animals and also help staff make cages and other housing units for new animals that are taken in. Don't come here if you're squeamish: There will be blood since many of the animals are wounded. The center welcomes anyone with an open heart who won't break down in tears at the animals' misfortune.

The center is about 6 miles (10 km) from Egina town at the foot of Mount Oros. Center employees pick up volunteers from the town about three times a day.

A fisherman returns to Idra harbor with a fresh catch.

Poros

⬜ 142 B2

Visitor Information

✉ City Hall, Poros

☎ (22980) 22250

**www.greeka.com/
saronic/poros/index
.htm**

NOTE: The high-speed ferry from Pireas to Poros ($$) takes about 70 minutes.

even today there are no cars on the island. In the summer, however, the population increases to around 4,500, as Athenian weekenders and other visitors flock to this secluded island.

The largest settlements on the island are **Angistri town** and **Skala,** the main port. Both are traditional, picturesque villages, surrounded by forests and beaches. Elsewhere on the island are the tiny villages of Metochi and Limenaria, where even the minimal tourist development seen on the rest of the island is absent. There are no notable historic sites or museums on Angistri,

but it does have miles and miles of beautiful beaches, relaxed and friendly tavernas, and an interior covered with cool forest.

Poros

A sea channel just 190 yards (200 m) wide separates Poros from the Peloponnese. Poros is two separate islands connected by a relatively modern causeway. The southern island, **Sphairia,** is only a fraction of the size of its northern neighbor yet is home to most of the island's roughly 4,000 inhabitants.

By contrast, **Kalavria,** to the north, is a quiet, rural island, whose population numbers only a few dozen. Archaeologists believe that the island has probably been inhabited since the Mycenaean period. In ancient times, Kalavria held an important Sanctuary of Poseidon, of which, sadly, almost nothing can be seen today.

Poros town is a lively and friendly place characterized by its fine neoclassical buildings. The most notable of these is the **clock tower** (built in 1927) that stands like a lighthouse on the highest point in the town. The island's history is documented in the **Poros Archaeological Museum,** which has artifacts from the Sanctuary of Poseidon, as well as reminders of the islands' more recent history.

Car ferries run every 30 minutes from Poros town to the mainland village of Galatas (about 450 yards/411 m away). The town is surrounded by the *lemondassos* (lemon forest)—an ancient plantation of about 30,000 fragrant lemon trees. It's a great spot for easy hikes or just an afternoon stroll in the shade of the old trees.

The 18th-century monastery of **Zoödochou Pigis,** on the eastern side of Poros, has a grand view of the sea as well as a spring that's reputed to heal ailments. Though the church is fairly plain, with few wall paintings, there is a 17th-century wood-carved icon from Cappadocia (present-day eastern Turkey) that's worth a look.

INSIDER TIP:

On these crowded islands the best beaches are almost always at the end of dirt roads or apparent dead-end tracks. Be prepared to explore.

—EVA VALSAMI-JONES
National Geographic field scientist

Idra

This long, narrow island was once a major commercial center; its fishing fleet plied their trade as far south as Egypt, while its merchants sailed as far away as Spain and France. Idra's rich shipping magnates helped fund their country's navy during the Greek War of Independence (see p. 34). Today the island is a sort of northern Mikonos, a hedonistic place where the interational jet-set go to party.

You don't have to own a pri-vate jet to live here, however, and it's also a popular haunt for artists.

Famous residents include the songwriter Leonard Cohen, who lived here throughout the 1960s, and the writer Henry Miller, who wrote about the island in his novel *The Colossus of Marousi* (1941).

One curious feature of the island, and probably the reason why it hasn't been overwhlemed by tourist development, is its lack of beaches. There are one or two sandy coves here and there on the island, but for the most part those who want to swim have to dive from the rocks on the shore. There are plenty of places to do this safely, however, including stone jetties and diving platforms, many within a few minutes walk of the harbor. The water is deep, clear, and clean. Close to the town, **Mandraki beach** is a small private beach with a wind-surfing center.

Visitors to the island arrive at the harbor in **Idra town,** whose houses are arranged like the seats in an amphitheater with the harbor as the stage. One of the first things you'll notice when you disembark is the absence of cars or motorcycles—visitors are greeted by a taxi-rank of donkeys, waiting patiently with their owners to take you and your luggage to your hotel. The lack of whirring mopeds or taxis gives the island a quiet, relaxed atmosphere that you'd expect from a much smaller and more isolated place.

Today, artifacts relating to the island's involvement in the Greek War of Independence are displayed in Idra's **Historical Archives Museum.** The museum, housed in a mansion owned

Poros Archaeological Museum

✉ Koryzis Square, Poros
☎ (22980) 23276
🕐 Closed Mon.
💲 $$

Zoödochou Pigis Monastery

🗺 142 B2
✉ Near Kalavria, Poros
💲 $ donation recommended

Idra

🗺 142 B1
Visitor Information
✉ City Hall, Idra
☎ (22980) 52210
www.hydra.com.gr

Historical Archives Museum

✉ Harborside, Idra town
☎ (22980) 52355
🕐 Closed Mon.
💲 $

Lazaros Koundouriotis House

✉ Idra town

☎ (22980) 52421

🕐 Closed Mon.

💲 $

www.hydra.com.gr /culture/lazaros -kountouriotis

Spetses

🅰 142 A1

Visitor Information

☎ (22980) 72225

www.greeka.com/ saronic/spetses/ spetses-tourist- information.htm

NOTE: The high-speed ferry from Pireas ($$) takes about 4 hours 30 minutes.

Bouboulina Museum

✉ Near Dapia, Spetses

☎ (22980) 72416

🕐 Closed end Oct.–end Mar.

💲 $$

www.bouboulina museum-spetses.gr

Mexis Mansion Museum

✉ Spetses town

☎ (22980) 72994

🕐 Closed Mon., afternoons, & winter months

💲 $$

by shipowner Gikas Koulouras, houses manuscripts relating to the war, old books and maps, traditional costumes, and relics from the two world wars and the Balkan wars. There is also the **Lazaros Koundouriotis House,** a museum devoted to a local hero of the Greek War of Independence, which also houses some examples of traditional local crafts and costumes.

Outside of the main town, those seeking nightlife usually go to **Molos,** located about 3 miles (5 km) southwest along the coast from Idra town. This small village consists of a number of bars and restaurants clustered around a small pebble beach. Not far from here is the fishing village of **Kamini,** from where you can see the Peloponnese coast on clear days.

The monasteries here are also notable. From Idra town, you can either hike or go by donkey to the summit of Mount Klimaki, which is topped by the **Profitis Ilias Monastery** and the nearby nunnery of **Agia Efrpraxia.** The most difficult hike is to **Zourvas Monastery,** but the views are unparalleled and there's also a secluded cove for swimming. To the southeast of Idra, the **Agios Nikolaos Monastery** has 16th-century icons and frescoes.

Spetses

A center of shipbuilding in the 18th and 19th centuries, Spetses is now a hideaway for the rich, who have summer homes here, and a popular weekend spot for Athenian tourists. The island,

INSIDER TIP:

Since Idra caters to an upscale clientele, expect to pay more than you would on neighboring islands.

—CLIVE CARPENTER
National Geographic contributor

which was known as Pityoussa in ancient times, remained quiet throughout most of its history. However, all that changed in the 1820s, when rebels met here to plan the revolt against the Ottomans, whose grip on their once-grand empire was weakening. On April 3, 1821, Spetses was the first island to raise the flag of revolution against the Turks at Agios Nikolaos cathedral.

The most famous Spetsiot revolutionary was Laskarina Bouboulina. She hailed from the ethnic Albanian community on nearby Idra. The mother of nine children and the possessor of a massive family inheritance, she used her money to purchase weapons, support rebel groups, and even build a large warship, the *Agamemnon* (which she bribed Ottoman officials to ignore). After the war began, she became the commander of her own naval fleet. With the *Agamemnon* as her flagship, she played a decisive role in the capture of the city of Nafplio (see pp. 128–129), modern Greece's first capital.

Her mansion, noted for its architectural flourishes, still stands and is now home to the **Bouboulina Museum.** The other notable museum on Spetses is the

Mexis Mansion Museum, which is housed in the former residence of the island's governor and has artifacts from the War of Independence as well as Bouboulina's bones.

Hotel Poseidonion *(Dapia, Spetses 18050, tel 22980/74553, www.poseidonion.com, $$$$$)* was built in 1914 by Sotirios Anargyros (1849–1918), a Spetsiot who left for New York as a penniless young man and returned a millionaire. The hotel became the scene of glamorous parties in the era between the two world wars. Anargyros also funded the Anargyros & Korgialenios School, an English-style boarding school opened in 1927. The school (closed to the public) became famous when a former teacher, John Fowles, used it as the setting for his 1965 novel *The Magus.*

Close to 4,000 people live on Spetses today, most of them in **Spetses town.** The town is small, but still divided into districts. **Kastelli** is the oldest quarter and is anchored by the 18th-century **Agia Triada church,** which is the town's highest point. The other quarter, **Kounoupitsa,** has cottages and lush gardens that are decorated in maritime motifs.

Other towns here include **Moni Aghion Panton, Ligoneri,** and **Kouzounos,** though only a few people live in each settlement. Spetses also has excellent hiking trails and good, low-key beaches, including **Scholes Kaiki** for the young and sporty, **Agii Anargiri** for the cosmopolitan and lounge-loving, and **Zogeria** for those who prefer a secluded, pine-lined space and deep blue water. The fishing village of **Analipsis** is also worth a visit, especially during Easter. To celebrate the resurrection, villagers set a boat on fire and push it out to sea. ∎

The lavishly decorated home of Spetsiot revolutionary Laskarina Bouboulina

Island-hopping in the Saronics

If you are trying to see as many of the islands as you can, but only have limited time, you'll be surprised how far you can get. With many quick ferries from Pireas and between the islands, there's more time to investigate the islands themselves.

A ferry leaves Poros beneath the gaze of the church's distinctive clock tower.

The Saronic Islands of Egina, Poros, Idra, Spetses, and Angistri are so close to Athens that locals flock to them on pleasant weekends in the summer. Nearly everyone arrives by ferry from the port city of Pireas. Hopping on ferries is easy and cheap and, if you go on a high-speed boat, very quick, too.

It's challenging to island-hop all of the Saronic Gulf sights in one day since timetables with ferries vary and you will barely have time to even step foot on some of the farther-flung islands like Spetses and Idra. You can do some short-scale island hopping from Egina to Angistri, or you can stretch out the itinerary to two or three days to fit in the rest of the islands.

Here's one itinerary that will give a traveler a good taste of the islands and a few good ferry rides, too.

NOT TO BE MISSED:

Visiting an Egina fish taverna • A quiet walk in Metochi • Swimming at dawn on Poros • A donkey ride on Idra

The first stop is **Egina** ❶ (see pp. 144–145), 19 miles (30 km) and a 40-minute ferry ride from Pireas. Several ferries leave for the island every day, from morning to early evening. Egina is known for its pistachios and its pottery, and also has some excellent fish taverns near the port. Try the **Aegean Flying Dolphins Pireas–Egina** ferry *(tel 22970/25800, 22970/91221, or 210/417 9822, www.aegeanflyingdolphins.gr, $$).* While on the

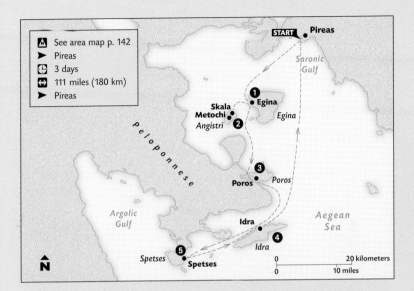

See area map p. 142
► Pireas
🕐 3 days
↔ 111 miles (180 km)
► Pireas

START ● Pireas

Saronic Gulf

Peloponnese

❶ ● Egina

Skala
Metochi ●
Angistri ❷

Egina

❸ ● Poros
Poros

Argolic Gulf

Aegean Sea

Idra ●
❹ Idra

Spetses ● ❺
Spetses

N

0   20 kilometers
0   10 miles

island, it's worth catching a local bus or taxi from Egina Town to the well-preserved yet little-known **Temple of Aphea** (see p. 145) on the island's east coast.

From Egina, you can also hop to nearby **Angistri** ❷ (Aegean Flying Dolphins, $). There are also water taxis that can shuttle you over for a bit more. The boat ride from Egina takes just 10 minutes. Milos (see p. 145), the main village on Angistri, is lively, though like nearby Skala, it can be a bit touristy during the summer months. The village of **Metochi** above Skala is lovely and quiet. The best way to explore the island is by mountain bike or moped. Check rental offices in Milos for more information.

If you get back to Egina by early evening, you can take a Hellenic Seaways ferry (www.hellenicseaways.gr, $$) to the lemon-scented island of **Poros** (see pp. 145–146) ❸ that night. The ferry ride lasts about an hour. It's quite an experience taking a ferry ride at night, when the seascape is shadowy and moody and the lights of distant coastal villages glimmer on the horizon. You will have to stay overnight in Poros (Poros Town and Kanali have the most options), but that's not a problem: Poros has

good beaches for a morning swim and some good hiking amid the citrus groves.

If you get an early start, you can catch a late-morning ferry ($$) to **Idra** (see pp. 146–148) ❹, the most beautiful of the Saronic islands. The ride will take about 30 minutes. Idra is a rugged island, with spare hills carved by paths that are traversed best by foot or on a donkey. It's also got notable architecture, with neoclassical mansions that are symbols of the island's shipowner wealth.

Return to the Mainland

From Idra, you can take an evening ferry to **Spetses** (see pp. 148–149) ❺ on Hellenic Seaways. This leg of the journey will take 40 minutes. Spetses is another paradise for Greece's shipowners, and so the island is well-maintained. There are plenty of places to stay here, but most hotels are pricey during the summer. Opt for a family-run pension instead (see Travelwise, p. 252). In the morning, you can explore the island by motorbike or by foot. You can return to Pireas on a late-afternoon ferry from Spetses (www.hellenicseaways.gr, $$$$$), a beautiful trip that will take about two hours.

Evia & the Sporades

Lush and mountainous, Evia and the islands of the Sporades are popular destinations for those who want an eclectic mix of nature, beaches, and culture. From the densely forested island of Evia—second largest island in Greece—to the scattered tranquil islands of the Sporades, this area offers a great deal of variety only a few hours from Athens.

Preparing the nets for another day's fishing on the island of Skiathos in the Sporades

Evia

⚑ 143 A3-C1

Visitor Information

✉ Hellenic Tourism Organization, Edipsos, Evia

☎ (22260) 22304

Evia is very easy to get to from Athens, either by driving over a bridge from Mikron Vathy on the mainland or via a short ferry to one of the port cities. Traveling to Skiathos and Skopelos is relatively easy by ferry or hydrofoil, though the service is less frequent during the November to April winter season. From Skiathos and Skopelos, you can also hire small boats to visit a number of tiny uninhabited islets in the Sporades. The ferry service to Skiros is irregular, though there is a weekly flight from Athens.

Evia

This long, mountainous island has been linked to the mainland by a road bridge since the 19th century. Like the towns of the Attica peninsula, the island of Evia is considered by many Athenians to be a kind of distant suburb. However, while there are some who commute to Athens from here, it has not been developed in the same way as closer islands like Salamina.

In ancient times, Evia's two principal cities were Chalkis and Eretria. Both were first settled by Ionian Greeks from Attica. The two cities were initially rivals, but later formed an alliance to fight against the Persians and later the Athenians. Their early autonomy came to an end in 446 B.C., when the island was brought under the control of Athens. Over the centuries the island has had many other rulers—including the Romans, Byzantines, and Ottomans—but has always managed to maintain its position as a prosperous trade hub and cultural center.

Halkida (the modern name for Chalkis) and **Eretria** are still the primary settlements on the island. Modern Halkida, located at the narrowest point of the Evvoikos Kolpos strait, grew after a railway connection was established with Athens. The city, now home to 70,000 people, is connected to the mainland by two bridges.

Athenians love vacationing in Evia because it is close to the capital and it is also one of the few places in Greece that hasn't been colonized by foreign tourists. The island's north is popular with hikers who like its quiet, lush trails and thickly forested vistas. Coastal towns such as **Agios Georgios,**

Artemision, and **Ilia** have small, traditional tavernas and warm, small-town vibes. The secluded **Lihadonisia islets,** just off the north coast of Evia, are popular with boaters and scuba-divers.

The central part of the island is home to Halkida, the administrative capital, as well as the rugged mountain of **Dirfys,** which is popular with climbers and mountaineers. The climb to the summit is for serious trekkers only. Most people start out at Steni Dirfyos, from where the peak is 10 miles (16 km). For more information, contact the Halkida Alpine Club *(Angeli Gouviou St. 22, Halkida, Evia, tel 22210/25230).* Eretria and **Amarinthos** are popular with families who like quiet beaches and lively vegetable markets. Southern Evia is mountainous and lined with creeks and has notable coastal towns such as **Karystos Marmarion,** and **Epsidos** (see sidebar below).

Skopelos

Legend says that Staphylus and Peparethos, sons of Diony- sus and the Minoan princess

Halkida
🗺 143 B2

Lihadonisia Islets
🗺 143 A3

Karystos
🗺 143 C1

Marmarion
🗺 143 C2

Edipsos
🗺 143 A3

Skopelos
🗺 143 B3-4
Visitor Information
✉ City Hall, Skopelos
☎ (22420) 22250
www.greeka.com/
sporades/skopelos/
skopelos-tourism
.htm

EXPERIENCE: The Healing Waters of Edipsos

According to mythology, the hero Hercules bathed in the hot springs of Edipsos, on the north end of Evia, to recharge before each of his labors. So many people sought out these hot springs that baths were built to accommodate the public. More recently, the springs attracted the likes of Aristotle Onassis, Greta Garbo, and Maria Callas.

The town is now a picturesque spa center with steam baths, hot tubs, and an Olympic-size pool with water from the hot springs and the sea. The water from the springs is said to have healing qualities. The **Thermae Sylla Spa and Wellness Hotel** *(Posidonos St. 2, Edipsos, tel 22260/ 60100, www.thermaesyllaspa hotel.com, $$$$$)* is the most luxurious place to stay. The hotel offers massages, facials, and physiotherapy, and it also has a restaurant and bar.

The Mamma Mia Effect

Skopelos likes being a low-key place, despite the hordes of tourists who come here solely because of its appearance in the film adaptation of the *Mamma Mia* musical, written by two former members of the Swedish disco/pop group ABBA. The film, released in 2008, was shot on location in the summer of 2007 on Kastani beach on the southwest coast of Skopelos.

The islanders did not want to cave in to Hollywood tourism after the movie. There is, however, one *Mamma Mia* boat tour every week, and islanders have also put up signposts pointing out highlights from the filming. These are fairly few and far between, though, as many of the film's locations were temporary sets. Nevertheless, thousands come to Skopelos every summer singing ABBA songs and trying to relive the sun, sea, and music of the movie.

Ariadne of Crete, founded this triangular island in the Sporades. Skopelos means "a sharp rock," but the island is actually very green. It covers about 47 square miles (122 sq km), most of it pine forests, olive groves, and orchards. Farmers in Skopelos are known for cultivating eight varieties of plums, though only three—the black, red, and yellow—are commonly used. The sweet black plum is cooked with chicken or pork as a local specialty, but Skopelos cooks go wild over the sweet-sour red plum, which is stewed with lentils, fish, squid, and octopus. The juicy yellow plum is usually picked before it is ripe and preserved whole in a sweet syrup for a popular Greek delicacy called *glyko tou koutaliou,* or "spoon sweet."

The island's main settlement, **Skopelos town,** overlooks a bay on the north coast. From the waterfront, it's a straight flight of stairs to the town. The climb is daunting, but there are several pretty churches on the way up, including the 11th-century **Agios Athanasios,** which has beautiful 17th-century murals inside. At the top of the stairs is a 13th-century Venetian **castle,** which stands on the ruins of a 2,500-year-old **acropolis.** The town is charming, full of whitewashed cottages contrasting with brightly painted balconies filled with blooming plants in ceramic pots. There's also a **Folk Art Museum** housed in a 19th-century mansion that has period furniture and traditional silk clothing stitched with intricate embroidery. The closest beach is **Staphylos,** which is fun but can be crowded.

Other towns on Skopelos include **Panormos Bay,** which is about 4 miles (6 km) west of Skopelos town. It's the smallest of the ancient towns of Peparethos, which were founded in the eighth century B.C. by colonists from Chalkis (now Halkida, on Evia; see p. 153). Panormos Bay is near a collection of traditional farmhouses called *kalivia,* which are surrounded by plum orchards. Farmers used to dry plums in giant outdoor ovens next to the kalivia. There's a beach called **Milia** just over 1 mile (2 km) away and another called **Adrina,** accessible through a hotel of the same name. Other villages include the quiet hamlet of **Elios,** about 6 miles (10 km) north of Panormos Bay, and **Glossa,** the island's second-largest settlement, which has a memorable vista of whitewashed homes topped with red roofs clustered into the hillside above the harbor of **Loutraki.**

Alonissos

Off the coast of Skopelos is the tiny but lush isle of Alonissos, surrounded by pretty islets such as **Peristera, Kyra Panagia, Gioura,** and **Piperi.** Most of its 3,000 people live in the capital, **Patitiri,** as well as the villages of **Rsoum** and **Votsi** and the seaside resorts of **Steni Vala** and **Kalamaki.** The beaches are covered by pebbles rather than sand, but the water is clean, clear and welcoming. The island remains a quiet and peaceful getaway, the islanders are warm and welcoming, and staff at the well-known marine park keep watch over the endangered Mediterranean monk seals.

Skiathos

The hilly and wooded island of Skiathos covers an area of only 16 square miles (42 sq km) but has more than 70 beaches and sandy coves. This inviting coastline makes it a popular destination for tourists on beach-and-bar holiday packages. As a result, this island is one of the most heavily developed in the region, and becomes one of the most crowded in the summer. Outside of peak season, however, the island takes on a more subdued, relaxed vibe.

The main town, also named

Alonissos
143 B4
Visitor Information
✉ Municipality of Alonissos, Patitiri, Alonissos
☎ (24240) 65555
www.alonissos.gr

Skiathos
143 B4
Visitor Information
✉ Skiathos City Hall, 12 Nikotsata, Skiathos
☎ (24270) 22022
www.skiathos.gr

A Mediterranean monk seal eating an octopus it has just caught

Alexandros Papadiamantis statue in Skiathos town

Skiathos, is more utilitarian than beautiful. The Nazis destroyed most of the buildings here in 1944, and postwar development has been of the concrete apartment block variety. The main street, Papadiamantis, has all the action: the banks, post offices, police stations, cafés, souvenir shops, and other tourist draws.

All the beaches around Skiathos town are crowded and very busy in the summer. The **Kalamaki peninsula** on the south coast has plenty of villas perched above secluded coves; some are available for rent. **Troullos Bay** is on the coastal road west of the Kalamaki peninsula. This is a resort area that gets very crowded in the summer. Its main beach, **Koukounaries,** used to be one of the most beautiful in Greece, but now it's full of beach umbrellas, sun chairs, refreshment stands, tavernas, and, of course, many, many people in the summer A better beach is **Mandraki,** which isn't far away and is far quieter. Mandraki is where the Persian leader Xerxes stopped on his way to the battles of Artemisium and Salamis, where the Greeks defeated his forces (see p. 29).

About 13 miles (20 km) northeast of Troullos is the cliff of **Kastro,** where islanders from Skiathos town built homes in the 16th century to protect themselves from pirates. They stayed until 1829, eking out a living. The only way to get to Kastro is by climbing steep steps; at the top are a couple of old churches and the remains of old homes. Returning to Skiathos town by foot is a pleasant three-hour hike through orchards, fields, and forests. About 1 mile (1.6 km) east of Kastro is **Lalaria beach,** the prettiest beach on the island. The beach is flanked by limestone promontories and is accessible only by water taxi or tour boat from the old port in Skiathos town.

Tour boats stop at the **Skoteini (Dark) Cave, Galazia (Azure) Cave,** and **Halkini (Copper) Cave.** Close to Lalaria beach is the **Evangelistria Monastery,** which monks from Mount Athos dedicated to the Annunciation of the Virgin Mary in the 18th century. It later became a base for revolutionaries in the war of independence against the Ottoman Turks. The monastery has a gift shop that sells locally made olive oil, preserves, wine, and icons.

Skiros

The island is craggy and rugged, especially in the south, and also somewhat isolated; there's nothing between Skiros and the northern Aegean island of Lesvos, near the Turkish coast. Skiros is the southernmost of the Sporades islands and also the largest, at 81 square miles (209 sq km). An isthmus ties verdant northern Skiros (or Meri, which means "tame") and the harsh southern part of the island (or Vouno, which means "mountain"). **Mount Kochilas** in the south is the highest point in Skiros. Because the south is so barren, a construction company involved in green energy

development partnered with a local monastery in 2007 to build some 85 wind turbines here on land owned by the Greek Orthodox Church. The idea was to harness the *meltemi*, the strong northern winds that whip the desolate landscape here. But residents and Athenians with summer homes here opposed the plan, saying that it would ruin their vistas of the island. Conservationists also nixed it, saying the turbines would harm the rare Skirian horses and migrating birds.

The west coast of Skiros has coves and bays dotted with islets. There are some 300 churches here, most owned by local families, but the pre-Lenten carnival is imbued with pre-Christian rituals, including one celebrating fertility and involving young men dressed as shepherds, women, grandfathers, and even goats,

Skiros
🅰 143 C3
Visitor Information
✉ Municipality of Skiros, Skiros
☎ (22220) 91929
www.greeka.com/
sporades/skyros/
skyros-tourist-
information.htm

Alexandros Papadiamantis Museum
✉ Skiathos town
☎ (24270) 23843,
🕐 Open Tues. only
💲 $

The Legacy of Alexandros Papadiamantis

The writer Alexandros Papadiamantis (1851–1911) is probably Skiathos's most famous son and also its most famous recluse. The son of an Orthodox priest, Papadiamantis studied and lived in Athens as a young man before returning to his home town to make his career as a novelist and short story writer.

This island of Skiathos appears frequently in his work, which often portrays the tough lives of the poor farmers who called this beautiful island home. The islanders are depicted with warmth and feeling. Because Papadiamantis was deeply religious, his stories often had a liturgical rhythm and mysticism and examined the essence of morality. His

masterpiece, a novella called *I Fonissa (The Murderess)*, tells the story of a midwife who kills female newborns to spare poor families who cannot provide them dowries. At the end of the book the midwife drowns in the sea after being found out, but Papadiamantis protrays her with sensitivity and nuance, inviting questions about ethics, misogynistic cultural values, and the desperate circumstances of many families in rural Greece.

Papadiamantis was known in Skiathos as a *kosmokalogeros*, or "worldly monk." He died of pneumonia in a humble three-room house in Skiathos town. The house is now a museum dedicated to his life and works.

Skiros Archaeological Museum

📧 Rupert Brooke Square, Sisyphos Agora, Skiros

☎ (22220) 91327

🕐 Closed Mon.

💲 $

Faltauïts Historical & Folklore Museum

📧 Plateia Rupert Brooke

☎ (22220) 91232

🕐 Closed afternoons & winter months

💲 $$

while singing racy songs (see sidebar p. 159). Skirians are also skilled artisans who make intricate furniture and embroidered linens.

Skiros town, called Chora by the locals, is built into a cliff that's topped by a fortified monastery. About 90 percent of the island's 3,000 people live here. Skirians often leave their windows open to show off the interior of their houses, which are decorated with porcelain, copper cooking utensils, wood carvings, and embroideries. The agora is called the **Sisyphos** here because its steepness recalls the myth of Sisyphus, who kept trying to roll a giant boulder up a mountain. The Sisyphos is home to travel agents, markets, pharmacies, artisanal shops, bars, and tavernas.

The tenth-century **Monastery of St. George** is at the Kastro, the town's highest point and the site of the ancient acropolis and a Bronze Age settlement. Built in 962 and massively overhauled in 1600, the monastery has a beautiful iconostasis inside, though the frescoes have sadly been covered by whitewash. Only one monk lives there. On the way to Magazia beach, there's also the small **Skiros Archaeological Museum** that has a collection of weapons, pottery, and jewelry from graves dating from Neolithic to Roman times. The **Faltauïts Historical & Folklore Museum** includes costumes, photographs, rare books, ceramics, paintings, and the

Local "goatmen" parade through Skiros town during the Goat Festival.

Goat Dancers of Skiros

Dressed in old-fashioned shepherd costumes, which include wooly coats and pants and traditional Skirian sandals, and carrying large staffs, the goat dancers are quite a sight during the pre-Lenten carnival celebration. But it's the sound of large bells clanging on the belts of the dancers that draws the most attention, especially when the men are dancing and singing to wake up the spirits of fertility.

A goat dancer is called a *geros*, which means "old man" in Greek, and some historians say the tradition dates back to the ancient cult of Dionysus. In addition to the shepherd costumes and bells, the goat dancers wear masks made from the skin of baby goats. During carnival, they walk around the village in gangs and stop at squares and monasteries to perform solo or group dances or to do primitive dance-off competitions, a kind of duel. As late as the 1960s, the goat dancers would go into homes to perform, but nowadays they dance in public spaces and villagers usually watch from tavernas, storefronts, or their home windows. Some goat dancers perform with belts of bells that weigh up to 100 pounds (50 kg) and try to show off their strength and virility by jumping onto tables while loaded with so much metal.

In recent years, women dressed in traditional clothes and wearing masks have joined the revelry, often joined by little boys wearing pint-sized versions of the men's shepherd costumes.

---

dazzling embroideries that feature the colorful, mohawked Eurasian bird called the hoopoe, as well as people with limbs and skirts blossoming into flowers.

The resort areas of **Magazia** and **Molos** are about half a mile (1 km) northeast of Skiros town. Once secluded and quiet, the beach areas are now growing fast. Beach-lovers can rent small rooms here and spend their days swimming and sunning and their nights sampling fresh fish and local wine at the seaside tavernas. If you're fit and up for an outdoorsy adventure, trek to **Vouno** for secluded beaches and sea caves. If you're lucky, you might catch a glimpse of a rare Skirian horse.

The Skirian Horse: Skiros is home to a unique breed of feral pony, the Skirian horse. Some scientists believe that the breed—which grows no taller than 4 feet (1.2 m)—is descended from horses brought to the islands by Athenian colonists between the fifth and eighth centuries B.C.

Skirian horses are usually friendly, sociable, and intelligent animals with a thick mane, a long tail, and strong legs. In the barren south of Skiros, the horses live in a semi-wild state. They used to be rounded up for work during the harvest but are rarely used these days. Today they are often cross-bred with donkeys or larger horses to supply the island with the stocky mules that pull many of the carts. The Greek government has designated the Skirian horse a protected animal. The Silva Project *(www.thesilvaproject.org)* wants to build its population by breeding the horse in other parts of Greece. ∎

Magazia
143 C3

Molos
143 C3

A scattering of spectacularly beautiful islands and whitewashed fishing villages, all set in a smooth azure sea

The Cyclades

The town of Oia, perched on the edge of Santorini's huge volcanic caldera

The Cyclades

The numerous small islands that make up the Cyclades are the highest peaks of a vast mountain range that lies beneath the Aegean Sea. Although the architecture and geography of the Cyclades changes little from island to island—think whitewashed homes built into steep cliffs, sparse and windswept vegetation, and dark, volcanic soil—the personalities of the islands vary greatly.

The Cyclades are steeped in myth and legend: These islands include the homes of gods and monsters, islands that rose from the sea to shelter ships from storms, and the location of a great battle between the gods. The real history of the Cyclades is no less fascinating, characterized by mysterious lost civilizations, mighty ruined temples, and an island that literally exploded.

A Little History

People may have lived on the Cyclades as far back as the fifth millennium B.C. Those who lived here were successful sailors and merchants who exported most of their products and resources, especially marble from the quarries at Paros and Naxos.

In the third millennium B.C., Cycladic-style marble figurines made it as far as Portugal. The Minoans imported the art to Crete, where it influenced sculpture on the island. In the second millennium B.C., the Cyclades were invaded by the Minoans, the Mycenaeans, and the Ionians, who incorporated the island-chain into their empires. In the fifth century B.C., the Persians conquered the Cyclades. After the Athenians defeated the Persians at the Battle of Salamis, the First Delian League (see p. 29) was founded on the island of Dilos, legendary birthplace of Apollo. The Cyclades were allied with the city-state of Athens for many centuries but revolted in 469 B.C., although the Athenians eventually took them back.

In more recent times, the Cyclades passed from the Venetians to the Ottomans, who largely ignored the islands and gave local leaders a good deal of autonomy. After the Cyclades became part of the modern Greek state, the French used marble from the long-forgotten quarries in Paros to build Napoleon's tomb. The maritime strength of the Cyclades dissipated after the Corinth Canal was built in 1893. Ermoupoli on Siros was considered Greece's second city before Thessaloniki became part of the Greek state in the early 20th century. During World War II, the Nazis blocked supplies to the islands, and many islanders starved. When a military junta took over the country from 1967–1974, the colonels, like the Romans, used Gyaros, a small and dry uninhabited isle near Siros, to exile prisoners.

After the junta fell, the islands (which had by now been equipped with electricity and phone lines) blossomed as tourist destinations.

AROUND
ATHENS
p. 124

ATHENS
Pireas ✈
Rafina
Karistos
3▷
Lavrion
Mount Kouvara
997m
Gavrio
Palaiopoli
Andros
Andros
Korissia
Kea
Gyaros
Pyrgos
Tinos
Tinos
Mikonos
Siros
Merichas
Kithnos
Ano Siros
Ermoupoli
Mikonos
Dilos
2▷
Aegean Sea
CYCLADES
Serifos
Serifos
Livadi
Naoussa
Paroikia
Marathi
Naxos
Donoussa
Adiparos
Lefkai
Moutsouna
Kamarai
Apollonia
Naxos
Sifnos
Paros
Aigiali
Chrysopigi
church
Erimonisia
Katapola
Kimolos
Amorgos
Plaka
Polyaigos
Paleokastro
1▷
Milos
Adamas
Sikinos
Ios
Trypiti
Ano Meria
Ios
Folegandros
△
A
Folegandros
Karavostasis
Iraklio
Oia
Santorini
✪ Thira
△
C
0   60 kilometers
0   30 miles
△
B
Iraklio
N

Area of map detail
Athens

And so began the modern mythology of the Cyclades as an exotic hideaway, home to dreamy blue seas and whitewashed cave houses built into dramatic rock faces. But if you find an old islander who remembers the harsh old times, you will hear a bit of the sadness that's hidden deep in the Cyclades, even against the most beautiful sunset on Earth.

The Cyclades Today

The best known of this chain of islands is Santorini, known for its excellent white wine, its sunsets, and for the active volcano that rumbles beneath the waters of its deep blue bay. Tinos is a pilgrimage site for Orthodox Christians and home to a community of marble sculptors and masons. Paros and Mikonos are party playgrounds for the rich and the restless. Tiny Sifnos is known for its potters, while Siros, the commercial center of the Cyclades, has stunning neoclassical architecture. Dilos is an archaeological mecca and legendary birthplace of Apollo, god of music and light. Naxos is the greenest of the Cyclades, a fertile land where farmers cultivate olives and fruit, and make fine cheeses and wines.

Despite the rapid growth of the tourism industry on many of these islands, they have, for the most part, maintained their traditionally rural and laid-back atmosphere. On most islands you'll be hard pressed to find a formal address for any building, or even a street name—on many islands the main settlement is called simply *Chora*, which translates as "the town." ■

The Northern Cyclades

Only around 50 miles (80 km) to the south and east of Athens, the northern Cyclades constitute some of the larger and more densely populated islands in the area. Despite their proximity to the Greek mainland, the islands maintain a unique cultural identity.

The medieval waterfront neighborhoods of Kastro and Little Venice on Mikonos

Mikonos

⚑ 163 C2

Visitor Information

✉ EOT Tourist Office, Paralia Mykonou, Mikonos

☎ (22890) 25250

www.mykonos-web .com

Curiously, the two islands closest to Athens, Kea and Kithnos, are probably the least touched by modern life. With a few exceptions these two islands are still rural, sparsely populated places, where the traditional island lifestyle continues largely untouched by tourism. They have few accommodation options and, with the exception of their beaches, even fewer sights to draw visitors. The islands that lie beyond, however, have numerous attractions to entice visitors farther out, including enigmatic ancient ruins, whitewashed towns, and stunning natural scenery.

Mikonos

Known as an island for the rich, beautiful, and hedonistic, Mikonos is characterized by smooth beaches, old-fashioned windmills, and a very expensive party scene. The island is 10 miles (16 km) by 7 miles (11 km) and was, according to myth, named for the grandson of Apollo and the nymph Rio.

The island has been inhabited for thousands of years and was, along with nearby Dilos, an important political center in ancient times. After the collapse of the Delian League, however, the island was forced to get by on the meager harvests its dry soil

INSIDER TIP:

The wooden water-taxis, or caiques, of Mikonos can take you to and from several beaches every morning and afternoon. Leave from Ornos Beach.

—CARSTEN STEHR
Staff, Starquest Expeditions tours

provided. During some periods of its history, Mikonos's residents resorted to piracy and raided nearby islands, but this was only ever a temporary solution.

The answer to the island's economic woes didn't come until the 1960s, when tourism transformed its economy (see sidebar below). Jackie Kennedy Onassis spent many holidays here in the 1960s, and she and other wealthy socialites turned the island into a summer paradise for the international jet-set.

Mikonos town is the main settlement on the island. It's one of the prettiest towns in the Cyclades, with its cobbled streets and whitewashed stone houses. As you explore the town, your eye is drawn to attractive decorative accents—such as brightly colored doors, lush green climbing vines, and weathered wooden balconies—that stand out against the background of white. The oldest part of the town is called **Kastro** and dates from the medieval period, while farther along the waterfront is the beautiful Little Venice neighborhood, filled with mansions that once belonged to shipowners and aristocrats.

On a high hill across from Little Venice are the old Mikonos **windmills** once used to grind the island's grain. Today almost all of these distinctive structures have been converted to private residences. One 16th-century windmill and its adjacent miller's cottage has been restored and opened to the public as the centerpiece of the island's **Agricultural Museum.** This open-air museum also includes a restored watermill,

Agricultural Museum

- ✉ Epano Myli, Mikonos town
- ☎ (22890) 26246
- 🕐 Open evenings only (4:30 p.m. –7:30 p.m.); closed Oct.– June.

Island Partying on Mikonos

Mikonos got its first taste of tourism when it became a playground for the international jet-set in the early 1960s, a development that lifted it out of centuries of poverty. It was not long, however, before this wealthy elite moved on to other fashionable resorts, leaving nothing but empty mansions and struggling jewelry stores in their wake. By the end of the decade the island had reinvented itself as a party island, enticing hippies and adventurers from across Europe.

Though crowds of young revelers mobbed the island in the 1990s, turning Mikonos into a rather tacky tourist trap, nowadays hoteliers and restaurateurs are focusing on boutique hotels, haute cuisine, and building a discreet, low-key atmosphere. The island has become a popular destination for gay couples from across Europe, who flock to the elegant bars, excellent restaurants, and white-sand beaches like Elia, the very popular nudist beach in the south.

Aegean Maritime Museum
- ✉ Parnassou Street 2, Tria Pigadia Maroussi, Mikonos
- ☎ (22890) 22700
- 🕐 Closed Tues.
- 💲 $

Mikonos Folk Art Museum
- ✉ Kastro, Mikonos town
- ☎ (22890) 22591
- 🕐 Closed Sun.

Mikonos Archaeological Museum
- ✉ Harborfront, Mikonos town
- ☎ (22890) 22325
- 🕐 Closed Mon.
- 💲 $

Monastery of Panayia Tourliani
- ✉ Ano Mera, Mikonos
- ☎ (22890) 71249
- 🕐 Open by appointment only.

a traditional outdoor oven, and an old-fashioned grape press (which still gets used every September).

In addition to the windmills, there are several other interesting little museums on the island, all located in small buildings dotted around the main town. These include the **Aegean Maritime Museum,** located down on the waterfront, which showcases the islands' nautical history; the **Mikonos Folk Art Museum,** which houses a fascinating collection of local crafts and art, as well as items that illustrate the traditional way of life on the island; and finally the **Mikonos Archaeological Museum,** where a small collection of local archaeological finds is kept, including a few ancient Greek statues and some items dating from the mysterious older civilizations that lived in the area.

About 5 miles (8 km), east of Mikonos town is **Ano Mera,** a hamlet in the central part of the island. The **Monastery of Panayia Tourliani** was founded here in 1580 and features a massive Baroque iconostasis that was made in 1775 by Florentine artists. The museum inside the monastery has embroideries, wood carvings, and vestments.

Dilos

Located only a 20-minute boat ride from Mikonos are the amazing ruins of the **ancient town** of Dilos. Although today it is hard to see what would have attracted anyone to this barren little island, it was once a thriving metropolis. From the ninth century B.C. to the late first century A.D., this island was home to was one of the holiest sanctuaries in the Greek religion, second only to Delphi. It was also a port of tremendous economic significance—thanks to its sheltered anchorage and position almost exactly halfway between Greece and Asia. During the years of the Delian

EXPERIENCE: Marble Workshops in Tinos

Marble-carving in the Cyclades goes back 5,000 years. On Paros, Naxos, and Tinos, marble was quarried and fashioned throughout antiquity for major public works. Between the Venetian and Ottoman periods, the marble workshops of Tinos rose in prominence as the island filled with master sculptors and artists. Many of the marble workers restoring the Parthenon today are from Tinos.

Tinos has several workshops where skilled artisans can help you work a piece of marble, but you will have to spend a lot of time there to make it worthwhile. Most sessions last five hours, split over

several days, though hurried tourists can try to squeeze it all in one day. Prices vary, but remember that sending a piece through customs is expensive.

Led by Greek sculptor Petros Dellatolas, the **Dellatolas Marble Sculpture School** (Spitalia, Tinos, 22830/23644, $$$$$, www.tinosmarble.com) offers one- to two-week courses for nascent marble carvers from May to October. **Trekking Hellas** (21033/10323, $$$$$, www.trekking .gr/en/selfguidedholidays/marblesculpture greece.html) offers five-day excursions to Tinos, with two days devoted to working in a marble workshop.

League it was also a political hub, home to a huge treasury and powerful government.

Today, the island's sole long-term inhabitants are archaeologists from the French Archaeological Institute that has controlled excavations here since the 19th century. Visitors can wander freely around the site, or sign up for one of the guided tours *($$$$)* before they board the ferry at Mikonos. The site's highlights include the **Sacred Way,** a grand colonnaded road that once led from the ceremonial harbor to the **Sanctuary of Apollo;** the **sanctuaries,** which include the ruins of temples and statues devoted to Apollo and Dionysos (the latter's temple is distinguished by a giant phallic statue); and the theater district, which contains the island's massive **public theater** (which seated an audience of around 5,000) as well as the remains of several beautifully decorated mansions.

Among the ruins there are a few simple facilities for visitors, including public restrooms, a restaurant, and the small **Dilos Archaeological Museum.** The museum contains an impressive collection of ancient artifacts gathered from the site, although the finest treasures have all ended up in the National Archaeological Museum in Athens (see pp. 94–95, 97). The museum houses models, maps, and illustrations showing how the site would once have looked.

Tinos

The island of Tinos is one of the largest islands in the Cyclades,

A student practices carving marble at Pyrgos School of Fine Arts in Tinos.

home to around 8,500 permanent residents and many more seasonal visitors.

The island's quarries have traditionally produced high-quality stone, particularly green marble, for sculptors and architects. This unique natural gift has attracted generations of sculptors and masons to the island, as well as encouraging many locals to take up the hammer and chisel themselves (see sidebar p. 166), and many still learn the mason's craft at the **School of Fine Arts** in the village of Pyrgos. It is not uncommon to see fantastic carved marble detailing on even the humblest homes on Tinos.

Apart from its sculptures, the island is best known as a religious center. The **Panagia Evangelistria** church in Tinos town lies at the heart of the island's religious culture. The church itself holds an icon of the Virgin Mary that is said to have miraculous properties.

Dilos
🄰 163 B2

Dilos Archaeological Museum
✉ Dilos
☎ (22890) 22259
🕐 Closed Mon.
💲 $$

Tinos
🄰 163 B2
Visitor Information
✉ Tinos Municipal Council, Tinos
☎ (22830) 23780
www.greeka
.com/cyclades/
tinos/tinos-tourism

Pyrgos School of Fine Arts
✉ Pyrgos, Tinos
☎ (22830) 31225
www.tinos.biz/
marbleschool_eng
.htm

Andros

 163 B3

Visitor Information

✉ Andros
Municipality,
Andros

☎ (22820) 25162

www.andros.gr

Basil & Elis Goulandris Museum of Modern Art

✉ P. Aravantinou
Street 6, Andros
town

☎ (22820) 22444

🕐 Closed Tues.
(summer)
& Tues.–Fri.
(Oct.–May)

💲 $$

www.moca-andros.gr

Legend has it that its existence was revealed in 1823 to a nun, Pelagia, who saw it in a dream. She dug the icon out of the earth near the town and it immediately began to heal people. On August 15 every year, the day of the Dormition of the Virgin, thousands of pilgrims come to Tinos and crawl on their hands and knees from the port to the church to show their devotion.

As with all of these islands, the remnants of the ancient past are never far from the surface. About 1 mile (1.6 km) away from the town, the hamlet of **Kiona** has a large **Sanctuary of Poseidon** that's virtually ignored. There's a small **museum** in the main town that features a sundial made by Andronikos of Kyrrhos, who also designed the Tower of the Winds in Athens (see p. 71).

Andros

The island, which is home to about 10,000 people, is the second largest—and most mountainous—of the Cyclades. Its highest point, **Mount Kouvara,** is 3,270 feet (997 m) above sea level. The island's chief claim to fame is that it was here, in 1821, that Greek revolutionary Theophilos Kairis delivered the speech that marked the beginning of the Greek War of Independence (see p. 34).

The town of **Andros,** on the island's east coast, is a picturesque hamlet of around 4,000 people. In addition to some small local museums, such as the seemingly mandatory **Archaeological Museum** and **Maritime Museum,** the town boasts one of Greece's best modern art galleries, the **Basil & Elis Goulandris Museum of Modern Art,** which exhibits work by new and daring Greek artists.

The island's densely forested and mountainous landscape is

Fishing boats moored in the harbor at Andros

popular with walkers, and the
island has some of the region's
finest beaches, hidden away in the
more remote parts of the island.

Siros

Standing at the center of the
Cyclades, the island of Siros is
the bustling commercial and
administrative heart of the
archipelago. By contrast with
its neighbors, whose fortunes
have waxed and waned in the
changing winds of Mediterranean history, Siros has always
occupied roughly the same role
and economic position that it
has today.

Siros's main settlement,
Ermoupoli, has a much more cosmopolitan atmosphere than most
island towns. Its architecture is a
little grander than its neighbors,
and it has a number of impressive
public buildings. The most striking
of these is the neoclassical **Apollo
Theater,** which was built as an
opera house in 1862. After lying
abandoned for several decades,
it is now nearing the end of a
lengthy restoration process and is

expected to open to the public in
the next few years.

The hill town of **Ano Siros,**
which is northwest of Ermoupolis,
has the typically Cycladic narrow
paths, whitewashed homes with
colored doors and blooms pour-
ing out of tiny balconies. The centerpiece here is the 13th-century
Catholic **Basilica of San Giorgo,**
from which there is a breathtaking
view of nearby islands, including
Tinos, Dilos, and Mikonos.

Serifos

Serifos is an important location
in Greek mythology. It is here
that the legendary hero-king
Perseus was raised and where
Odysseus saved his men from
the monstrous Cyclops. Local
legend asserts that the many
ancient walls scattered around
the island are the work of
the one-eyed giant, while the
island's boulder-strewn earth
is said to be a consequence
of Perseus bringing the head
of Medusa—which could turn
people into stone—to the island.

The main town (also called
Serifos) has windmills and an
attractive neoclassical **town hall**
on Agios Athanasios Square. Not
far from the town hall are the
Island's two museums, the **Folklore Museum,** which gives a fascinating insight into local culture
and customs, and the **Archaeological Museum,** which houses
a collection of ancient—but sadly
headless—statues. Another impressive sight is the heavily fortified
Monastery of Taxiarches, whose
high walls guard the monastic
community from pirates. ∎

The Southern Cyclades

The landscape of the outhern Cyclades varies from the verdant fields of Naxos to the bone-dry hills of Paros, while each island's main town can be anything from a humble farming village to spectacular, gleaming white town like Fira, which is perched on the rim of a volcanic caldera on Santorini.

Workers bring in the grape harvest on Santorini.

Santorini

🅰 163 C1

Visitor Information

✉ Tourist Office, Santorini National Airport

☎ (23104) 71170

www.greeka.com /cyclades/santorini

Santorini

Around 3,500 years ago Santorini was a large island with a tall volcanic mountain in the center, similar to Maui or Saint Vincent today. This all changed around 1600 B.C., when, during an eruption, the volcano exploded with many times more force than even the largest nuclear bomb. It blew apart the island, leaving just Santorini and four nearby islets: Thirasia, Aspronisi, and the "Burnt Isles" of Nea Kameni and Palea Kameni. The explosion also created the caldera that lies beneath the bay today. This blast was a cataclysmic event, often associated with the myth of Atlantis, the city that sank beneath the sea, an association reinforced by the discovery in 1967 of the ancient town of Akrotiri buried beneath layers of ash in the south of the island.

The first settlers called the island Kallisti, or the "loveliest one," though the Greeks nowadays often call it Thira, for Thiras, the ninth-century Dorian leader. The name Santorini comes from St. Irini of Thessaloniki, the Byzantine empress who is the patron saint of the island.

Civilization on Santorini dates as least as far back as 3000 B.C., though its heyday was between 2000 and 1580 B.C. Like the Minoans in Crete, the people of Santorini worshipped a fertility goddess, disliked weapons, and built their towns without defenses. In ancient times, there is evidence that agriculture flourished here, but today the island is chronically water-deprived, like the rest of the Cyclades. Locals collect rainwater in cisterns for irrigation and drinking.

Thira & Around: Tourism is by far the biggest industry on the island. The capital, Thira, is the most packed, especially in summer. The local priests of **Panagia Ypapantis,** the Greek Orthodox cathedral here, wander the summer streets with sunburned tourists in shorts or bikinis. The **Museum of Prehistoric Thira** features the amazingly well-preserved frescoes from Akrotiri. The Akrotiri site itself has been closed to the public since 2005, when a huge roof structure, designed to cover the whole site, collapsed. It is hoped that the site will reopen in 2011 or 2012. The section of the city called **Kato Thira** overlooks the caldera, so accommodations here are especially pricey. Near Thira are the suburban villages of **Firostefani,** where traditional cave houses are quickly becoming little boutique hotels and pensions, and **Imerovigli,** the caldera's highest point. On the other side of the island, two charming (continued on p. 174)

Museum of Prehistoric Thira

- ✉ Mitropoleos, Thira, Santorini
- ☎ (22860) 23217
- 🕐 Closed Mon.
- 💲 $$

EXPERIENCE: Sampling Santorini's Wines

In the vineyards of Santorini, plants receive no more water than what falls on them as rain or settles as dew—there are no rivers nor enough water for intensive irrigation. This dry environment is overcome by inventive methods of cultivation that yields grapes and wines with a unique flavor. The best way to discover these wines is to sample them at their source.

The residents of Santorini were likely making wine as far back as the second millennium B.C., when a catastrophic volcanic eruption buried the Minoan settlement of Akrotiri and devastated the island. Excavations show evidence of viticulture, including carbonized seeds. Today ancient grape varieties such as Athiri, Assyrtiko, Nykteri, and Mandelaria are raised here. The wines range from the dry white Athiri to the sweet Vinsanto, though some wineries also make red wine.

Santo Wines (Pirgos, Santorini, tel 22860/22596, www.santowines.gr) housed in a beautiful building with a terrace overlooking the caldera, is one of the island's largest wineries, welcoming some 80,000 visitors a year. The **Antoniou Winery** (Megalochori, tel 22860/23857), housed in a lovely cliff-top buildling, is a popular venue for weddings and holds frequent wine-tastings.

Canava Roussos (Episkopi, Santorini, tel 22860/31349, www.canavaroussos .gr) has been run by the Roussos family since 1836 and is one of the oldest wineries on the island. The adjoining taverna here features Santorini specialties such as fava, tomato fritters, and salads dotted with local cheeses, sun-dried local tomatoes, and wild capers. Giorgos Koutsogiannopoulos of **Volcan Wines** (Vothona, Santorini, tel 22860/23182, www.volcan wines.gr), near Vothona en route to Kamari beach, is a fourth-generation winemaker whose grandfather began cultivating grapes here in the 1880s. Volcan Wines also has a museum that tracks the history of Santorini winemaking from 1660 to today.

Santorini's Caldera by Boat and on Foot

The Cycladic island of Santorini has the largest volcanic caldera in the world and, some would say, the most beautiful. It's possible that the legend of Atlantis, the land that sank into the ocean, has its roots in Santorini's geological history.

Boaters on Santorini's water-filled caldera

NOT TO BE MISSED:

A stroll down to Thira's old harbor • Bathing in Palea Kameni's thermal springs • A bite to eat in one of Korfos's tavernas

Caldera is Spanish for cauldron, which describes the crater of collapsed land after a volcanic explosion. This is what happened on Santorini after the Minoan eruption of circa 1645 B.C., leaving the island with the shape of a back-to-front C. The villages of Oia, on the caldera's northern tip, and Thira, in the south, are two popular points from which to view the deep-blue basin.

Begin in Thira, the lively island capital, on a winding path of stone steps that leads to **Mesa Gialos Bay ❶**, where the old harbor sits and where many of the cruise ships stop. If the 20-minute downhill hike is too daunting, you can also hire a donkey or take a cable car. From the

harbor, you can hire a boat to take you to the two small, uninhabited volcanic islands, Nea Kameni and Palea Kameni.

The boat will first head to the harbor of **Nea Kameni ❷**, the larger of the two islets. Nea Kameni, which means the "new burnt" isle, is practically round and just over a mile (2 km) in diameter. It was formed after a series of volcanic eruptions that ended in 1711, creating a black island that, after more eruptions, united with **Mikra Kameni** ("small burnt" isle) by 1870. The oft-visited active volcano is here, so it's a magnet for both travelers and scientists. The Institute for the Study of Monitoring of the Santorini Volcano is here, and if you're lucky, you might find a vulcanologist on duty who will fill you in on its geological history.

The Climb to the Crater

Once you get off the boat at the small harbor on Nea Kameni, you will notice the water is a muted green from the sulfur in it. From the harbor, you will need to walk for 30–45 minutes across a dusty moonscape of brown and black gravel. It can get very hot along this walk in the summer, so make sure to wear a wide-brimmed hat and plenty of sunscreen—and to bring drinking water. As you climb to the top of the 410-foot-high (130 m) crater, the smell of sulfur will get stronger. The **volcano's vent** ❸ is in a basin of sand and sulfur crystals, and a thin but steady stream of steam will be issuing forth. Tour guides like to warn that the volcano can blow its top at any time, but the last noted eruption was 1950.

To Thirasia

After walking down the rim of the crater, retrace your footsteps and return to the harbor. From here, most boats set off for **Palea Kameni** ❹, the smaller and older of the two uninhabited volcanic islets. This islet is known for its thermal springs, where temperatures can reach 98°F (36°C). Swimmers love lingering here, especially in the early part of the summer when the sea is still cold.

Take time to have a swim if you wish, then the boat will set off for **Thirasia,** a larger—but still small—island northwest of Nea Kameni and in the heart of the caldera. On the way the boat will pass the southernmost island in the caldera, **Aspronisi.**

Only about 300 people live on Thirasia, but the community does cater to visitors. Several fish tavernas line the harbor at **Korfos** ❺, but be careful: They tend to be overpriced. If you want to eat with the locals, climb the steep path from the harbor to the village on the cliff above. Any tavernas there will offer better food and at a more reasonable price. The summit also will give you a great view over the caldera. The last part of your adventure will be the boat trip back to Thira.

ⓐ	See area map p. 163
►	Thira
⏱	6–7 hours
⤢	8 miles (13 km)
►	Thira

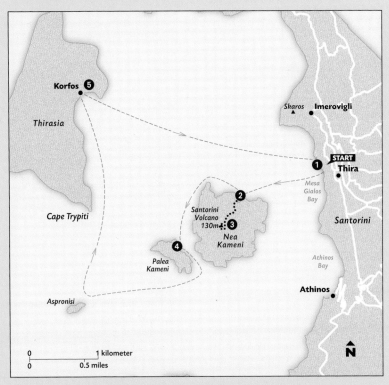

Milos

▲ 163 A1–B1

Visitor Information

✉ Milos Municipal
Tourist Office,
Quayside

☎ (22870) 22445

🕐 Closed
Oct.–May

www.greeka.com/
cyclades/milos

and quiet towns—Pyrgos and Megalochori—are home to two excellent wineries.

Oia: The island's centerpiece is Oia, the second-largest town, and surely the most photographed hamlet in the Aegean. It's much quieter than Thira, though in summer it's packed with tourists angling for a view of the sunset on the caldera. The town is also full of rental cave houses, the most luxurious located in the southern end, and very good restaurants, especially the stalwart **1800** (*Nikolaou Nomihou, Oia, tel 22860/71485, www.oia-1800.com, $$$$*), a pricey but outstanding bistro located in an old captain's house. The eclectic bookstore **Atlantis Books** (*Nikolaou Nomihou, Oia, tel 22860/72346, www.atlantis books.org*), run by an enterprising

collective of young writers and bookworms mostly from the United States and Great Britain, is one of the best in Greece. Oia also has a small port, called **Ammoudi,** which has excellent fish tavernas. The volcanic ash soil here nurtures some standout produce. The tiny cherry tomatoes of Santorini are deep-red, sweet, and bursting with flavor. The yellow split-pea here makes what is considered the world's best *fava*. The small, white eggplants have few seeds; locals eat them raw.

Milos

The trove of obsidian here made Milos a manufacturing center for stone tools in ancient times, though the Bronze Age made those tools somewhat obsolete. Still, the island was able to maintain its wealth during the

The Venus De Milo

In the spring of 1820, a farmer named Giorgos Kentrotas was digging in the ruins of the ancient city of Milos. He was not there out of archaeological curiosity, but simply because he needed some building materials to repair his house. He uncovered a well-preserved statue of the Greek goddess Aphrodite (known to the Romans as Venus).

By a lucky coincidence, he was not the only one digging on the site that day. A French naval officer and amateur historian, Olivier Voutier, was also exploring the site. Together they uncovered the two halves of the broken statue and reassembled them for the first time in thousands of years, although they could find no trace of the statue's missing arms.

A few weeks after the discovery, Voutier persuaded an eminent French classicist to examine the statue. He agreed to buy it from Giorgos Kentrotas and ship it to the Louvre in Paris. Once it was put on display, the statue caused a sensation. It was hailed as a masterpiece and a rare surviving work of the great fourth century sculptor Praxiteles. This latter assertion was proved embarrassingly wrong, however, when the inscription on the plinth (now lost) was translated and found to name the sculptor as Alexandros of Antioch, a traveling craftsman who lived in the first century B.C. The statue continues to attract thousands of visitors every day and is known throughout the world for its beauty.

Relaxing in the shade by the harbor on Naxos

Minoan period through the sixth century B.C., when Dorians from Laconia settled here and turned it into a hub for ceramics. Milos refused to fight the Spartans alongside Athens in the fifth century B.C., as the islanders claimed they were descended from Spartans. The Athenians attacked soon after, sold the women into slavery, and killed many of the men. Today, the horseshoe-shaped island has about 5,500 residents and is known for its colorful volcanic rock and 70 beaches.

The hilltop town of **Plaka** is the main settlement on Milos. The **Archaeological Museum** has various interesting finds from the ancient city of Milos, as well as an exact replica of the Venus de Milo. The local **Folk Art Museum** has a small but interesting collection of local crafts and artwork. The village of **Trypiti,** about 1 mile (1.6 km) south of Plaka, is notable for

its miles of winding catacombs. These were built by an early Christian community on the island and contain several shrines and the tomb of a local saint. From the harbor at **Adamas,** you can catch a ferry to the tiny and peaceful island of **Kimolos,** just a short boat ride to the north.

Naxos

According to myth, this island was the home of Dionysius, the god of wine and theater. It is also where the womanizing hero Theseus abandoned Ariadne, daughter of the Minoan King Minos. People have lived here for 6,000 years, forming a small but prosperous farming community as early as the eighth century B.C. It was once the richest island in the Aegean.

The island boasts a breathtaking landscape of ravines and mountains, some of the finest beaches in Greece, and many

**Plaka
Archaeological
Museum**

- ⊠ Plaka, Milos
- ☎ (22870) 21629
- 🅢 $$
- 🕒 Closed Mon., afternoons, & winter months

Naxos

- 🅰 163 C2

Visitor Information

- ⊠ Naxos Tourist Information Center, Quayside, Naxos town
- ☎ (22850) 25201

www.greeka.com /cyclades/naxos

Naxos Archaeological Museum

✉ Kastro, Naxos town, Naxos

☎ (22850) 22387

💲 $$

🕐 Closed Mon. & winter months

Domus Venetian Museum

✉ Kastro, Naxos town, Naxos

☎ (22850) 22387

🕐 Closed afternoons

💲 $$

relics of its long and fascinating history, including classical temples, medieval monasteries, and Byzantine churches.

The whitewashed houses of **Naxos town,** the island's main settlement, are clustered on the slopes of a hill that rises up from the harbor, with the imposing walls of the Venetian castle at its top. This castle is a symbol of the island's past as the capital of the Venetian Duchy of the Archipelago. Today the castle houses the **Naxos Archaeological Museum.**

The town is an important regional transportation hub, with serivices running frequently to other islands in the Cyclades, as well as the Greek mainland at Pireas, which is about seven hours away. From the harbor visitors can walk a short distance along the breakwater to Naxos's most famous landmark, located on the nearby islet of Palatia. Here there

INSIDER TIP:

Moutsouna, the sleepy fishing village on the east coast of Naxos, has traditional caiques you can hire to visit the small Cyclades: Koufonisia, Skhoinousa, or Irakleia.

—CASTEN STEHR
Staff, Starquest Expeditions tours

is a ruined temple believed to have been devoted to Apollo and a vast monumental doorway, the **Portara,** which faces toward the sanctuary on Dilos. The Portara is a striking sight: a weathered, square stone doorway that stands completely alone—the building it was intended to be part of was never finished.

Other sites include **Domus Venetian Museum,** which

EXPERIENCE: Natural Mud Baths on Paros & Santorini

The ancients bathed in therapeutic mud to heal skin and soul. Spa tourism has become trendy in Greece in recent years, with whole centers devoted to beauty-by-mud in resorts as far north as Kavala in the northeastern part of the mainland. The Cyclades has its own mud baths, and you don't have to pay for them.

In Palea Kameni, the islet next to Nea Kameni, the volcanic islet off Santorini that's in the center of the caldera (see pp. 172–173), the heat congregates in a patch of sea off the muddy shore. In the summer, tour boats stop nearby, leaving tourists in swimsuits to jump off the boat

and swim to the mud. Many stay there for up to an hour, covering their hair and faces in thick, warm mud. After rinsing it off, they return to the boats claiming to feel refreshed and glowing.

In Paros, the mud baths are near Molos Bay at a beach called Vigla. The beach is pebbly, but the nearby cliffs are soft with red mud that people scoop out with shovels and spread on their bodies. They sun their mud-frosted bodies until the mud gets a little hard and turns green, then run into the sea to wash it off. Locals say the ritual makes skin soft and smooth.

Fishing nets dry in the sun outside a Paros church.

shows off historic Venetian residences, the **Naxos Folklore Museum,** and the ruins of the **ancient town** of Naxos, where you will see remains dating to the Mycenaean era.

Paros & Adiparos

Until the tourism boom of the late 20th century, the fortunes of Paros were closely linked to the value of the high-quality marble found throughout the island. The sculptors Praxiteles and Scopas, whose works defined the style of Greek and Roman sculpture from the fourth century B.C. onward, both preferred to work only with marble from the mines at Paros, making it popular with generations of sculptors and patrons. In ancient times, more than 150,000 people lived on Paros, many of them slaves who labored in the marble quarries

around the town of Marathi. They cut away blocks of the white, granular marble that was prized for its ability to absorb light. This was shipped all over the ancient world from the island's jetties.

The main town and port is **Paroikia** (or Paros town), which is very crowded in the summer. The waterfront here is lined with travel agencies, rental offices for cars and mopeds, fast food shacks, cafés, and shops selling touristy souvenirs. In the evening, families hang out in the lovely marble-paved plaza in the town center, but in the blazing heat of the day, it's usually deserted. The spectacular **Panagia Ekatondapiliani** (Hundred Doors Church; see p. 178) is one of the oldest unaltered churches in the world (built in A.D. 328 by Emperor Constantine the Great in honor of his mother). It was fitted with a stunning dome

Naxos Folklore Museum

✉ Old Market St., Naxos town, Naxos

☎ (22850) 25561

🕐 Closed Mon. & winter months

💲 $

www.naxosfolk museum.com

Paros & Adiparos

🗺 163 B2

Visitor Information

✉ Paros Tourist Office, Paroikia, Paros

☎ (22840) 24772

www.parosparadise .com

Panagia Ekatondapiliani

✉ Paroikia, Paros

☎ (22840) 21243

Island Churches & Monasteries

The churches and monasteries of the Cyclades offer fascinating relics of Greece's unique Orthodox Christian heritage and culture and vantage points to admire the rocky islands jutting from a deep blue sea. These places are still popular pilgrimage destinations, attracting thousands of devout travelers every year.

A show of piety at Panagia Evangelistria

One of the major landmarks on Paros is the **Panagia Ekatondapiliani** (Hundred Doors Church), built in 328 by Emperor Constantine the Great as a homage to his mother, St. Helen, who had a vision when her ship stopped here en route to the Holy Land. Justinian the Great added the dome two hundred years later. The Greeks, who still call Istanbul Constantinople, say only 99 of the 100 doors have been discovered because the last one will only be revealed after Constantinople is part of a Greek Orthodox empire again. The church, which has frescoes and a fourth-century iconostasis, is dedicated to the Dormition of the Virgin and celebrates its feast day on August 15. Located in Paroikia, not far from the dock, it is open daily from 8 a.m. to 10 p.m.

On Amorgos, the 11th-century **Panagia Hozoviotissa** monastery clings onto a rock promontory and celebrates its feast day on November 21. Founded by Alexius Comnenos I to honor the Virgin Mary, it houses an icon that is said to have floated in on an empty boat from Palestine. Inside, there are portraits of monks and icons including the 15th-century Panagia Portaitissa, produced by the Cretan school of icon painters that is also said to have inspired the Renaissance painter El Greco, who was born in Crete (see sidebar p. 187). There's a beach about a 40-minute, downhill walk from the monastery that's a good spot to cool off with a swim afterward.

The most dramatic religious experience on Tinos is at the **Panagia Evangelistria,** or the Church of the Annunciate Virgin. The magnificent church was built in 1823 on the site of a Byzantine chapel where an icon was unearthed that, according to nun-turned-saint Pelagia, was sent from the Virgin herself. Locals here say the icon has healed many people over the years, and thousands of people are believers. Those who are tending the sick often crawl on their hands and knees on a padded path from the port to the church in a sign of piety. There's usually a very long line to see the icon, which is encrusted with jewels.

Hiking up to some of the remote monasteries can be very hard work, espcially in the early afternoon sun, so bring a bottle of water and wear sunscreen and a protective hat. Most churches and monasteries require modest dress, so if you're in a swimsuit and shorts, the attending nun or monk probably won't let you in. Some monasteries provide skirts or robes that you can wear over your skin-baring summer clothes.

INSIDER TIP:

Some of the best parts of any trip to the Cyclades are to be had lazily cruising from one island to another, past the rocky outcrops of the region's hundreds of tiny islets.

—CLIVE CARPENTER
National Geographic contributor

by Justinian the Great, who ruled the Byzantine Empire from A.D. 527–565. The **Archaeological Museum** here contains a big chunk of the Parian chronicle, which cataloged the culture of Greece from 1500–260 B.C. Also in the museum are artifacts from the Aegean's oldest known settlement, Saliagos, an islet between Paros and Adiparos, and a marble slab featuring a depiction of the poet Archilocus, who invented iambic meter and wrote the first signed love lyric.

The pretty hamlet of **Naoussa** is about 6 miles (10 km) northeast of Paroikia. Ringed by villas and fancy hotels, its quiet port is lined with *ouzeries* (traditional bars) and brightly painted fishing jetties. **Marathi,** which holds the ancient marble mines, lies about 6 miles (10 km) east of Paroikia. The largest village in the interior of Paros is **Lefkai,** which is about 4 miles (6 km) south of Marathi. Scented with jasmine and dotted with restored mansions and olive groves, the

village is built into a steep hillside surrounded by mountains.

The tiny island of **Adiparos,** sister to Paros, used to be the secret hideaway for Parians, but no more. Today, ferries run to and from Paroikia to the Antiparian settlement of **Pounta** every day. On the way, there's a small, lush islet that belongs to heiress Dolly Goulandris. Adiparos has one town, also named Adiparos, and a seaside cave once visited by British poet and adventurer Lord Byron, who carved his signature inside, and long, sandy beaches.

Ios

Located between Naxos and Santorini, this hilly island is only 12 miles by 5 miles (19 km by 8 km). The island was once a magnet for young backpackers, who used to gather around the beaches at Mylopotomas for night-time parties in the 1970s, but it is now home mostly to European families on summer vacations.

From the port of Ormos, where ferries dock, you can walk or take a donkey up the steep path that leads to Ios town. This settlement is a typical Cycladic village, with simple whitewashed homes, blue-domed churches, and tiny, winding paths. Just to the north of the town, perched high above the sea, is the stunning **Panagia Gremiotissa** (Our Lady of the Cliffs), a church built to house an icon of the Virgin Mary that washed up on the island hundreds of years ago. This site provides views of the town, the ruined castle, and the coastline.

Ios is home to one of the most impressive ancient sites in the

Paros Archaeological Museum

✉ Behind Panagia Ekatondapiliani, Paroikia, Paros
☎ (22840) 21231
🕐 Closed Mon. and winter months
💲 $

Ios

🅰 163 C1
Visitor Information
☎ (22860) 91002
www.greeka.com /cyclades/ios

Panagia Gremiotissa

✉ Chora, Ios

Paleokastro

163 C1

Near Psathi, Ios

Amorgos

163 C1

Visitor Information

www.greeka.com
/cyclades/amorgos

Panagia Hozoviotissa

Profitis Ilias mountain, south of Amorgos town

(22850) 71274

By arrangement

A ceramic chimney on Sifnos

Cyclades, the huge bronze age hill-fort of **Paleokastro.** Within its massive defensive earthworks lie the ruins of generations of settlements, dating from the Bronze Age to the Byzantine era..

Ios is traditionally associated with the ancient poet Homer (see p. 40), and many locals maintain that **Homer's Tomb** is among the ancient ruins on the north coast. The authenticity of this claim is dubious, but it's an atmospheric and peaceful site, surrounded by olive groves and vineyards, all within sight of the sea.

Amorgos

The easternmost island in the Cyclades, Amorgos has long served as a stepping stone for traders and migrants going from the Greek mainland to Asia Minor and the islands of the Dodecanese. Originally settled by the Minoans, it was later colonized by the Ionians as they migrated to the Greek mainland. In the 19th and early 20th centuries, the island became a haven for Greek refugees leaving the Ottoman Empire, many of whom settled in the island's towns. Today, about 1,800 people live in this easternmost Cycladic island. There are two ports here, **Katapola** and **Aigiali,** and three notable mountains, the highest being Krikelos, at 2,697 feet (822 m). In Aigiali port there's a long and sandy beach that begins at the fishing village Ormos.

Throughout its history, the settlements on Amorgos have been highly vulnerable to raids by pirates. The constant fear of pirate attacks has had a profound effect on the architecture of the island; many buildings here look like fortresses, and some of the older homes on the island have hidden strong rooms or escape routes. One of the most spectacular examples of this defensive architecture is the Byzantine **Panagia Hozoviotissa,** a striking white structure built into the side of a cliff high above the coast. The monastery boasts awe-inspiring views out to sea and a fascinating collection of holy texts and icons (see p. 178). This is still an active monastic community, so dress modestly. The beach below is a stunning expanse of dark sand and inviting, shady caves.

Folegandros

Like the rest of the Cyclades, this tiny island has dramatic cliffs with whitewashed homes built into them. Its three main villages are the port **Karavostasis, Folegandros town,** and **Ano Meria,** which are all connected by a paved road. Ano Meria is filled with lime trees, bougainvillea, and hibiscus. It is closed to traffic and has three main squares in its center. The **Kastro** is a Venetian-era fortress with the ruins of a medieval village. Ano Meria has a few cafés and tavernas, as well as a **Folklore Museum.** The port of Karavostasis has the best selection of shops and tavernas. **Katergo beach** is a beautiful and secluded place that's reached only via boat from Karavostasis.

Sifnos

Sandwiched between Serifos and Milos, Sifnos was wealthy in ancient times because of its gold, silver, and lead mines. *Sifnios* is still the local word for potter, an appropriate word considering hundreds of them used to live here. The island loves its intricately painted pottery, which is among the best in Greece (see sidebar below). Its central town, **Apollonia,** is home to about 950 people and has a folklore museum. The small village of **Kastro** is built on the site of the ancient city of Sifnos and has the island's **Archaeological Museum.** The soft, fine-sand beach at **Vathi** is one of the loveliest in Greece.

Sifnos has 365 churches, the most recognizable being **Chrysopigi.** Built in 1650 on the ruins of an earlier church, the brilliant white walls of this monastery contrast with the rock of the narrow peninsula on which it sits. ∎

Folegandros

🅰 163 B1

www.folegandros .com

Folegandros Folklore Museum

✉ Ano Meria, Folegandros

Sifnos

🅰 163 B1-2

Visitor Information

✉ Sifnos Municipal Tourist Office, Kamarai

☎ (22840) 31977

🕐 Closed Nov.–Easter

Sifnos Archaeological Museum

✉ Kastro, Apollonia, Sifnos

☎ (22840) 31022

🕐 Closed Mon., afternoons, & winter months

Traditional Pottery on Sifnos

Sifnos has been a potter's paradise since ancient times. The Greek peripatetic philosopher Theophrastus mentioned the island's pottery as far back as the third century B.C. Archaeologists have discovered pottery here dating to the Proto-cycladic period. In modern times, during the 18th century, Sifnos potters traveled the country selling their wares, and a few even settled in Marousi, now a suburb of Athens.

The island is rich with clay, water, and sunshine, the best resources for ceramicists, and so the tradition continues today. The first pottery workshops, called *tsikaladika* in Greek, were set up in the hamlets of Artemonas and Ano Petali to keep the artists safe from pirates. The potters made pots, crocks, jugs, pitchers, and other domestic utensils as well as decorative bowls and statues.

There are more than a dozen pottery workshops in Sifnos today, including that operated by the Atsonios family, who are among the finest ceramicists. **Peristeriona** (*www.atsonios.gr*), their workshop and gallery, is in the port of Kamarai near Koulouris Square. Their ceramics are intricately painted masterpieces that include plates, lamps, and owl statues.

Archaeological sites that evoke ancient myths, great walking country, and some of Greece's most spectacular wildflowers

Crete

The dramatic Samaria Gorge, a great place for a hike

Crete

Rugged and ensconced in tradition, Greece's largest island has a mountainous backbone cut through by gorges and caves, and miles of shoreline. Rich in a history highlighted by the ancient Minoan civilization that ruled here between 4,000 and 3,000 years ago, modern Crete now subsists largely off the tourists who flock to its sandy beaches and picturesque mountain villages.

A long and thin island of richly varied geography, Crete stretches 155 miles (250 km) from Elafonisos in the west to Palaikastron in the east, yet on average it is only 20 miles (32 km) wide. About 610,000 people live on this temperate island, which straddles the Mediterranean and North African climatic zones. Crete is well connected with the Greek mainland: It has three airports for passenger flights—at Iraklio, Hania, and Sitia—and three major ports, in Iraklio, Hania, and Rethimno.

Crete's history stretches back to the Minoans, who ruled Crete between 2600 B.C. and 1450 B.C. No one is sure what happened to them, but several earthquakes devastated parts of Crete between 1700 B.C. and 1450 B.C., the last of which was the Santorini tsunami. The Minoans left an important legacy: Excavations show they left behind outstanding art, architecture, and an early form of writing called Linear A and Linear B.

Crete's culture remains stubbornly true to itself: Mustachioed men sing rhymed couplets called *mandinadhes* over a fierce distilled spirit called *tsikoudia*, or raki, while tall, strong women dance to *lyra* music, their feet moving faster and faster to the rhythm of the quickening songs. Older men still wear traditional dress such as tall black riding boots, black shirts, and gauzy black kerchiefs, often weaved like fishnets, wrapped around their heads. Sheep and goats fill country lanes, black-clad priests tend their monasteries, and revelers at all-night, big-family Cretan weddings still shoot pistols into the air.

Art & Culture

Music is a fundamental part of life here; most young men, and now young women, learn to play the *lyra*—a pear-shaped, three-stringed instrument played with a bow—or the *laouto,* a long-necked lute that sounds like an oud. At weddings, musicians play laouto, lyra, guitar and, sometimes, with delight, the *askomandoura,* a type of bagpipe that's popular in mountain villages. Cretan songs are about crazy love and crushing loss, war, and rebellion, and the Cretans still love to sing them today.

The Renaissance painter El Greco was born Domenikos Theotokopoulos in Crete,

NOT TO BE MISSED:

The ruins of the Minoan palaces of Knossos and Phaestus 187, 190

Rethimno's Venetian old town 190–191

Arkadiou Monastery, southeast of Rethimno 191

A hike through the spectacular Samaria Gorge 193

Swimming in deserted coves on Crete's eastern coast 197

and the 20th-century master novelist Nikos Kazantzakis, who wrote *Zorba the Greek* and *The Last Temptation of Christ*, was also born here. The Cretans still revere both men, especially Kazantzakis. The Nikos Kazantzakis Foundation has a museum devoted to him in the village of Myrtia near Iraklio, and Kazantzakis's epitaph, "I hope for nothing. I fear nothing. I am free," has graced thousands of T-shirts and coffee mugs at tourist shops.

Cretan Cuisine

The famously healthy cuisine here makes the most of pulses, fish, and the island's wild greens, though fatty fast food has compromised the Mediterranean diet in recent years. Resort towns along the coast tend to cater to tourist tastes, so don't expect to find the best of Cretan food there. Cities such as Hania and Rethimno have a few fancy restaurants fusing old and new traditions, but for the most authentic experience of Cretan food, go out of your way to visit some mountain villages. That's where you will most likely find staples such as *chortopites* (pies made of wild greens), *hohlous boubouristi* (snails fried in olive oil, vinegar, and rosemary), and fresh salads made of wild greens, soft Cretan cheese, and pomegranate seeds.

Though the north coast cities of Iraklio, Rethimno, and Hania have grown so quickly that they have lost some of their charm, Crete has done a relatively good job balancing its complex identity with modernity. ∎

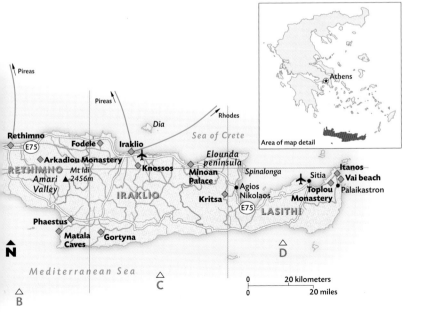

Iraklio & Central Crete

A bustling, sometimes maddening city of 150,000 people, Iraklio became the capital of Crete in 1971 and has attracted much of the island's commerce and industry. On bad days locals derisively refer to the place as "Little Athens," a reference to the traffic and haphazard urban planning.

The loggia above the Throne Room at Knossos, as restored by Arthur Evans

Iraklio

⚑ 185 C2

Visitor Information

✉ Tourism Directorate, Xanthoudidou 1, Iraklio

☎ (2810) 228225

www.greeka.com /crete/heraklion /heraklion-tourist- information.htm

Iraklio

Iraklio's port, where ferries from Pireas dock, is the island's busiest. It is lined with touristy cafés and tavernas, as well as offices for car and motorbike rentals. Modern Greece's best-known novelist, Nikos Kazantzakis, author of *Zorba the Greek* and the controversial *Last Temptation of Christ,* was born here.

Founded in 824 by Saracene invaders, Iraklio was named Chandax by the Byzantines and then Candia by the Venetians, who bought it in 1204 and fortified it with thick walls and high

fortresses. All that defense work failed to keep away the Ottoman Turks, who took over the city after a 21-day siege in 1669. More than 200 years later, in 1889, the Cretans were rebeling regularly to free themselves from Ottoman rule, and by 1898 they had succeeded in freeing themselves with the assistance of the British. The capital city was re-named Iraklio for the Roman port of Heracleum that was once nearby. The British left when Crete joined Greece in 1913.

The **Archaeological Museum of Crete** (*Xanthoudidou 2, Iraklio,* *tel 2810/279000, closed Mon. a.m., $$, www.heraklion-crete.org/archaeological-museum.html)* traces much of the island's ancient history through artifacts from the excavations at Knossos—seal stones inscribed with Linear B (see p. 189), including the Phaestus Disk, and vibrant frescoes show daily life. For later history, the **Historical Museum of Crete** has a collection of early Christian and Byzantine sculptures, Venetian and Ottoman stonework, weapons, and folk art.

Knossos & Phaestus

Central Crete, which is anchored by Iraklio, has several notable sites with storied pasts. The most famous is the palace of **Knossos,** which was excavated by the British archaeologist Sir Arthur Evans at the turn of the 20th century. Like Heinrich Schliemann with his excavation of Troy, Evans challenged

the idea that King Minos and his people were purely myth. His team unearthed the massive complex and also reconstructed parts of it with concrete. Though many archaeologists now severely criticize the reconstruction as inaccurate, their recriminations are lost on visitors, who love the majestic painted pillars and delight in photographing themselves amid Egyptian-style frescoes and reconstructed thrones.

Another major Minoan site, **Phaestus,** located on a hill near Mount Ida, was first excavated by the Italian School of Archaeology in Athens in 1884. Most of the site has been preserved but not restored, so it's harder to orient yourself without a guide. In 1908, the Italian archaeologist Luigi Pernier discovered the so-called

(continued on p. 190)

Historical Museum of Crete

- ✉ 27 Sofokli Venizelou Ave., Iraklio
- ☎ (2810) 283219
- 🕐 Closed Sat. p.m. & Sun.
- 💲 $

www.historical-museum.gr

Knossos

- ✉ 3 miles (5 km) SE of Iraklio
- ☎ (2810) 231940
- 💲 $$ (E6)

www.heraklion-crete.org/knossos.html

Phaestus

- 🅰 185 B1
- ☎ (28920) 42315
- 💲 $

www.heraklion-crete.org/knossos.html

El Greco's Birthplace

The Renaissance painter known as El Greco (1541–1614) was born on Crete as Domenikos Theotokopoulos, but Iraklio and the nearby village of Fodele have been quietly dueling over his exact birthplace for years. In the farming village of Fodele, 17 miles (27 km) west of Iraklio, many of the 650 inhabitants claim some relationship to the painter. The village gets a significant chunk of its income from El Greco-related tourism. Tourists even photograph themselves with some Fodele natives who have the painter's thin face and almond-shaped eyes. Fodele has a tiny **El Greco museum** *(tel 28105/21500, $)* housed in a cottage that once belonged to a Theotokopoulos, decorated with

poster-sized prints of his work. There's also an El Greco statue in the square, and he is said to have painted his first icons in a nearby monastery.

Others say that El Greco spent only a few years in Fodele, painting on the beach there. Iraklio's historians point to two documents from a trial in 1606 that give his place of birth as Candia, the Venetian name for Iraklio. (Fodele natives say he likely gave his birthplace as Candia because it was the city closest to unknown Fodele.) Iraklio has an El Greco square and bust, and its Historical Museum has both the painter's "Landscape of the God-Trodden Mount Sinai" and a recently discovered altarpiece.

Uncovering the Minoans

Crete was inhabited by Neolithic farmers as far back as 7000 B.C., but the civilization known today as Minoan did not flourish until between 2700 and 1500 B.C. It's not known what the early Cretans called themselves, but today we call them the Minoans because of Arthur Evans, a British archaeologists who, like other archaeologists of his era, loved Greek myths.

An ancient wall painting from Knossos

Born in England in 1851, the Oxford University-educated Evans had been interested in prehistoric Crete for years. His interest intensified when merchant and antiquarian Minos Kalokairinos discovered the important ruins at Knossos in 1878. Evans began excavating there in 1900, using local Cretan laborers, and uncovered what appeared to be a palace complex. He finished excavating in 1905, uncovering

the ruins of an advanced city with artwork, primitive plumbing, sturdy architecture, and an unknown form of writing.

Evans claimed the palace belonged to the mythic King Minos, who had built a labyrinth below it where a half-man, half-bull called the Minotaur lurked. The Minotaur was born to Minos's wife, Pasiphae, and a beautiful white bull she had seduced in frustration over her husband's infidelity.

Myth or Reality?

Was the myth real? Many history books say that the Cretan sea-kingdom of the Minoans, with their capital at Knossos, delivered Egyptian civilization to Greece. That assessment is based entirely on the work of Evans, who wanted to believe the myth was based on reality. In his excavations, he pointed to wall paintings in the palace complex that showed numerous scenes with bulls, hence assuming that the Minoans did worship the bull. He declared a room with a throne-like stone chair the "throne room" and asked two artists, Emile Gillierons and his son (also Emile), to paint it. Evans claimed that the frescoes painted by the Gillieronses had their origins in archaeological evidence, but they were actually invented by the artists. Based on his excavations, Evans concluded that the civilization on Crete existed long before those discovered at Mycenae and Tiryns (Troy) by Heinrich Schliemann, the amateur archaeologist who was also deeply besotted with myths.

Evans also discovered some 3,000 clay tablets and tried to transcribe them. The Linear A script, apparently the official script

The Battle to Control Knossos

In 1878, Minos Kalokairinos, who discovered the site of Knossos, had already unearthed western portions of the palace and its store-rooms. However, Turkish authorities, who ruled Crete at the time, stopped the excavation and instead let American ambassador W. J. Stillman onto the site. It was Stillman who first claimed that Knossos was actually the lair of the Minotaur. But the Turks soon kicked him out, too, leaving an opportunity for German adventurer and amateur archaeologist Heinrich Schliemann, who arrived here with his colleague Wilhelm Dorpfeld in 1886. Schliemann tried to buy the site but couldn't make a deal with the landowners, who wanted too much money, in Schliemann's opinion. Andre Joubin, a French archaeologist, tried to buy the land in 1891 but also failed.

In 1897, Arthur Evans obtained a firman, or royal decree issued by the Ottoman state, to excavate at Knossos. After Crete became independent from the Ottoman Empire in 1898, Evans bought the entire site. He did his main excavations between 1900 and 1905 but continued to work nearly annually (with an interruption for World War I) until 1932.

When Evans named his new find, some observers hoped that the term "Minoan" referred to Minoas Kalokairinos, who had discovered the site and who had been killed by the Turks in 1898. However, it was Evans's love of the mythical Minos of Crete that coined the name—and so a myth became "history."

for the palaces and religious cults, was dated to immediately before the collapse of the Minoan civilization in the 15th century B.C. In *Scripta Minoa*, his writings on the issue, Evans argued that the Phoenician alphabet strongly resembles the Cretan hieroglyphs discovered at Knossos. He was not so sure about Linear B, which was later studied by a London architect named Michael Ventris.

Archaean Civilization

In 1911, Arthur Evans was knighted for his contributions to archaeology. He was 90 when he died, 30 years later, revered by archaeologists around the world. Arthur Evans's legacy, like that of Schliemann before him, is a contentious and ambiguous one. While he was undoubtedly a pioneer in his field, his dubious methods have attracted harsh criticism from later generations of archaeologists.

In 1952, Michael Ventris, who studied the Linear B tablets after Evans's death, concluded that Linear B script was actually an early form of Greek, which upended Evans's version of Minoan history by establishing that ancient Crete had been part of Mycenean Greece. Ventris argued that the Achaeans, who were actually a literate people 700 years before Homer, traveled to Crete instead of the other way around. In 1960, after reading a daybook by Evans's assistant, Oxford philologist Leonard R. Palmer, another philologist discovered that Evans had made changes to his assistant's records to support his theory that Cretan culture is older than that of Greece.

Today, many archaeologists say much historical information was lost because of Evans's excavation and shoddy restoration. Some scholars also resent that Evans is often credited with discovering the site since Minos Kalokairinos actually unearthed it first. But Evans chose instead to honor the mythic king of Crete and so drew history out of a fable.

However, Arthur Evans's name will forever be associated with Knossos, and his bust is located on the south side of the west court of the palace.

Cretan Cuisine

The Cretan diet was once among the healthiest in the world. It emphasized legumes, grains, olive oil, fresh fruits and vegetables, and fish, which lowered cancer rates and helped people live longer. Though vestiges of this diet still exist, at least in cookbooks and in the kitchens of stubborn Cretan grandmothers, an increasing number of young Cretans now subsist on a less healthy diet.

If only they would listen to their grandmothers! Traditional Cretan food is among the best in Greece. In her seminal cookbook, *The Glorious Food of Greece,* the food writer Diane Kochilas describes tasty mezes such as green olives steeped in bitter orange juice, baked dried figs dipped in grape must, and a sheep's milk cheese called *tis tripas,* or "from

the hole," because it's aged in mountain caves. Wild greens are everywhere in Crete, and one of the most interesting is called *stamnagathi,* which is foraged in the spring when its leaves are most tender. It's tossed raw with pomegranate seeds, soft goat cheese, and olive oil or slow-cooked with lamb. Wild leeks, fennel, and aromatic greens are often used to make savory pies. The savory or sweet little cheese pies called *kallitsounia* have roots that go back to the era of Homer. The Minoans savored peas, lentils, broad beans, and the area's abundant wild herbs and greens. They sweetened their food with honey and loved barley, the main ingredient in the ubiquitous rusks called *paximadia,* which grace nearly every Cretan table today.

Gortyna

- 185 C1
- 28 miles/45 km south of Iraklio
- (28920) 31144
- $

Minoan Palace

- 2 miles/3 km east of Malia
- (28970) 31597
- Closed Sun.–Mon.
- $

Rethimno

- 185 B2

Visitor Information

- Municipal Tourist Office Eleftheriou Venizelou
- (28310) 29148
- Closed Sat.–Sun. & Oct.–Mar.

www.rethymno.org

Phaestus Disk, a round ceramic disk with hieroglyphics thought to be Linear A. Farther south is **Matala,** home to giant **caves** first carved out in the Neolithic era. The Romans used the caves to bury dead soldiers. In modern times, during the 1960s, hippies from around the world lived in the caves and frolicked on the nearby beach. The hippies were kicked out by the military junta that gripped Greece in 1967, but they returned after the dictators fell in 1974.

Nearby is the archaeological site of **Gortyna,** which has remains from Minoan times to the sixth century A.D., the latter including the **Basilica of St. Titus,** which stands at the spot where St. Titus was martyred. He worked with the Apostle Paul, proselytizing the Christian Gospel in Crete.

The **Minoan Palace** near the town of Malia is still magnificent, though the once-beautiful village that was lined with traditional homes, grandmothers working on looms, and vibrantly colored embroideries and rugs has now been transformed into a dreary trap of fast-food restaurants and cheap bars.

Rethimno & Environs

The seaside town of Rethimno was founded in antiquity as Rithymna, and though it never became a Minoan stronghold, it grew big enough to mint its own coins. Now a teeming city of 40,000, it's home to an increasing number of resorts as well as the University of Crete.

The Venetians loved the town, and they have left their imprint in scores of monuments in the city as well as a beautiful old Venetian quarter with the fortified **Fortetsa.** Next to the foot of the Fortetsa, the **Archaeological Museum of Rethimno** has a collection of artifacts dating to Neolithic times. The Venetian harbor, easily the loveliest spot here, has a restored 13th-century lighthouse and is lined with tiny fishing boats and tavernas.

In Ottoman times, Rethimno was the capital of Crete, and a collection of **wooden Turkish houses** still stands here, as does the **Neratze Mosque,** now a concert hall and one of the few surviving Ottoman mosques in Greece. Nearby, the **Historical & Folk Art Museum,** housed in a restored Venetian palazzo, features weaving, furniture, and tools. The city has also produced some of Crete's notable writers, including the dramatist Giorgos Chortatzis

(1545–1610), who wrote *Erophile*, a bloody Romeo-and-Juliet-style love story set in Egypt, and the poet and essayist Pandelis Prevelakis (1909–1986), whose statue now graces the front of Rethimno's city hall.

About 14 miles (23 km) southeast of Rethimno is **Arkadiou Monastery,** a landmark of the Cretan revolt against the Ottomans. The 16th-century church, which mixes Roman and Baroque elements, used to be a center for Cretan rebels and intellectuals. During a battle with Ottoman forces in 1866, nearly 1,000 Cretans sought refuge here. After a three-day siege, the rebels and those hidden in the monastery blew themselves up with barrels of gunpowder rather than surrender. Today, Arkadiou Monastery is open to the public. ■

Archaeological Museum of Rethimno

- ✉ Fortetsa, Rethimno
- ☎ (28310) 29975
- 🕐 Closed Mon.
- 💲 $

Historical & Folk Art Museum

- ✉ Manouil Vernardou 28–30, Rethimno
- ☎ (28310) 23667
- 🕐 Closed Sun.–Mon.
- 💲 $

Arkadiou Monastery

- 🗺 185 B2
- ✉ Arkadiou
- ☎ (28310) 83116
- 💲 $

www.crete-kreta .com/arkadi-monastery

Arkadiou Monastery was the scene of a terrible massacre in the 19th century.

Hania & Western Crete

Once the sleepy capital of Crete, Hania is now the second-largest city on the island, and its metropolitan area is home to about 81,000 people. Scores of resorts have sprouted along the western tip of Crete, and there is great hiking country inland.

Tavernas crowd around the harbor in old Hania.

Hania

 184 A2

Visitor Information

✉ Information Office, Kriari 40, Megaro Pantheon, Hania

☎ (28210) 92943

www.greeka.com /crete/chania/ chania-tourist-information.htm

✉ Hania Municipal Tourist Office, Kydonias 29, Hania

☎ (28210) 36155

Hania

Settled during the Minoan era, Hania was originally known as Cydonia, which means "quince," the apple-like fruit which grows in abundance here. The Venetians made Hania their capital and so fortified it, but the Ottoman Turks took the city in 1645 after a two-month siege. In 1898, after the Ottomans fell, Hania became the capital of independent Crete. The Greek flag was first raised at Fort Firca in Hania in 1913. Hania remained Crete's capital until

1971, when it moved to Iraklio.

Hania has a good-sized **old town** that reaches the harbor, lined with restored Venetian houses, fishing boats, Venetian arsenals and warehouses, and a lot of touristy cafés and tavernas. The city also has excellent markets, including a covered spice and meat market. Behind the city is **Kastelli Hill,** where the Venetians first settled. The 17th-century **Janissaries Mosque** (Yiali Tzamisis) is at the foot of the hill; it's now used for art exhibitions and trade shows. Nearby, the old

EXPERIENCE: Hiking in Western Crete

South of Hania, the landscape of western Crete becomes much more rugged, as it descends from the high White Mountains to the southern coast in a series of narrow, densely forested gorges. This landscape is loved by hikers and cyclists for its dramatic landscapes, diverse wildlife, and charming villages. The most popular hiking route in the area is the **Samaria Gorge** (*15 miles/24 km south of Hania, tel 28250/67179, closed mid-Oct.– Apr., $$*)—a 6-mile (10 km) canyon that runs from the tiny village of Xyloskalo to the south coast.

The Samaria Gorge is one of the most striking landscapes in Crete, with densely forested sides, jagged rockfaces, and sparkling streams. About halfway down the canyon lies the abandoned village of Samaria (the last residents left in the mid-1960s), with its rustic farmhouses gradually being overrun by vegetation. The gorge ends at the lovely, isolated village of Agia Rhoumeli. From there you can catch a boat to nearby Chora Sfakion, and from there a bus or taxi back to Hania.

The gorge is a national park, so there is an entrance fee and camping is not permitted. It is also on the excursion programs of several resorts so it can get crowded. Alternatively, hikers can head to the nearby **Agia Irini Gorge**—which runs from Agia Irini to the coastal village of Sougia. It is equally impressive but much less busy. The gorges are closed in spring when the rivers swell with snowmelt.

Turkish prison of Firka is now the **Maritime Museum.** The **Byzantine and Post-Byzantine Collection,** which features artifacts including mosaics, icons, and coins, is housed in a 15th-century church (*Church of San Salvatore, Theotokopoulou St. 82, Old Town, Hania, tel 28210/96046, closed Mon., $*). The 17th-century **Etz Hayyim Synagogue** used to serve the Jewish community here; many of them died during World War II. The **Archaeological Museum** features artifacts from western Crete dating from the Minoan era.

Western Crete

On western Crete's rugged southern coast there are a couple of picturesque little villages that have never been linked to the rest of the island by road. The only way to reach Loutro and Agia Rhoumeli is by hiking through the gorges or by getting a ferry from Chora Sfakion. Because of the constant traffic from the Samaria Gorge (see sidebar above), the town of **Agia Rhoumeli** is the busier of the two but is still a quiet and peaceful place.

Loutro feels completely cut off from the world, despite being only a few miles from some of the area's busy tourist resorts. Life in Loutro moves at a slow pace, and even the sea here in this sheltered bay seems relaxed. Loutro doesn't have much by way of nightlife, but it does have a few good hotels and some excellent restaurants. Those looking to stay can spend their days on quiet beaches within a few minutes' walk, or if you're feeling more active, take a course at the **Notos Mare Diving Center** (*Chora Sfakion, 28250/91333, www.notosmare.com, $$$$$*). ∎

Janissaries Mosque
✉ Akti Tompazi, Hania

Hania Maritime Museum
✉ Akti Koundourioti, Hania
☎ (28210) 91875
$ $
www.crete-kreta. com/maritime-museum-crete

Archaeological Museum of Hania
✉ Halidon Street 30, Hania
☎ (28210) 90334
$ $$

Agia Rhoumeli
🗺 184 A1

Loutro
🗺 184 A1
Visitor Information
www.loutro.gr

Bike Ride Across Crete

This journey of discovery, from Kalyves to Chora Sfakion, is a relatively easy one-day adventure through a lovely section of western Crete. You cycle on a small ashphalt road, and the route highlights the area's small, attractive villages and its rugged scenery, not least the stark, snow-covered White Mountains.

Crete has some excellent routes for cyclists.

Travel from Hania to Kalyves, a few miles to the east, by bus and rent a bike from outdoor enthusiast **Vangelis Stavrokoulis** (*Trekking Plan, Agia Marina-Nea Kidonias, Hania, tel 28210/60861, info@cycling.gr, www .cycling.gr, $–$$$*). If you aim to start cycling at around 9 a.m. and ride slowly, you should be at your destination, Chora Sfakion, by 4 p.m. Most of the ride is flat or downhill, but there is a gradual uphill stretch that will last about two hours if you're cycling slowly. You can set out from Kalyves on your own (Vangelis can supply a map), or go out with a bike guide.

NOT TO BE MISSED:

The orange groves of Nio Chorio • Admiring the spring flowers • The yogurt in Vrisses • The White Mountains

Cyclists will want to stop at villages along the way for a coffee or some homemade yogurt with honey, but the abiding memory of the day will be the unforgettably rugged beauty of the scenery.

Cycling South

From **Kalyves,** a popular tourist resort on the coast at the entrance of Souda Bay, your route takes you in a generally southerly direction to **Armeni ❶,** a farming village that lies amid groves of avocados, olives, and orange trees. The village square, like so many in Greece, is shaded by a large plane tree. Before and after Armeni the route is virtually flat, though there is a gentle climb into the quiet village of **Nio Chorio,** which lies in a lush valley amid orange and olive groves. You will find some cute cafés here.

The next opportunity to rest and get refreshment is **Agioi Pantes ❷,** a small village with good tavernas and blooming wildflowers in the spring. The track then swings to the southeast before your next port of call, **Vrisses ❸,** a lively village known for its goat cheese and thick, creamy yogurt. A river runs near the main square; nearby are frescoed churches. You will now cycle through one of the loveliest parts of Crete, the **Askifou Plateau** (the plateau resembles a cup, which is *skyphos* in

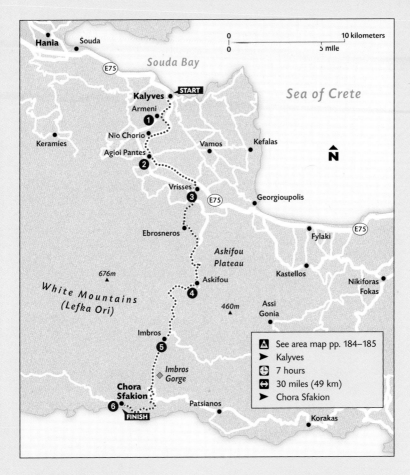

ancient Greek—hence the name), a fertile stretch that's surrounded by the **White Mountains** (Lefka Ori).

As you head south once more, toward Askifou, you encounter the only strenuous part of the ride, as the track winds more steeply uphill. The village of **Askifou** ❹ has a private war museum dedicated to those Cretans who died during World War II (*Georgios Hatzidakis War Museum, Askifou, tel 28250/95289*). Just after the village is the highest point of your journey, at 2,625 feet (800 m). Now, it's all downhill, and the descent is much steeper than the ascent has been, with the road swinging first one way, then the other as you head toward

the south coast. **Imbros** ❺ is a tiny village of stock breeders and farmers who cultivate walnuts and grapes for wine and the strong grape-must spirit called *tsikoudia* (also known as raki). Great honey is found here, too. The village is near the popular **Imbros Gorge.**

You end up at **Chora Sfakion** ❻, a small and beautiful coastal village surrounded by tamarisks and pine trees. Tourism, fishing, olive oil production, and sheep and goat herding are big here. Chora Sfakion also has excellent fish tavernas, which are known for their outstanding *kakavia* (fish soup). Vangelis will arrange to pick up your bike from the village, and you can catch a bus back to Hania at 6 p.m.

Agios Nikolaos & Eastern Crete

Eastern Crete, anchored by Agios Nikolaos, stretches from green farming plateaus to dry crags overlooking blue bays. Though some parts of this region have the usual beach resorts overrun with sunbathing tourists, the eastern tip is quiet, unexplored, and scented with wild oregano, bay, and sage plants. It's a place to catch a glimpse of a disappearing Crete before the resorts spread here, too.

Colorful pottery for sale in Agios Nikolaos, eastern Crete's biggest town

Agios Nikolaos
🅰 185 D1
Visitor Information
✉ Information Office, Akti S. Koundourou 21A, Agios Nikolaos
☎ (28410) 22357
www.agiosnikolaos .com

Archaeological Museum of Agios Nikolaos
✉ Konstantinou Paleologou St. 74
☎ (28410) 24943
🕐 Closed Mon.

Agios Nikolaos

A pretty town of 20,000, Agios Nikolaos was settled in the late Bronze Age by Dorian explorers. It's situated on a peninsula along the Gulf of Mirabello, a geographic mix of balding mountains and tiny islets engulfed by the sea. The town has all the requisite cafés and tavernas to serve travelers and locals alike, as well as the **Archaeological Museum,** featuring the Goddess of Myrtos, a statue that dates to 2500 B.C., and late-Minoan pottery. Two good beaches, Kitropolatia and Ammos, are a 10-minute walk

from the town center. A lagoon called Lake Voulismeni has a park, amphitheater, and cafés.

About 7 miles (11 km) north of Agios Nikolaos is the **Elounda peninsula,** which has great views of the Gulf of Mirabello and pebbly beaches with clean, clear water. The shore south of the gulf is populated with some of Greece's luxury hotels, so don't go there unless you want to rub elbows with rich internationals.

Farther East

The traditional village of **Kritsa** is about 13 miles (20 km) south of Elounda. Kritsa has

INSIDER TIP:

April is the peak flowering time for the native flora of Crete and the other southern islands.

—NICHOLAS TURLAND
National Geographic field scientist

an old-fashioned town square, where local grandfathers play backgammon over tiny cups of Greek coffee while admiring views of the valley and sea. There's also a notable Byzantine church, **Panagia Kera,** which was constructed during the early years of Venetian rule. It has well-preserved 13th-century medieval frescoes.

The town of **Sitia** is low-key and focused on agriculture, especially the cultivation of small, fat, and fragrant Cretan bananas. Cafés and tavernas line its sandy beach, and there's the Venetian **Kazarma Fortress,** which offers great views of the bay. Not far

away is the fortified **Toplou Monastery,** which has few monks but a lot of money. Toplou helped bring wind farms to this part of the island.

Vai, noted since classical times, is a beautiful place but extremely crowded in the summer—people flock to its fine **beach.** Farmers selling bananas and cold-press olive oil often set up small stands outside the beach. The town of **Palaikastron,** the easternmost settlement of any size, is close to Kouremenos Bay and has old-fashioned cafés and tavernas with grandmothers' home-cooking. Nearby is a Minoan-era settlement that archaeologists say may have approached the size of Knossos. A dirt road leads from Palaikastron to the Minoan archaeological site of **Roussola-kos,** which is cordoned off by a rusting metal fence.

The ancient town of **Itanos,** also called Erimoupolis ("deserted city"), has beautiful, deserted coves that offer some of the most satisfying swimming in Crete. ∎

Kritsa
- 🅰 185 C1

Panagia Kera
- ✉ Agiou Nikolaou Kritsas, Kritsa
- ☎ (28410) 51525
- 🕐 Closed Sat. p.m. & Sun.
- 💲 $

Kazarma Fortress
- ✉ Sitia
- 🕐 Closed Mon.
- **www.explorecrete .com/crete-east/ EN-Sitia-fortress-kazarma.html**

Toplou Monastery
- ✉ 8 miles (13 km) northwest of Palaikastron
- ☎ (28430) 61226
- 💲 $$

Palaikastron
- 🅰 185 D1

Itanos
- 🅰 185 D1

Spinalonga and *The Island*

From 1903 to 1957, the island of Spinalonga in eastern Crete was one of the last active leper colonies in Europe. When the lepers first arrived here, they went through a tunnel they called Dante's Gate because they were so anxious about what lay ahead. But compared to what they were used to, the patients were treated well: They received food, water, medical attention, and social security payments. Before Spinalonga, the afflicted were often banished to caves.

Spinalonga was founded during the Venetian period, and the Ottomans eventually took control in 1715. When the Turks lost power at the end of the 19th century, Ottoman families, fearing Christian reprisals, took refuge here. The last Turks left the island in 1903.

Nowadays, Spinalonga is a tourist attraction that's getting more attention since the release of *The Island,* Victoria Hislop's wildly successful novel about the leper colony. Tourist boats depart daily from Elounda for the 15-minute trip to the island, which also has nice pebble beaches.

The UNESCO World Heritage site of Rhodes, medieval monasteries and knights' castles, Mediterranean bird-watching at its best, and the ouzo distilleries of Lesvos

Dodecanese & Northeastern Aegean

A sun-dappled passage in Rhodes's Old Town

Dodecanese & Northeastern Aegean

The Dodecanese literally means the "twelve islands," though the island chain actually includes many more, smaller islands. Of the total of 163, only 26 islands are inhabited, the largest of which is Rhodes, a powerhouse in ancient history and a magnet for foreign travelers in modern times.

Flour-grinding windmills on the island of Karpathos

Dodecanese

The Dodecanese has a rich history that has left remnants of Byzantine churches and medieval castles on even the smallest islets. These islands hug the shores of Turkey and Asia Minor, and—with the exception of Crete—are the southernmost Greek islands. Besides Rhodes, other major islands include Kos, known in antiquity for its powerful healing center, the Asklepio; Patmos, where St. John wrote his Revelation and which became known as a monastic center; and dramatic, rugged Karpathos. Though the major Dodecanese islands have gotten very touristy over the years, there are still spots to swim, hike, and explore with abandon.

Northeastern Aegean Islands

The Northeastern Aegean islands blend a strong shipping history with ecotourism, tradition, and a homegrown entrepreneurship that has sent products made from an aromatic resin called mastic to boutique stores around the world.

The biggest of the islands, Lesvos, produces olive oil as well as half of the world's ouzo.

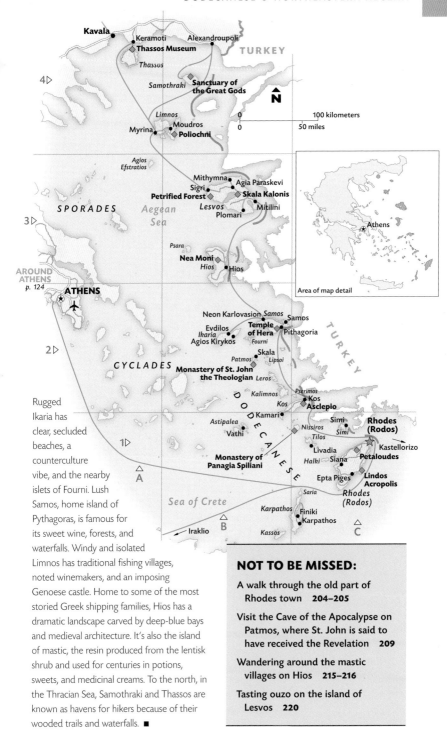

Kavala
Keramoti
Alexandroupoli
Thassos Museum
TURKEY
Thassos
Samothraki
Sanctuary of the Great Gods
N
0   100 kilometers
0   50 miles
Limnos
Moudros
Myrina   Poliochni
Agios Efstratios
Mithymna   Agia Paraskevi
Sigri   Skala Kalonis
Petrified Forest   Lesvos   Mitilini
Plomari
SPORADES   Aegean Sea
Psara
Nea Moni
Hios   Hios
AROUND ATHENS
p. 124
ATHENS
Athens
Area of map detail
Neon Karlovasion Samos
Samos
Evdilos   Temple   Pithagoria
Ikaria   of Hera
Agios Kirykos   Fourni
Skala
Patmos   Lipsoi
CYCLADES   Monastery of St. John the Theologian   Leros
Kalimnos
Pserimos
Kos   Kos
Asclepio
Kamari
Astipalea   Simi   Rhodes (Rodos)
Vathi   Nissiros   Simi
Tilos   Kastellorizo
Livadia   Petaloudes
Monastery of Panagia Spiliani   Halki   Siana
Epta Piges   Lindos Acropolis
Saria   Rhodes (Rodos)
Sea of Crete
Karpathos   Finiki
Iraklio   Karpathos
Kassos

Rugged Ikaria has clear, secluded beaches, a counterculture vibe, and the nearby islets of Fourni. Lush Samos, home island of Pythagoras, is famous for its sweet wine, forests, and waterfalls. Windy and isolated Limnos has traditional fishing villages, noted winemakers, and an imposing Genoese castle. Home to some of the most storied Greek shipping families, Hios has a dramatic landscape carved by deep-blue bays and medieval architecture. It's also the island of mastic, the resin produced from the lentisk shrub and used for centuries in potions, sweets, and medicinal creams. To the north, in the Thracian Sea, Samothraki and Thassos are known as havens for hikers because of their wooded trails and waterfalls. ∎

NOT TO BE MISSED:

A walk through the old part of Rhodes town **204–205**

Visit the Cave of the Apocalypse on Patmos, where St. John is said to have received the Revelation **209**

Wandering around the mastic villages on Hios **215–216**

Tasting ouzo on the island of Lesvos **220**

Rhodes

Today, Rhodes is one of Greece's biggest draws for vacationers. This, the fourth-largest Greek island, lies just 11 miles (18 km) off the coast of Turkey, so it is hardly surprising that the island's landscape and coastline resemble that country. Its history is extremely rich: Settled in Neolithic times by metal-workers from Asia Minor, it was an important link between Europe and the Near East for thousands of years.

Shops in Rhodes Old Town at dusk

Rhodes

🅰 201 C1

Visitor Information

✉ Municipal
Tourist Office,
Plateia Rimini,
Rhodes town

☎ (22410) 35945

🕐 Closed Sat.–Sun.

✉ South Aegean
Tourist Office,
Makariou/
Papagou,
Rhodes town

☎ (22410) 44333

🕐 Closed Sat.–Sun.

www.visitgreece.gr

A Little History

Rhodes was settled by many peoples, including the Minoans, Mycenaeans, and Achaeans. The Dorians founded the powerful naval towns of Lindos, Ialysos, and Kamiros. The Persians invaded Rhodes, but the islanders fought back and eventually drove them away. Alexander the Great defeated the Persians in 332 B.C., and the Rhodians helped with the sacking of Tyre.

After Alexander's death, Rhodes formed an alliance with Ptolemaic Egypt. King Antigonus

of Syria sent his son Demetrios Poliorkitis ("The Besieger") to capture Rhodes but the islanders put up such a fight that after a year he gave up. He signed a peace agreement with Rhodes and left many of his war-related inventions (including a battering ram and a so-called "siege tower") to the islanders, who in turn sold them to finance the building of a monumental statue called the Colossus of Rhodes. The statue, more than 95 feet (30 m) tall, depicted the Greek god Helios and was erected between

292 and 280 B.C. Considered one of the Seven Wonders of the Ancient World, it stood for only 54 years until it was toppled by an earthquake in 226 B.C. It lay on the ground for the next 800 years until Arabs sold off the pieces to a Jewish trader.

During the Roman era, Rhodes became a center of education, and in medieval times, St. Paul converted the island to Christianity. The island fell to the Arabs in 672 B.C. and in 1090 to the Seljuk Turks, but it returned to the Byzantines during the First Crusade of Emperor Alexius Comnenus. The Ottomans took over the island in the 16th century and ruled here until 1912, when the Italians invaded. Rhodes did not become part of Greece until 1948.

INSIDER TIP:

The Old Town of Rhodes becomes crowded with tourists in the late morning. Go sightseeing as early as you can to avoid the crowds.

—CLIVE CARPENTER
National Geographic contributor

Rhodes Island

The island of Rhodes has beautiful fine-sand beaches such as **Elli,** which is just north of Rhodes Old Town, near Rhodes Yacht Club. But beware, the coastline is heavily developed with resorts and the beaches can be crowded during summer. This is particularly true of the east coast of the island, which is lined with white-sand beaches. To get away from the crowds, head to the island's west coast, which has fewer fine-sand beaches but is full of vineyards, archaeological ruins, and quirky small-town traditions, food, and drink, such as *souma,* a grape-flavored schnapps made in the village of **Siana.**

Other towns include **Epta Piges,** or Seven Springs, a pristine village where the lush foliage is nurtured by mountain springs, and the ancient town of **Lindos,** which was the island's main harbor and capital in antiquity. Much of the 15th-century architecture here is very well preserved, and there's an impressive **acropolis,** which rises high above the town and was fortified successively by the Greeks, Romans, and Byzantines, the Knights of St. John, and the Ottomans. Within the acropolis is the huge **Temple of Athena Lindia,** finished around 300 B.C., a 14th-century **castle,** and the remains of a Knights of St. John **chapel,** although all that remains of the last is the outside wall. In the summer, Lindos gets very crowded.

Rhodes Town

The main town is also called Rhodes, and it's divided into two parts, the old and the new. The medieval **Old Town** is a UNESCO World Heritage site with Orthodox and Catholic churches and Ottoman *(continued on p. 206)*

Siana
🅰 201 C1

Epta Piges
🅰 201 C1

Lindos
🅰 201 C1
Visitor Information
✉ Lindos Municipal Tourist Office, Plateia Eleftherias, Lindos town
☎ (22440) 31900

(continued on p. 206)

A Walk in Rhodes's Old Town

Volumes of history are packed into the tightly packed streets of Rhodes's Old Town. Leave behind the most popular tourist attractions and you'll be pleasantly surprised to find some real historic gems.

Begin at the **Palace of the Grand Masters** **❶**, built by the Knights of St. John and located in the medieval city's highest spot. In 1856, the palace was heavily damaged by an ammunition explosion, but the Italians later rebuilt it. You can walk through moody Amboise Gate from the palace across the moat. You can also follow the lush Moat Walkway from near the end of the gate.

In front of the palace court is the **Loggia of St. John,** where the aforementioned knights were buried. From there, walk south along Orfeos, passing a **clock tower** on the left. The 16th-century **Suleiman's Mosque** and 18th-century **Turkish Library** **❷** are still used by the island's small Turkish community (both the mosque and library are on Sokratous Square). Capped by a pink dome, Suleiman's Mosque was built in 1522 to honor the Ottoman victory against the knights. The bare but appealing **Rhodes Hammam** **❸** in Arionos Square is still very popular with locals, who come here to the Turkish-style public baths to ease their muscle aches. A wood fire warms the water for the steam room, and afterwards you rinse off in a shower and settle down for a massage.

Head south along Ippodamou and look at the **Agiou Athanasiou Gate** **❹**, then return to Omirou and walk east along the inside of the city walls to the **Gate of St. John** **❺**.

Toward the Harbor

A stroll north along Pithagora takes you toward the harbor, but before you get there make a small detour to **Ibrahim Pasha**

NOT TO BE MISSED:

Palace of the Grand Masters
• Town walls • Ippoton (Street of the Knights) • Eleftherias Gate • Plateia Ippokratous

---

The Knights of St. John

Also known as the Knights Hospitaller, the Knights of St. John grew out of a seventh-century papal hospital for pilgrims in Jerusalem. The Arab Caliphs destroyed the hospital, but later had it rebuilt on the grounds of Jerusalem's monastery of St. John. From there, the hospital evolved into a safe haven for pilgrims, who later formed a militia—supported by the papacy—that fought Muslims.

The Muslims forced the knights out of the Holy Land in 1291; the knights resettled on Cyprus and, from there, decided to relocate to Rhodes. The knights secured the island on August 15, 1309, and spent the next 200 years fighting off attacks from the Ottoman empire, pirates, and other invaders. The knights financed buildings such as the Palace of the Grand Masters (which eventually served as a summer palace for both an Italian King and Benito Mussolini, though the latter never actually stayed there).

In 1522, the Knights of St. John fell to Suleiman the Magnificent. Rhodes's 7,000 knights, however, were able to hold off Suleiman's 200,000 troops for six months before finally being overpowered by the Ottoman's enormous army.

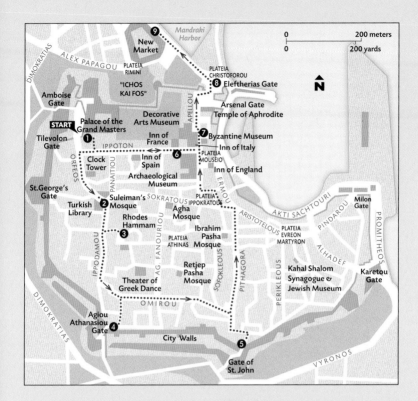

Map labels:
Mandraki Harbor
New Market
9
PLATEIA RIMINI
DIMOKRATIAS
ALEX PAPAGOU
"ICHOS KAI FOS"
Amboise Gate
Decorative Arts Museum
Palace of the Grand Masters
START
Tilevolon Gate
ORFEOS
IPPOTON
Inn of France
Clock Tower
Inn of Spain
Archaeological Museum
St. George's Gate
PANAITIOU
Turkish Library
Suleiman's Mosque
2
Rhodes Hammam
3
IPPODAMOU
AG. FANOURIOU
SOKRATOUS
Agha Mosque
PLATEIA ATHINAS
Ibrahim Pasha Mosque
Retjep Pasha Mosque
Theater of Greek Dance
OMIROU
Agiou Athanasiou Gate
4
DIMOKRATIAS
City Walls
Gate of St. John
5
SOPROKLEOUS
PITHAGORA
PERIKLEOUS
Kahal Shalom Synagogue & Jewish Museum
PLATEIA EVREON MARTYRON
ALHADEF
Karetou Gate
PROMITHEOS
Milon Gate
PINDAROU
AKTI SACHTOURI
ARISTOTELOUS
ERMOU
PLATEIA IPPOKRATOUS
6
Inn of Italy
PLATEIA MOUSEIO
Inn of England
7
Byzantine Museum
Arsenal Gate
Temple of Aphrodite
8
Eleftherias Gate
PLATEIA CHRISTOFOROU
APELLOU
N
0   200 meters
0   200 yards
VYRONOS

Mosque on the left. This is the town's oldest mosque, built in 1531. Continue north past **Plateia Ippokratous** to Inn of England.

From here, the **Ippoton (Street of the Knights)** climbs to the west, away from the commercial port, flanked by the Inns of the Tongues, where the knights met and dined. First you will see the knights' former hospital, finished in 1489 and now an **Archaeological Museum** 6 (*Plateia Mouseio, Rhodes Old Town, tel 22410/27657, closed Mon., $$*) that holds ancient pottery and sculpture. Two of the finest pieces are the Aphrodite of Rhodes and an Aphrodite Thalassia. The Ippoton was divided into seven "tongues" based on the knights' place of origin: Aragon, Auvergne, England, France, Germany, Italy, and Provence. Each tongue was responsible for policing and protecting that section. They all reported to a ruling Grand Master, who lived in the palace.

See area map p. 201
► Palace of the Grand Masters
🕐 1–2 hours
↔ 1.2 miles (2 km)
► New Market

Opposite the Archeological Museum is the **Inn of France** (now the French consulate), which dates to the 15th and 16th centuries and was a key gathering spot for the knights.

Take a look inside the **Byzantine Museum** 7, housed in a Gothic church and containing 14th-century wall paintings and icons from the late Byzantine and post-Byzantine period. Almost next door are the ruins of the **Temple of Aphrodite.** Then pass through the **Eleftherias Gate** 8 and end your walk on the quayside at **Mandraki Harbor** 9, with the **New Market** adjacent.

Palace of the Grand Masters

⊠ Ippoton, Rhodes Old Town

☎ (22410) 23359

🕐 Closed Mon.

$ $$

www.travel-rhodes .com

Museum of Decorative Arts

⊠ Plateia Argyrokastrou, Rhodes Old Town

☎ (22410) 72674

🕐 Closed Mon.

$ $$

Suleiman's Mosque

⊠ Orfeos Street, Rhodes town

$ $

Petaloudes

△ 201 C1

architecture. The influence of the medieval Knights of St. John is everywhere, but there is much of more recent interest, too. The old city walls were built in the mid-14th century and subsequently reconstructed after the Ottoman siege of 1480 and a severe earthquake the following year. The walls are punctured by several gates, including the **Amboise Gate** in the northwest, and the **Gate of St. John** and the **Agiou Athanasiou Gate** to the south of the old city.

At the top of the Ippoton (or Street of the Knights) is the **Palace of the Grand Masters.** Originally built by the Knights of St. John in the 14th century, it was very badly damaged by a gunpowder explosion in the 1850s. The palace was sympathetically rebuilt between 1937 and 1940, and visitors can now look around more than 20 rooms. The ballroom, music room, and grand reception

INSIDER TIP:

Rhodes town has a good beach, but pick your spot carefully. The most sheltered places, protected from the prevailing wind, are usually along the eastern side.

—CLIVE CARPENTER
National Geographic contributor

hall—along with their exhibits of antique furniture, frescoes, carpets, and sculpture—are now open to the public.

At the other end of the Ippoton, in a domed structure that was once part of the knights' arsenal, is the **Museum of Decorative Arts.** This features fine embroidery, traditional costumes, hand-crafted wooden vessels and pottery, and a reconstruction of a traditional Rhodian home. Elsewhere,

Valley of the Butterflies

Located about 15 miles (23 km) southwest of Rhodes town, the Valley of the Butterflies, or **Petaloudes,** is a popular summer visitor attraction. In late May, thousands of Jersey tiger moths, gather on the branches of the pungent oriental sweetgum (or storax) plant in the Pelekanos river valley. According to lore, the river is named for a servant to the Byzantine emperor Alexandros Ypsilantis who guarded the emperor's ailing daughter here. The servant and the daughter fell in love, but when Ypsilantis refused to give his blessing, the servant killed himself.

The valley is lush and has several beautiful waterfalls. You will hear chirping birds, spot tiny lizards on the rocks, and see crabs in the cool spring water. The air is humid and scented with the resin from the storax trees. Watching the ascent of so many pairs of wings is both beautiful and primal.

A 45-minute bus ride from Rhodes town, Petaloudes is best visited from July to September. For a different take on a spectacular experience, book yourself on a cycle tour of the valley. Contact **Bicycle Greece** *(Falirou Street 15, 11742 Athens, tel 21092/18160).*

Tiger moths in Rhodes's Valley of the Butterflies

Jewish Synagogue Museum

✉ Kahal Shalom Synagogue, Dosiadou, Jewish Quarter, Rhodes town

🕐 Open weekday mornings only.

www.rhodesjewish museum.org

Suleiman's Mosque, Ibrahim Pasha Mosque, and **Rhodes Hammam** (see p. 204) are impressive reminders of the many centuries that this town spent as part of the Muslim Ottoman empire.

Within the Old Town is the **Jewish Quarter,** which is well worth a visit. Once home to a thriving Jewish community, it had six synagogues, although only the **Kahal Shalom Synagogue** is still used for services today. Built in 1577, it is probably Greece's oldest surviving synagogue. The **Jewish Synagogue Museum** offers the history of the community, which in the 1920s was 4,000 strong. In 1944, the Nazis deported 1,673 of its Jews to Auschwitz concentration camp and **Plateia Evreon Martyron (Square of the Jewish Martyrs)** is dedicated to them.

Rhodes is not all about history, however. There are plenty of tavernas and restaurants, some better than others. Try **Symposium** *(Archelaou St. 3, Old Town, Rhodes, tel 22410/28598)* for mousaka, tasty salads, and Greek coffee; or **To Steki to Xeila** *(Chatziagou/ Dendrinou corner, tel 22410/29337)* for its fresh fish. ■

Other Dodecanese Islands

Every one of the Dodecanese islands has its own charm. All have traditional villages with cube-shaped white-painted houses, little fishing harbors, and—often—the remains of a hilltop fort built by the Knights of St. John. The most famous of the "other" islands is probably historic Patmos, sometimes called the "Jerusalem of the Aegean."

The walled Monastery of St. John dominates the brilliant white buildings of the Chora on Patmos.

Patmos

⛰ 201 B2

Visitor Information

✉ Municipal Tourist Office, Skala, Patmos

☎ (22470) 31666

🕐 Closed winter months

www.patmos-island .com

Patmos

Small, rocky, and stark, the island of Patmos covers only 21 square miles (34 sq km) but it carries a weighty history. According to myth, the moon goddess Selene asked Artemis to raise the sunken island of Patmos. Artemis obliged and, with her brother Apollo's help, brought the island to the surface.

In the first century A.D., St. John, exiled from Ephesus, wrote his *Revelation* under a temple to Artemis. In 1088, St. Christodou-

los founded the **Monastery of St. John the Theologian** (see sidebar p. 209) on the same site as the temple to Artemis. The locals heavily fortified the monastery to protect it against pirate raids. Many other basilicas were built on the island after St. John's death, and the church held jurisdiction on the island during the Byzantine Empire. After Constantinople fell in 1453, Greek refugees filled the island. The Ottomans, Venetians, Russians, and Italians took turns to control the island until after

EXPERIENCE: On the Trail of St. John

St. John the Theologian was exiled to Patmos in A.D. 95 as the emperor Domitian was cracking down on Christians. During his two years on this rocky, bare island, St. John found his purpose. It was here that he heard a booming, otherworldly voice commanding him to write a book of gospel and disperse it to the churches.

St. John is said to have written the text of *Revelation* in a little cave called the Sacred Grotto, now built into the **Monastery of the Apocalypse** *(tel 22470/31234, closed Mon., Wed., Fri., & Sat., $$ for Treasury)*. Today, the grotto has 12th-century wall paintings. In late August or early September, the monastery also hosts an open-air festival of Byzantine and ecclesiastical music. The Byzantine Emperor Alexius Komnenos

gave Patmos to the soldier-priest of Ioannis Christodoulos in 1088, who went about building an enormous Monastery of St. John the Theologian on the ruins of an ancient temple to Artemis. Today it is the most magnificent site on Patmos.

To experience a St. John-inspired pilgrimage, go to the Chora, an immaculate, whitewashed village organized around the **Monastery of St. John the Theologian** *(tel 22470/31398, closed Mon., Wed., Fri., & Sat.)*. Attend a service here if you can; the chants and the incense seem otherworldly. Then walk up the Byzantine path that begins on the Skala–Hora road and ends at the Monastery of the Apocalypse. The monastery is built around the cave where St. John received his divine revelation.

Kambos beach is a great place to swim and socialize. Tourists and locals get together at George's Place to play *tavli* (Greek backgammon), sip *freddos* (coffee drinks), and sample fresh apple pie.

—MICHAEL CHARLES SCOTT
Classicist & TV presenter

the Second World War, when Italy ceded the island to Greece. Today, Patmos is a UNESCO World Heritage site and is one of several Greek islands that report to the Ecumenical Patriarchate of the Greek Orthodox Church. **Skala** is the main town here, and

it's popular as a cruise-ship stop. Overlooking it is the old part of town, the Chora. A 20-minute walk up to **Kastelli,** on a hill overlooking Skala, offers a great view.

The **Chora,** built around the walls of the Monastery of St. John the Theologian, has become a magnet for rich foreigners who have built beautiful summer homes here. It has about 40 churches. The monastery itself has courtyards, chapels, stairways, arcades, galleries, and roof terraces, a magnificently well-preserved example of medieval monastic architecture. The buildings here include the 17th-century **Chapel of the Holy Apostle,** the 12th-century **Chapel of the Virgin,** a **treasury,** and a **library.** Five minutes' walk west of the Monastery of the Apocalypse (see sidebar, this page) is the **Holy**

Skala
🗺 201 B2

Kos

⚠ 201 C2

Visitor Information

✉ Tourist Office, Vasileous Georgiou, Kos town

☎ (22420) 24460

🕐 Closed Sat. afternoon & Sun.; closed Nov.–Apr.)

Archaeological Museum

✉ Near Platanou Square, Kos town

☎ (22420) 28326

💲 $$

Monastery of Zoodohos Pigi, which features beautiful frescoes.

The island has at least two dozen beaches, and though most are rocky, the water is beautiful and clear. **Kambos beach** is the most popular beach and has neighboring tavernas and watersport facilities. The loveliest beach on the island is the sandy stretch called **Psili Ammos,** which is about nine miles (14 km) from Skala in the south. You can take either a 20-minute hike along a footpath or a 45-minute caique ride.

Kos

Originally settled by the Carians, Kos was a member of the Delian League during the Peloponnesian War and a strategic base for Athenians after Rhodes dropped out of the League. Rhodes was once an important stop on the Silk Road—a trade route that carried goods between Europe and the Far East. Kos thrived during the Hellenistic Age as a center of education, especially relating to medicine, partly because of the influence of Hippocrates (see sidebar this page). Control of Kos passed through the Byzantines, Venetians, Knights of St. John, Ottoman Turks, Italians, Germans, and British before becoming part of modern Greece in 1948.

The third-largest of the Dodecanese islands, Kos is blessed with green fields, forested mountains, and sandy beaches. However, mass tourism has taken its toll on the island; the beaches are packed, and resorts overpower the villages and towns. **Kos town** is flanked to the west by a **fortress** where Hippocrates is said to have taught in the shade of a plane tree. Near **Platanou Square,** which is named for the tree, you will find the 15th-century **Castle of the Knights,** a drop-off point for ancient funerary monuments, and the **Archaeological Museum,** which has Hellenistic and Roman sculptures by Koan artists, including a statue of Hippocrates. About two and a half miles (4 km) west of Kos town, the **Asclepio** was once considered one of the great healing centers of antiquity, and its ruins still stand today.

Other notable spots on Kos include the **Castle of Andima-**

The Hippocratic Oath

Hippocrates of Kos (460–377 B.C.) was an ancient Greek physician widely considered to be the father of Western medicine. He founded the Hippocratic School of medicine and established medicine as a profession in Greece. He is also believed to have written the Hippocratic Oath, which is a creed based on the ethics he is said to have followed as a physician.

The oath, called *orkos* in Greek, was first written in the 4th century B.C. and required a new doctor to swear to the healing gods that he would be an ethical practitioner of medicine. Hippocrates, however, believed that disease could be explained rationally and was not due to the whims of the gods.

The Hippocratic Oath is still used today, though it's not required by medical schools and it has also been dramatically updated to suit various cultures. The basic idea, however, is still there: Doctors do all in their power to cure patients and never knowingly harm them.

Megisti town's waterfront, including the slender minaret of the former mosque

cheia, a medieval fortress where you can see the remains of a ruined settlement, and the beach town of **Kamari**, which is near **Paradise beach**, a long, sandy stretch of shoreline that, at its northern end, is secluded and, as such, often full of nudists.

Kastellorizo (Megisti)

About 70 miles (110 km) east of Rhodes, and almost within swimming distance of the Turkish coast, Kastellorizo is the easternmost Greek island. Connected with Rhodes by ferry, it also has an airport. The only town, **Megisti**, has a beautiful waterfront where the former Ottoman mosque is now a **museum**. The island has been ruled by Rhodes, Turkey, France, and Italy, and only became part of Greece in 1948. About 400

people live there today, a fraction of its former population. There is a beautiful sea cave called the **Blue Grotto** on the south coast of the island and the third-century B.C. ancient settlement of **Palaiokastro** on the eastern side of the island.

Kassos

The southernmost island in the Aegean, rocky little Kassos, has about 900 people and, for such a tiny island, an impressive history as a maritime port. The island was founded as a Philistine harbor and was settled by the Venetians, Franks, Genoese, Albanians, Turks, and Russians. The Kassiots were known as strong seamen even in classical times; Homer wrote that their ships were used in the Trojan War. Early in the 20th century,

Asclepio
🔺 201 C2

Kamari
🔺 201 B1

Kastellorizo
🔺 201 C1
Visitor Information
☎ (22460) 49269
www.megisti.gr

Kassos
🔺 201 B1
Visitor Information
✉ Maritime and Tourist Agency, Plateia Iroön Kasou, Kassos
☎ (22450) 41495
www.kassos-island .gr

Simi

201 C1

Visitor Information

Municipality of Simi, Simi town

(22460) 70110

www.symi.gr

Karpathos

201 C1

Visitor Information

Tourist kiosk, near Karpathou-Kipou, Karpathos town

(22450) 23835

Closed Sept.– June

many Kassiots emigrated to Egypt, Turkey, Greece, South Africa, and the United States. The largest villages are Fry, Aghia Marina, Panagia, and Arvanitohori.

Simi

Named for Poseidon's wife, the nymph Syme, this mountainous island was once a center of the shipbuilding and sponge industries. In medieval times, the Knights of St. John turned the island into a prosperous trading post that pivoted on natural sponge production. At the end of the 19th century, more than 22,500 people lived here.

Today, Simi relies primarily on tourism and has a population of about 2,500. The island's main settlement—also called **Simi**—is located around the harbor, while the smaller village of **Ano Simi** sits on the slopes of a nearby hill. The island has lovely, secluded beaches, numerous churches, and several archaeological sites. The beautiful 18th-century **Monastery of Taxiarchis Michael Panormitis,** in the lush hills around the **Gulf of Panormitis,** has an ornate bell tower, a mosaic in the courtyard, and elaborate frescoes and iconostases. From July to September, the **Simi Festival** (www.symigreece.com/festival) has dance, music, theater, and cinema offerings for free.

Karpathos

The second-largest of the Dodecanese islands, Karpathos is remote enough to have retained its unique sense of

dress, tradition, and even local dialect. Located about 30 miles (47 km) southwest of Rhodes, Karpathos has 10 villages, including the ports of Karpathos town and Diafani.

There is an airport in the south of the island, which is connected to all neighboring islands by ferries. The island is a popular locale for European tourists, who admire the Karpathians' sense of tradition and independence. About 6,500 people live here, but in the summer the population hikes to 20,000 due to summering Europeans and Athenians. The biggest celebration here is the August 15 festival called the **Panageia,** which celebrates the Assumption of the Virgin Mary.

The capital, **Karpathos town,** or Pigadia, has most of the island's eateries, bars, cafés, and accommodations. About 3 miles (5 km) away, **Ammoopi** is a resort center that has great opportunities for snorkeling. Nearby **Afiartis Bay** is popular with windsurfers. **Arkasa** has forgone tradition to embrace sun-and-sea tourism, though the nearby **Basilica of Agia Sophia** is worth a stop. Two miles (3 km) north, the fishing village of **Finiki** has good seafood tavernas.

Nissiros

A volcanic island located between Kos and Tilos, Nissiros (see sidebar this page) can be reached by ferry from the former. Tourism development is limited, and its main settlement, **Mandrakion,** has a population of less than 700. The **Monastery of Panagia Spiliani** sits beside a 14th-century Knights of St. John **castle** in Mandrakion. The traditional local almond-flavored *soumada* can be sampled in one of the town's waterfront tavernas.

Halki

A tiny island near Rhodes, Halki was a thriving island of 7,000 people during the fourth and fifth centuries B.C. Named for the copper it produced, its residents also farmed wheat. Water shortages have blunted any agriculture nowadays, so Halki is now a quiet islet for relaxation, swimming, and exploring picturesque villages. Hikes are scented with wild oregano and marjoram and brightened by the many herds of goats that graze here. The port village of **Emborios** is full of Venetian-style villas that once belonged to sea captains.

Tilos

A little more than 500 people live on this tiny island, but it's becoming increasingly popular with travelers seeking natural beauty in the quietest of settings. Birders catch glimpses of

Eleonora's falcons (the island is home to up to 10 percent of the world's population of this species) and Bonelli's eagles here. Hikers like the mountain trails, while swimmers who have grown weary of loud, crowded beaches can revel in isolation. The island is also home to rare orchids and endangered sea turtles, and Mediterranean monk seals can be seen from its

Volcanic Nissiros

The active volcano on the island of Nissiros has five craters in the caldera, with a trail leading to the largest crater. Along the way, you will see the kaleidoscopic fumaroles and smell the hiss of sulfur emitted as vapors. Be sure to wear good, thick shoes, since the surface is hot and malleable. According to myth, Poseidon cut off a piece of Kos and threw it on a Titan named Polyvotis, who had been irritating the sea-god. That piece of Kos trapped the Titan; the sounds of the volcano—groans, hisses, sighs—are said to be the vocalization of Polyvotis trying to escape from his imprisonment. The volcano's second crater is named Polyvotis, for the Titan. The last eruption, a steam explosion, took place in 1888, though there were also small ash eruptions in 1871 and 1873. There are also occasional earthquakes here.

shores. Most of the population lives in **Livadia,** the main village and port where you will find most of the cafés, tavernas, and places to stay. The capital, **Megalo Horio,** means "big village," but it's actually tiny—only 50 people live there. It's got a **museum** that's only open in summer, a **Knights' Castle,** and an **ancient settlement.** ■

Nissiros
◮ 201 C1

Visitor Information
✉ Municipality of Nissiros, Nissiros town
☎ (22420) 31330

Monastery of Panagia Spiliani
◮ 201 C1
✉ Mandrakion, Nissiros

Halki
◮ 201 C1

Tilos
◮ 201 C1

Livadia
◮ 201 C1

Northeastern Aegean Islands

Lesvos, Greece's third largest island, Hios, and Samos are connected to the Greek mainland and Turkey by regular ferry services, but the traveler has to use these islands as stepping stones to reach some of the smaller islands. A hydrofoil serves Samothraki, although in rough seas it can't always dock, since the island lacks a natural harbor. Reach Ikaria via Samos.

Thassos has some of the Aegean's most wonderful sandy beaches.

Ikaria
201 B2

Visitor Information

www.greeka.com
/eastern_aegean
/ikaria

Ikaria

This relaxed island, between the Cyclades and the Turkish coast, has an emerging counterculture vibe. It was named for a mythical but infamously hapless idealist named Icarus, the son of the Cretan inventor Daedalus, who made wings of wax, flew too close to the sun, and fell to his death in the sea when the waxen wings melted. People have lived here since 7,000 B.C. In the 14th century, Ikarians destroyed their own harbors to repel invaders and used a system of cisterns and watchtowers as a warning system for invading pirates. Impoverished for centuries, the Ikarians were essentially left to manage on their own, and they did. In 1912, they made the island into a free state, though it was incorporated into modern Greece after just five months.

Ferries from Samos, Limnos, and Lesvos serve the ports of **Evdilos** and the capital, **Agios Kirykos.** If you don't have the time or inclination to wander far from your port of arrival, the **Archaeological Museum of Kambos** (*Kambos village, west of Evdilos*) has tools dating back to the Neolithic period and coins, pottery, and grave carvings from the Classical, Geometric, and Hellenistic periods. And in Agios Kirykos is the **Archaeological & Folklore Museum.** Explore inland and you may encounter a **Byzantine fortress** (*Koskina village*).

Samos

Samos is closer to Turkey than any other Greek island; only a 2-mile (3 km) strip of sea separates it from the Turkish mainland coast.

Most people live in **Samos town,** the island's main port. The town's harbor is unremarkable, but the old quarter of **Ano Vathi** has tiny, steep streets winding around 19th-century homes and lovely old tavernas. The main attraction in the town is the **Archaeological Museum of Samos** (*Samos town, tel 22730/27469, closed Mon., $*), a highly regarded institution whose collection is split between two buildings—the Old Museum and the New Museum—separated by a few streets. The prize exhibit (in the new building) is an almost perfectly intact 18-foot-tall (5.5 m) kouros excavated from the Temple of Hera.

The area around the coastal town of **Pithagoria,** at Samos's southeast corner, boasts several fascinating ancient sites. The **Tunnel of Eupalinos** (named for the engineer who designed it) is a 2,500-year-old underground aqueduct cut into the hillside just north of the town. It is more than 1,000 yards (1 km) long. The remains of the **Temple of Hera** (*near Heraion, 4 miles/6 km west of Pithagoria, tel 22890/22325, $*) are nearby. This gigantic structure was built in several phases between the eighth and fourth centuries B.C., but never completed.

Hios

The island of Hios is located just a stone's throw from the Turkish coast. Arriving by ferry at Hios town, the concrete buildings

Archaeological & Folklore Museum
- ✉ Agios Kirykos, Ikaria

Samos
- 201 B2
Visitor Information
- ✉ Tourist Office, Plateia Pythagorou, Samos town
- ☎ (22730) 28530
- www.greeka.com /eastern_aegean /samos

Hios
- ▲ 201 B3
Visitor Information
- ✉ Municipal Tourist Office, Kanari 18, Hios town
- ☎ (22710) 44389

EXPERIENCE: Learn to Cook Greek Food in Ikaria

The Greek-American food writer **Diane Kochilas** is legendary in Greece both for her incisive restaurant reviews and for her thoroughly researched and innovative cookbooks on Greek cuisine. Every summer, she and her husband Vassilis Stenos host cooking classes in the ancient village of Agios Dimitris on Ikaria. Participants are brought to a lovely old stone house with immaculate kitchens and a stunning ocean view for their lessons.

Students learn about the local cuisine through visits to food artisans and then cook various Greek meals—including vegetarian, phyllo-based, meze, and seafood—in the afternoon for a full dinner in the garden outside the house. Kochilas and Stenos also teach students about the country's wines, cheeses, honey, and olive oil varieties. To book a cooking class on Ikaria with Diane Kochilas, visit her website: www.dianekochilas.com.

The Hios Mastihohoria

The aromatic resin from the mastiha (or tentisk) shrub has flavored potions and sweets in the eastern Mediterranean for thousands of years. In southern Hios, the *mastihohoria,* or mastic villages, are the centers of production. The largest is Pirgi, a scenic village of stenciled architecture set amid tiny, winding streets, and the most striking is Mesta, which has a gorgeously preserved medieval center with labyrinthine streets and thick fortress walls. Surrounding the villages are groves of mastiha shrubs, white halos of resin around their roots.

The Hios Gum Mastic Growers Association has turned mastiha production into an international enterprise. Mediterra, an outgrowth of the association, runs the mastihashops, which are located all over the world.

Mastiha tastes like a fresh burst of sweetness, with a slight hint of bitter aftertaste. It flavors chewing gum, coffee, candy, pasta, and ouzo. The shrubs begin to produce resin after about five years. Most of the product is exported, mainly to Arab countries, where it is sold in chewy crystals or powder. The first **Mastihashop** opened in Hios town (*Mastihashop, Leoforos Egeou 36, Mytilene, Hios, tel 22710/81600, www.mastihashop .com*) and is still open for business.

Hios Byzantine Museum

- ✉ Plateia Vounakiou, Hios town
- ☎ (22710) 26866
- 🕐 Closed Mon.
- 💲 $

Nea Moni Monastery & Museum

- ✉ Omiroupoli, Hios
- ☎ (22710) 79370
- 🕐 Closed Mon.
- 💲 $

Lesvos

- 🅰 201 B3

Visitor Information

- ✉ Hellenic Tourist Organization, Aristarchou 6, Mitilini, Lesvos
- ☎ (22510) 42511

www.lesvosonline.gr

along the waterfront don't make the best first impression. Beyond this, however, the island is beautiful, calm, and peaceful.

In the center of town, in a 19th-century Ottoman mosque, the **Hios Byzantine Museum** chronicles the rich history of Orthodox Christianity on the island. The museum contains several beautiful Byzantine frescos and mosaics that have been moved to the museum from some of the island's ruined churches. The collection of sculptures in the courtyard dates from the early Christian period to the Ottoman occupation.

The highlight of any trip to Hios, however, is the UNESCO World Heritage site of **Nea Moni.** This Byzantine monastery was founded in the 11th century and, thanks to the generosity of a succession of local rulers, soon became one of the largest and wealthiest monasteries in the

Aegean. Between the 13th and 19th centuries, the monastery commissioned the finest artisans and artists to beautify the site.

Sadly, the monastery was sacked by Ottoman forces in 1822 and further damaged by an earthquake in 1881. What remains, however, is still one of the finest examples of Byzantine art and architecture in the Aegean. The on-site **museum** houses a fantastic collection of material recovered from the site and a full history of the monastery.

Lesvos

Lesvos is the third largest island in Greece, with an area of 630 square miles (1,632 sq km), and has 90,000 permanent residents.

The island's capital, **Mitilini,** on the Turkey-facing east coast of the island, is an elegant town, filled with grand neoclassical mansions known as *pyrgelia.* One of these mansions today houses

INSIDER TIP:

In early spring, take a walk through the pine forest near Achladeri on Lesvos's Gulf of Kalloni to reach the beautiful spring and waterfall of Pessa.

—POLINA PATSI
National Geographic contributor

the **Archaeological Museum of Mitilini,** which has a small but comprehensive collection of ancient Greek, early Christian, and Byzantine artifacts.

Outside the island's capital, Lesvos is an island of tremendous natural beauty and peaceful island villages, where there are few concessions to the pace of modern life. Near Mitilini the **Teriade Museum** *(Varia, Lesvos, tel 22510/23372, closed Mon., $$)* has paintings by Picasso, Chagall, and Matisse. The museum is named for Lesvos native Stratis Eleftheriadis, an artist and critic who changed his name to Teriade when he moved to Paris.

The village of **Agia Paraskevi,** with its lovely architecture and authentic tavernas, is an attraction in itself and well worth exploring. However, the main interest here is the **Museum of Olive Oil Production** *(Agia Paraskevi, Lesvos, tel 22530/32300, closed Tues., $),* which gives visitors an inside look at how this product is made. Housed in a former communal oil mill, the museum walks visitors through the fundamental steps of olive-oil making.

On the north coast lies the lovely fishing town of **Mithymna,** also known by its ancient name, Molyvos. It is home to the beautiful 16th-century **Leimonos Monastery** *(Kalloni, Lesvos, tel 22530/22289),* which houses 40 chapels and an impressive library of handwritten manuscripts, documents, and books—some of which are more than 1,000 years old. The monks are currently in the process of digitizing their remarkable collection for their website.

In the far west of the island, near the fishing village of **Sigri,** stands the remarkable **Petrified** *(continued on p. 220)*

Archaeological Museum of Mitillni

- ✉ Agryri Eftalioti Street, Mitilini, Lesvos
- ☎ (22510) 28032
- 🕐 Closed Mon.
- 💲 $

Natural History Museum of the Petrified Forest

- ✉ Sigri, Lesvos
- ☎ (22530) 54434
- 💲 $$

www.lesvos museum.gr

Limnos

- 🅰 201 A4, B4

Checking the vats in an ouzo distillery on Lesvos

Outdoor Life on Lesvos

Greece's third-largest island is a haven for birdwatchers, hikers, snorkelers, and sea-kayaking enthusiasts. Its varied landscape—which alternates between craggy hillsides and verdant farmland—is home to challenging hiking routes and fascinating habitats, while the sheltered coast is safe and easy to explore in a kayak.

Kayaks and canoes are an excellent way to tour the coastal villages and beaches of Lesvos.

When you reach the warm, sunny coast of Lesvos, you soon understand why neither the locals nor visitors spend much of their time inside. Why should they when they can bask in the sunshine and sea breezes? It is no surprise that the island has an unrivaled reputation for outdoor activities. Even in winter, when the temperature doesn't often get above 60°F (16°C), visitors will have plenty of company outdoors, as many island-ers will be working on the olive harvest and preparing the ground for spring.

Bird-watching

The island is a haven for thousands of migrating birds in spring and fall, as they make their way to and from Central Asia and Africa. Conveniently, this is also the time when Lesvos's weather is especially lovely. The island is filled with marshlands, swamps, springs, and rivers that appear after the heavy rains in the spring.

Skala Kalonis is a favorite spot for bird-watchers, where you can see flamingos, herons, bitterns, storks, avocets and other shorebirds, terns, bee-eaters, and buntings in the spring and more shorebirds, kingfishers, and many warblers in the fall. Kalonis also has elevated hides and watchtowers where you can watch the birds without disturbing them. You'll also be able to spot storks' nests on the chimneys of abandoned buildings Other good birding spots include the main marshlands and flatlands around Kalloni, Skala Eresos, and **Sigri,** and in the hills around Eresos, **Mithymna,** and Agiasos.

Do-it-yourself bird-watching is easy on Lesvos. To find out what's been seen, and where, check the bird news provided by resident birders Eleni Galinou and Terry Robinson (http://athene-birdinglesvos.blogspot.com). Alternatively, several companies offer bird-watching tours of Lesvos. One of the most experienced guides is British ornithologist and writer **Steve Dudley** (www.lesvosbirding.com). He has been a regular visitor to the island for more than ten years, and organizes birdwatching trips to Lesvos several times a year.

Hiking

You can hike year-round on Lesvos, but fall and spring are the best times to enjoy the scenery without getting too hot. In the spring, the countryside is enlivened by seas of blooming flowers, including daffodils, red anemones, blue hyacinths, as well as blossoming citrus and other fruit trees. In the fall, the land has the burnished glow of leaves turning colors. You'll see chestnut, fig, walnut, and quince trees everywhere. Hiking is a great way to see the less well-known parts of the island—the hilltop

communities whose lifestyles have remained largely untouched by the island's tourism boom. These traditional villages are shrinking every year as more and more young people leave behind their island homes and head for the lights of Athens.

There are several trails around the island. One popular, but long, hike is a 10.5-mile (17 km) adventure that begins in Lambou Myli, passes the **Roman Aqueduct** (Lambou Myli, 10 miles/16 km west of Mitilini) and ends in Agiasos (16 miles/26 km west of Mitilini), a lovely hilltop village. You will walk along simple country roads, through groves of olives and walnuts and past old watermills, whitewashed churches, and farms. The trail has its share of steep, uphill sections, but gives hikers a spectacular view of the local countryside.

The **Lesvos Natura Network** (Skala Kaloni, tel 22530/24024, closed Sun., www.lesvos-natura .com), run by Giorgos Eleftheriou, offers guided hiking tours throughout the island with many more itineraries. His company also leads expeditions by jeep, arranges for tourists to join in winter olive harvests, and even offers a few sailing tours around the island.

EXPERIENCE: Sea Kayaking off Lesvos

The warm, sheltered waters around the coast of Lesvos are an ideal location to go sea kayaking. Unlike sailing or touring in a larger boat, traveling by sea kayak allows you to explore tiny, shallow coves and stop off whenever and wherever you feel like it, while still giving you enough space to carry food, spare clothing, or even a tent.

Adventure guide Nektarios Paraskevaidis offers daily ($$$$) and weekly ($$$$$) rentals through his company **Lesvos Adventure** (Nektarios Paraskevaidis, Mantamados, Lesvos, tel 22530/61172, www.lesvosadventure.com). For those who don't want to go it alone, Nektarios also schedules guided tours around the islets

off Lesvos, which combine sea kayaking with other activities such as snorkeling and archery. These tours range from short day trips to nearby islets, to longer explorations of the island's coast.

A typical day tour starts at the beach of Avlaki on the mainland, where you begin a kayaking tour of two small islets near Lesvos. On one, Rabbit Island, you can take a break and hike, snorkel, or take an archery lesson. You return to Lesvos by late afternoon.

Multi-day tours allow for additional activities such as dolphin-watching, visiting ancient sites on Lesvos's coast, or even paddling over to the nearby coast of Turkey.

EXPERIENCE: Ouzo Tasting on Lesvos

In the 19th century, Lesvos became the primary producer of the iconic—and very strong—anise-flavored liquor called ouzo. Although many of the major commercial brands are now made elsewhere, Lesvos remains the mecca for ouzo connoisseurs.

Most of the island's distilleries are based in or around the town of Plomari. The largest distillery in town, **Ouzo Barbayanni** (www.barbayanni-ouzo.com), is still run by the Barbayannis family, who have been making ouzo for five generations. In Plomari, the family also runs the

Ouzo Museum (Mytilene Road, Plomari, tel 22520/32741, closed Sat.–Sun.) next to its distilleries. Visitors can see early distillery equipment and also sample the family's ouzo, among the finest in the country.

There are also dozens of other distilleries on the island, ranging from medium-sized artisan companies like the excellent **Ouzo Giannatsi** (Leoforos Michalelli, Plomari, tel 22520/32822) to tiny village stills. As it lacks the anise flavor, the ouzo produced by the latter might perhaps be more accurately described as moonshine.

Samothraki

📍 201 B4

Visitor Information

✉ Tourist Office, Samothraki town

☎ (25510) 41218

www.samothrace .gr/index

Sanctuary of the Great Gods

📍 201 B4

✉ Palaeopoli, Samothraki

☎ (25510) 41474

🕐 Closed Mon.

💲 $$

Forest. The curious stone trees are a reminder of the island's volcanic past, since this forest was buried in a volcanic eruption 20 million years ago. The development of the site can be studied at the **Natural History Museum of the Petrified Forest.**

Limnos

Limnos is isolated but its lonely spot in the northeastern Aegean has kept it largely free of the tourist development that has both enriched and degraded some Greek islands. Limnos gets very windy in the summer, and seems to attract jellyfish, which put off many visitors.

The island's capital, **Myrina,** is about the only place touched by tourism, and even here it's mostly only Greek families from the mainland. High above the town is an old **Genoese fortress,** which is open to the public. There has not been any attempt to restore or showcase the ruined castle, but the views from its walls are

worth the climb up from town.

The fishing village of **Moudros** is a beautiful place filled with old-fashioned tavernas and cafés. A short distance to the south of the town there are a number of stunning beaches, while 4 miles (7 km) to the east lies the fascinating ruined city of **Poliochni,** which thrived around 6,000 years ago as a trading city connected with Minoan Crete.

Samothraki

This island is the most north-easterly of them all. Because it had no harbor or cultivable land, Samothraki sat in obscurity for most of classical Greek history.

One of the rockiest Greek islands, Samothraki is completely dominated by **Mount Fengari,** which rises to 5,285 feet (1,611 m). Northwest of the peak, and overlooking the north coast, is the **Sanctuary of the Great Gods,** one of the great Hellenic religious sanctuaries where, some time between 250 and 170 B.C., the famous Winged Victory (Nike of Samothrace, now in the Louvre in Paris) was sculpted. The site has a **theater, necropolis,** the **Altar of Hekate,** and a small **museum.**

Thassos

This is probably the most "un-Greek" of all the islands. Often described as the "emerald isle," it is famous for its relatively lush vegetation. It is a well-watered island, possibly unique in the Aegean for the sounds of springs and running water.

Lore says that Demeter was born here and taught the locals the art of agriculture in this lush, forested island. Inhabited since the Paleolithic era, Thassos was first colonized by the Phoenicians, who mined gold here. The island's mines made it wealthy, though wars in the fifth century B.C. eventually depleted the treasury. The Macedonians, Romans, and Genoese ruled the islands before the Turks captured it in 1455. Egypt got the island after the Greek Revolution, though the Greeks regained control of it during the Balkan Wars of 1912–13.

About 14,000 people live here today, and the capital is **Thassos town.** The island produces honey and olive oil and still makes money from mining lead, zinc, and marble, though a major industry is now tourism. **Thassos Museum** has interesting collections of pottery and sculpture, including a colossal statue of a young naked man carrying a ram, dating to about 600 B.C. ∎

Thassos
🅜 201 A4
Visitor Information
✉ Municipality of Thassos, Thassos town
☎ (25390) 22118

Thassos Museum
🅜 201 A4
✉ Megalou Alexandrou St. 18, Thassos town,
☎ (25930) 22180
🕐 Closed Mon.
💲 $
www.gothassos.com

Part of the Sanctuary of the Great Gods on Samothraki

An island whose architecture has as much in common with Venice as with Greece, and another where the heroic actions took place that inspired *Captain Corelli's Mandolin*

Corfu & the Ionians

Greek Orthodox clergy prepare for a holy day in Corfu's old town.

Corfu & the Ionians

Lying off the west coast of Greece, Corfu and the other Ionian islands have been popular vacation destinations for hundreds of years, and although they now see more visitors than ever before, there are still many unspoiled places for those who wish to avoid the crowds.

A glorious sunset over the Ionians, viewed from Kefalonia

The culture of the Ionian islands is heavily influenced by the various foreign powers that have occupied the islands over the years, particularly the Venetians, who ruled in Corfu from the 13th to 19th centuries. For many, however, it is their much older history that defines these islands. It was on Ithaca that Homer's hero Odysseus ruled.

Cosmopolitan Influences

The island that displays its foreign influences most prominently is Corfu, where the locals speak a dialect that mixes Greek with words and phrases taken from Italian, French, and English. Most of the other islands bear the marks of these foreign occupiers and many take great pride from the fact that they are the only Greeks who were never conquered by the Ottoman Empire.

The islands are known for their mild climate, which is typically cooler than that of southern Greece or the Aegean islands,

and their beautiful verdant landscape. Unlike the parched islands in the south, the Ionians experience significant rainfall, with spring and summer's brief showers giving way to crashing storms in the late fall and winter. With the arrival of spring, these wet months blossom into a glorious period when the islands are bathed in warm sunshine and carpeted with wild flowers. Many rare species of orchid blossom in the meadows and wooded hillsides, and numerous breeds of bird come here to nest.

The Southern Islands

There are seven notable islands in the Ionian chain. Traveling south from Corfu these are tiny Paxi (with its even tinier satellite,

---

NOT TO BE MISSED:

Watch a game of cricket in Corfu town **226**

Admiring the Venetian church architecture of Corfu's ancient heart **228**

Relaxing in the beautiful village of Ano Korakiana **229**

A rowboat trip from Paxi to the wooded islet of Agios Nikolaos **230–231**

Bathing on one of Lefkada's secluded, pristine beaches **232**

Marveling at the stalactites in Kefalonia's magnificent Caves of Drogarati **233**

Dine al fresco in the hilltop village of Kerion, on Zakinthos **235**

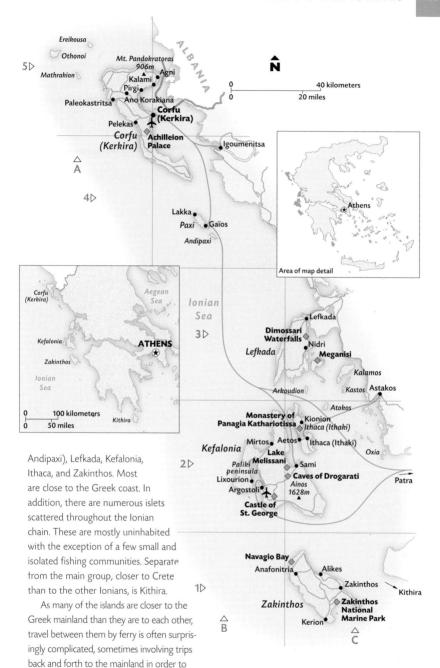

Andipaxi), Lefkada, Kefalonia, Ithaca, and Zakinthos. Most are close to the Greek coast. In addition, there are numerous islets scattered throughout the Ionian chain. These are mostly uninhabited with the exception of a few small and isolated fishing communities. Separate from the main group, closer to Crete than to the other Ionians, is Kithira.

As many of the islands are closer to the Greek mainland than they are to each other, travel between them by ferry is often surprisingly complicated, sometimes involving trips back and forth to the mainland in order to visit an island you can see from your starting point. The island of Corfu serves as a transport hub for the northern islands in the chain, while Kefalonia serves a similar role in the south. One

of the Ionian islands, Lefkada, is so close to the Greek mainland that it is accessible by road from Athens, thanks to a long causeway that links it to the national highway system. ∎

Corfu

With hints of Venice in its architecture, and scenery that is more lush than is typical on the Greek islands, it is hardly surprising that the island of Corfu (Kerkira) has become a haven for European vacationers. However, even on this heavily developed island, there is still a range of destinations and activities that lie beyond the tourist trail.

A sheltered, sandy beach on Corfu's north coast

Corfu

🗺 225 A4–5, B4–5

Visitor Information

✉ Tourist Office, corner of Voulefton St. & Mantzarou St., Corfu town

☎ (26610) 37520

www.corfu-town .com

Palaio Frourio (Old Fortress)

✉ Corfu town

☎ (26610) 48310

💲 $$

Corfu Town

With its well-preserved neoclassical houses, blooming with wisteria and washed with pastel colors, the island's only big center of population, Corfu town, is one of the most attractive in the region. The town is the commercial and cultural heart of the island, and its airport and seaport make it only a short journey from Athens and mainland Greece.

The historic heart of the city is located on a broad peninsula that juts out from the island's east coast. At the tip of this peninsula, separated from the town by a man-made channel, lies the old Venetian citadel of **Palaio Frourio (Old Fortress)**—an imposing stone bulwark that offers commanding views over the old city and the harbor.

Just beyond the walls of the citadel is the pleasant greenery of the esplanade, a neat little park that includes a slightly incongruous **cricket pitch** that is regularly used. At the northern end of the park is the **Palace of St. Michael & St. George**, a grand neoclassical

INSIDER TIP:

On Sunday mornings, rival village cricket teams play in the shadow of Corfu town's Palaio Frourio. It's very English, except that they never have to stop because of rain.

—TOM JACKSON
National Geographic contributor

building erected using white stone imported from the other British possession in the Mediterranean, Malta. Once the home of the island's British governor—a man who was given the grand title of Lord High Commissioner of the Ionian islands—the building today houses the island's tourist office. Its high-ceilinged rooms also contain the **Museum of Asian Art**—a collection of art from Japan and China.

On the western side of the park rise the densely packed houses and winding streets of the **Campiello,** the medieval walled settlement that stands in the heart of Corfu town. Some areas of the old town look so strikingly like Venice, with their tall colonnaded houses, that you expect to see gondolas floating down the streets. In other parts of the town, the British or French influence is more apparent. Towering over the Campiello is the **Neo Frourio,** another massive fortress built by the Venetians to defend the city from land-based forces. The fortress's high bastions offer

commanding views out over the town and surrounding coastline.

The most popular attraction in the Campiello is undoubtedly the town's modern **Archaeological Museum** *(Vraila Armeni Street 1, Corfu town),* whose collection includes a well-preserved frieze depicting snake-haired Medusa as well as numerous ancient sculptures. The museum was renovated in early 2011. Also located in the streets of the old town is the Panagia Antivouniotissa, a 15th-century church now used as the **Byzantine Museum,** housing a collection of icons and other religious artifacts. Among the maze of Venetian streets lies the **Church of St. Spiridon,** a beautiful little building easily identified by its red-domed bell tower. The church houses the remains of Saint Spyridon, a Cypriot shepherd who later became a bishop.

Palace of St. Michael & St. George (including Museum of Asian Art)

✉ Corfu town
☎ (26610) 30443
💲 $$

Byzantine Museum

✉ Panagia Antivouniotissa, Arseniou St., Corfu town
☎ (26610) 38313
🕐 Closed Mon.

Church of St. Spiridon

✉ Agios Spiridon St., Corfu town

The Durrell Brothers

The British naturalist Gerald Durrell (1925–1995) grew up on Corfu. He was fascinated by the animals that lived on the island and wrote extensively about his youth on Corfu in *My Family and Other Animals*, the most popular of the 34 books he wrote during his career as a naturalist. His more famous older brother Lawrence (1912–1990) was the one who first brought international attention to the island, however. Lawrence wrote novels, poems, verse plays, and short stories, and his Greek trilogy included the 1945 novel *Prospero's Cell*, in which he describes his life in Corfu in the late 1930s. The Durrells lived in the seaside village of Kalami, which is as lovely now as it was then—though it gets very busy during the summer.

Venetian Corfu

The Ionian islands were once all ruled by the Venetians, and their culture still bears many marks of this period. However, one aspect of Venetian culture—its beautiful architecture—has been lost on most of the islands. The devastating earthquake of 1953 bought down the great buildings on every major island except Corfu, which was far enough from the epicenter for its architectural treasures to survive.

The distinctive style of Venetian architecture owes much to the city in which it was born. Land (or water shallow enough to build in) has always been at a premium in Venice, and no architect could ever be certain of their foundations. As a result, Venetian-style buildings were never as heavy or stout as their northern European cousins.

Although there has never been a risk of Corfu's buildings sinking into the sea, the limited space within the town walls meant that

INSIDER TIP:

Even if your interest isn't architecture, make sure you visit Town Hall Square, with its great variety of buildings.

—CLIVE CARPENTER
National Geographic contributor

compact Venetian buildings were well suited. The clearest example of a Venetian-style urban building is the **Ionian Academy** *(Akadimias, Corfu town)*, a five-story mansion constructed in the early 18th century. It has a simple, perfectly symmetrical design, with regularly placed windows, a central balcony, and a pair of staircases leading down on either side of the main entrance. It is finished with stucco and painted pastel pink.

Freed from the restricting circumstances of their home city, Venetian architects were free to incorporate other popular Italian styles into their work. The most prominent of these was the school of architecture developed by the

Italian Andrea Palladio (1508–1580). Palladio was born in Padua, a city under Venetian rule, and became fascinated by the architectural principles of ancient Rome. He developed his classically-inspired style into a set of strict rules for architectural composition characterized by strict symmetry and a lack of ostentatious decoration—many of his grandest buildings are quite strikingly plain. In 1570, he was appointed chief architect of the Republic of Venice. Although Palladio never worked in Corfu, his popularity among Venetians meant that the town has no shortage of Palladian-style buildings.

The finest examples of these are located on Town Hall Square, in the heart of Corfu's old town. On its northern side stands the **Dimarcheio,** or town hall. This lovely little building was constructed in 1663, originally as an opera house. It continued to be used for this purpose until replaced by a larger theater space in the 19th century (the newer theater was destroyed during the bombing raids of the Second World War). Today it is the island's town hall and houses several public offices and information centers. On the opposite side of the square is the 17th-century **Cathedral of San Giacomo** *(Town Hall Square, Corfu town),* a small but perfectly formed church building that has a symmetrical pair of bell towers on either side of the main entrance.

The construction of these Venetian-style buildings did not stop with the departure of the Venetians, however. The French decided to emulate the great promenades of Venice and Paris by building the **Liston** *(Liston Square, Corfu town)*–a long, colonnaded row of buildings.

Southern Corfu

Just south of Corfu town is the **Palace of Mon Repos**. This grand residence was built by Sir Frederick Adam as a summer residence and later became the summer residence of the Greek royal family until their overthrow and exile in 1967. It now houses the **Paleopolis Archaeological Museum.**

One of Corfu's most interesting sights is the lavishly decorated **Achilleion Palace** (map p. 225 A5; *Gastouri, 7 miles/10 km south of Corfu town, tel 26610/56210, $$*), built by Empress Elizabeth of Austria in 1890. The palace is a grand if rather pretentious neoclassical building, adorned with dozens of sculptures that depict scenes from Greek mythology. The interior features a replica Byzantine chapel and a series of frescoes depicting scenes from the *Iliad* and the *Odyssey.*

Northern Corfu

The mountainous northern half of Corfu is dominated by the 2,972-foot-tall (906 m) peak of **Mount Pandokratoras.** Those who are willing to tackle the twisting mountain road that leads to the top will be treated to stunning views of Corfu, as well as across the sea to Albania and mainland Greece. Optimistic visitors claim that on a clear day you can see the east coast of Italy.

At the foot of the mountain is the quaint village of **Ano Korakiana,** renowned for its lovely Venetian architecture. This quiet village is a great place to stop and

The distinctive Italianate architecture of the belltower of one of Corfu town's Venetian Catholic churches

take in the slow place of rural Corfu. Farther west is **Paleokastritsa,** a small town set by a rugged peninsula that is topped by **Moni Theotokou,** a 13th-century monastery. The fishing village of **Agni** on the northeast coast is also worth a visit, if only for its excellent seafront restaurants. Try **Taverna Agni** (*Agni Bay, Corfu, tel 26630/91142*) for its seafood. ■

Palaeopolis Archaeological Museum

✉ Palace of Mon Repos, Kanoni, 2.5 miles (4 km) south of Corfu town

☎ (26610) 56254

🕐 Closed Mon.

💲 $$

The Ionians

Extending south from Corfu, the islands of the Ionian chain offer a varied and fascinating range of sights and experiences. From the popular tourist destinations of Kefalonia and Paxi, to the quiet shores of distant Kithira, this region of lush green Islands and sparkling blue water has a unique atmosphere matched nowhere else in Greece.

The lighthouse of St. Theodoroi at Argostoli, Kefalonia, was rebuilt after the earthquake of 1953.

Paxi
🅼 225 B4

Andipaxi
🅼 225 B4

Paxi Folklore Museum
✉ Waterfront, Gaïos, Paxi
☎ (26620) 32566
🕐 Closed during winter months
💲 $

Paxi

According to myth, Paxi was formed when Poseidon struck Corfu with his trident and cracked off this islet, one of the smallest of the Ionian islands. The god of the sea was said to have gone here to relax with his favorite nymph, Amphitrite. Throughout its history, Paxi has remained a place for lovers; Marc Antony and Cleopatra also apparently stayed here, and its secluded atmosphere make it a popular honeymoon destination.

Visitors to Paxi arrive by ferry in the port of **Gaïos,** where services run to and from the mainland, Corfu, and the small islet of **Andipaxi,** just off the southeast tip of Paxi. Although it is the largest settlement on the island, Gaïos is only a village. There's a small **Folklore Museum** here, but the main attraction, as with the rest of Paxi, is just the slow, relaxing pace of life. There are several cafés and bars down on the seafront, as well as a few good restaurants, and it is only a short taxi ride to pretty much anywhere on the island from here.

Gaïos harbor is sheltered by the wooded islet of **Agios Nikolaos,** a beautiful spot that can be reached via one of the many rowboat ferries that can be found on the seafront. The island has a small but lovely beach, and its cool forested interior is a great

INSIDER TIP:

The novel *Captain Corelli's Mandolin* is despised by many Kefalonians, who say that the book's depiction of the Greek resistance is unfair and untrue.

—SALLY MCFALL
National Geographic contributor

place to explore. There are two picturesque old churches and a crumbling Venetian fortress hidden among the trees.

North of Gaïos is the attractive little village of **Lakka,** which can be reached easily by bus, taxi, or, or course, by boat. The clear blue waters of its harbor are always filled with sailing yachts, and in the summer the open-air cafés and bars stay open until very late. The coast on either side of this village is dotted with some of the finest beaches on the island and features some stunning rock formations and sea caves like the mysterious cave of **Ypapanti.**

Lefkada

Named for the white *(lefko)* rocks in the island's south, Lefkada is actually connected to the mainland by a causeway and—since 2002—a tunnel *($ toll).* The island's main settlement, Lefkada town, is located in the northeast of the island, close to the causeway to the mainland. The town was badly damaged by the devastating Ionian earthquake of 1953, so much of the present-day settlement is less than 60 years old.

Concerned over the effects of future earthquakes, the townsfolk rebuilt their homes in a style that

Lakka
🗺 225 B4

Lefkada
🗺 225 B3, C3
Visitor Information
✉ Municipal Tourist Office, Municipal Building, Aggelou Sikelianou, Lefkada town
☎ (26450) 23000
www.lefkada.net

EXPERIENCE: Touring Captain Corelli's Kefalonia

During World War II, an Italian General named Antonio Gandin was in charge of more than 12,000 Italian troops on Kefalonia. The Acqui division, as they were known, stayed there even after Mussolini was overthrown in 1943. The Nazis began taking over Italian positions throughout Greece and tried to make Italians join their forces. But the Italians resisted, and the Nazis executed thousands of them. The writer Louis De Bernieres adapted the true story into the 1993 novel *Captain Corelli's Mandolin,* which became a bestseller. In 2001, De Bernieres's book was adapted into a film starring Nicolas Cage and Penelope Cruz.

The film was shot throughout the island. A few key locales include **Sami,** where the main set was built around the Kastro Hotel and recreated to resemble wartime Argostoli; **AntiSamos beach,** where the Italian encampment was based; the village of **Dikhalia,** where home life was portrayed; the **Sia Monastery** in Mirtos, where the love scene between Corelli and Pelagia was filmed; and **Mirtos beach,** where La Skala, Corelli's musical ensemble, danced as Corelli blew up an old Turkish mine.

Other must-sees include the seaside village of **Farsa** and Argostoli, where you can eat a Kefalonian meat pie at the **Captain's Table** *(Main Square, Argostoli).*

Agia Maura

- ✉ Just north of Lefkada town
- 🕐 Closed every afternoon
- 💲 $

Nidri

- 🅰 225 C3

Kefalonia

- 🅰 225 B2, C2

Visitor Information

- ✉ EOT Hellenic Tourism Office, Ioannis Metaxas, Argostoli, Kefalonia town
- ☎ (26710) 22248

www.greeka.com /ionian/kefalonia /kefalonia-tourism .htm

makes it like no other in Greece. The houses are mostly made from timber, sheet metal, and clapboard—light, flexible materials that fare well in earthquakes—and these humble materials are enlivened with liberal applications of vibrant colors and climbing plants. The obvious exception to this rule is the fortress of **Agia Maura**— built by the Franks in 1300 to protect the island from pirate raids—and several old churches. The sturdy walls of these buildings were largely unaffected by the earthquake. In addition to plenty of lively cafés and bars, the town also has a small **archaeological museum.**

The fishing village of **Nidri,** on the east coast of the island, is one of the most popular destinations on the island. The village is close to some beautiful beaches and has several excellent restaurants and bars. Just north of the town are the wonderful **Dimossari Waterfalls,** where underground streams pour out of the rocks into clear pools and channels. The water here is always cool. From Nidri you can take a day-long boat tour that winds around the many small islands that are scattered in the sea around Lefkada. These tours stop at secluded island monasteries, beautiful, pristine beaches, and inside the gigantic sea caves of **Meganisi Island.**

Kefalonia

The largest of the Ionian islands, Kefalonia offers a wide variety of activities from lounging on the beach to hiking up a windswept mountain or exploring massive

INSIDER TIP:

Catch a boat tour from Nidri and you'll see the lair of a secret submarine and the private island where Aristotle Onassis married Jackie Kennedy in 1968.

—TIM HARRIS
National Geographic contributor

cave systems. Although it is often filled to capacity with sunseekers, during the off season, it's a charming place to visit.

Kefalonia is thought to have been an important colony of the ancient city-state of Mycenae as long ago as 1500 B.C. It has long been argued that Kefalonia— not the nearby island known as Ithaca today—is the real location of Homer's Ithaca (see sidebar p. 233).

The Venetians ruled the island between the 1200s and 1797, and exerted a strong influence on its culture. After brief periods of French and then British rule, the island was ceded to Greece. For most of its history Kefalonia made its money from the export of currants. Although they lived a peaceful existence, most of the island's people inhabited fortified hilltop villages to protect themselves from pirate raids. In 1943, the island was the scene of the massacre of the Acqui division, the killing of thousands of Italian soldiers by the German occupying force, an event later chronicled in the novel *Captain Corelli's Mandolin* (see sidebar p. 231).

In 1953, Kefalonia, which is on a geological fault line, was hit by a series of four major earthquakes measuring between 6 and 7 on the Richter scale. These earthquakes brought down almost every building on Kefalonia, Lefkada, and Zakinthos. Kefalonia was the hardest hit and struggled for many decades to recover.

Today, tourism has revived the island's economy. The population has returned to pre-earthquake levels and is supplemented every year by tens of thousands of

Most visitors quickly get into taxis or buses and head off to see the island's sights. Around 17 miles (27 km) northeast of Argostoli, close to the village of Sami, are the island's most impressive natural wonders, the **Caves of Drogarati** and the breathtaking **Lake Melissani.** The deep and extensive cave system at Drogarati is one of the most impressive caves in Greece, with its multicolored stalactites and stalagmites, winding tunnels, and gigantic underground caverns.

Argostoli
🅰 225 B2

Argostoli Archaeological Museum
🅰 225 B2
✉ Rokou Vergoti, Argostoli
☎ (26710) 28300
🕓 Closed Mon.
💲 $

Caves of Drogarati & Lake Melissani
🅰 225 C2

The Geography of Homer's *Odyssey*

Is the island of Ithaca, off Kefalonia, the real home of Odysseus? This question has been debated for centuries. Homer's descriptions are so detailed, the prospect that the *Odyssey* may have been based on real events is tantalizing. Beginning with the first-century A.D. Greek geographer Strabo, scholars have long speculated that the island we call Ithaca may be Odysseus' home.

A passage in the *Odyssey* describes "a mountain there, high Neriton, covered in forest. Many islands lie around it, very close to each other. Douchlichion, Same, and wooded Zacynthos, but low-lying

Ithaca is farthest out to sea, toward the sunset, and the others are apart, toward the dawn and sun." Because these details do not describe modern-day Ithaca, some scholars say that Homer's Ithaca lies elsewhere, perhaps the neighboring islands of Lefkada or Kefalonia.

Interest in this theory has recently been renewed by British historian Robert Bittlestone, whose study of the region's violent seismic history led him to conclude that Paliki, the western peninsula of Kefalonia, may have been a separate island at one point and may, in fact, be the original Ithaca.

European tourists. Most of the island's visitors arrive by ferry at the island's capital and main port, **Argostoli.** This town is on the island's west coast, opposite the port of Lixourion on the Paliki peninsula. There isn't a lot to see in Argostoli barring the interesting **Archaeological Museum,** but there are several good restaurants and cafés around the main square and the harbor.

The nearby Lake Melissani is the real highlight for most visitors. It is located at the bottom of a deep sinkhole whose sheer rock walls descend 98 feet (30 m) from ground level to the water's edge. Boat tours (tel 26710/22997, $$) leave from a small jetty at the foot of the access tunnel and work their way around the beautiful turquoise waters of the lake. Oddly, the waters in this lake are partly

EXPERIENCE:
Helping Sea Turtles

Beach development and fishing have drastically reduced the population of loggerhead turtles. Zakinthos is one of their few remaining nesting grounds.

Visitors can help the turtle by volunteering at the **National Marine Park of Zakinthos** (www.nmp-zak.org), located in the island's south. **Archelon**—the Sea Turtle Protection Society of Greece (www.archelon.gr) and the **Katelios Group** (www.kateliosgroup.org) run programs to patrol beaches, count turtles, and make sure the animals are not disturbed while nesting. Yiannis Vardakastanis is a conservationist who runs **Earth Sea & Sky** (www.earthseasky.org), a nature-loving organization that specializes in green tourism. Vardakastanis's organization also minds the turtles but offers many other ecotourism options in Zakinthos.

Castle of St. George
🅰 225 B2

Ithaca (Ithaki)
🅰 225 C2

Visitor Information

www.greeka.com
/ionian/ithaca
/ithaca-tourism.htm

Monastery of Panagia Kathariotissa
🅰 225 C2

Zakinthos
🅰 225 C1

Visitor Information

☎ (26950) 48073
(Hellenic Tourism Office)

www.zakynthos.net.gr

seawater from nearby Katavothres. How the water travels a third of a mile (500 m) inland and two feet (1 m) up from sea level to surface in the lake is still a mystery.

Visitors heading south should stop by the lush inland village of Metaxata, where Lord Byron wrote his epic poem, *Don Juan*. Above the village of Travliata perches the stunning **Castle of St. George,** a majestically ruined Byzantine fortress with great views over the island.

Ithaca

A pretty island with a famous name, Ithaca (Ithaki) is located off the northeastern coast of Kefalonia. It is reputed to be the home of Homer's hero, Odysseus (see sidebar p. 233). The island's capital, **Ithaca town,** has been inhabited since the second millennium B.C. and was occupied by the Romans, Byzantines, Ottoman Turks, and Venetians.

Although many of the island's visitors are drawn here by the descriptions in the *Odyssey,* there are few ruins or historic sites on the island and none that can be definitively linked to the events of the story. The island's main attractions are its two main settlements: Ithaca and the picturesque northern fishing village of **Kionion.**

Although the buildings of both towns were destroyed by the 1953 earthquake, the townsfolk have rebuilt many in the original Venetian style, preserving the towns' charming atmosphere. Inland, at the summit of one of the island's peaks, stands the **Monastery of Panagia Kathariotissa.** This 16th-century building still houses an active monastic community so visitors are requested to dress modestly.

Zakinthos

Zakinthos (also known as Zante) is the third largest Ionian island, and the farthest south of the main group. Like the rest of the Ionians, it was ruled by the Venetians for most of its history before passing to the British and finally uniting with the rest of Greece.

The island's capital, **Zakinthos town,** is located on the east coast of the island. As on Kefalonia, Ithaca, and Lefkada, most of the town's old buildings were destroyed in the 1953 earthquake. Some parts of town have been restored to their former glory, however, particularly in the area around **Solomos Square** where—along with **St. Mark's Square**—most of the town's popular bars and restaurants are.

The most famous sight on the island is **Navagio Bay,** or "shipwreck bay," in the northwest. The isolated sandy cove is where the rusting hulk of the smuggling ship *Panagiotis* sits on the beach where it ran aground in 1980, while being chased by the Greek navy.

In the south of the island the hilltop village of **Kerion** remains largely untroubled by tourist development. The charming stone houses and cobbled streets are clustered around the main square and the lovely Venetian bell-tower that stands at the edge. There are a few good cafés in the town, but few accommodation options.

Kithira

The small island of Kithira lies off the southern coast of the Peloponnese, closer to Crete than to the other Ionian islands.

The island's capital, **Kithira town,** is a delightful village of whitewashed houses and narrow streets on a high hill by the sea. The ruins of the **Venetian Castle** perch on the edge of the cliffs near the town. Inside its walls are numerous churches, some ruined, dating back to the Byzantine period. The north of the island has many beautiful beaches, including stunning **Agia Pelagia.** These can be crowded in the summer, but are still quieter than those on the northern islands. Those who need to cool down can head to the slightly eerie **Cave of Agia Sofia,** where a small church stands in a cavern near the village of Kapsali. ■

Navagio Bay
🗺 225 C1
✉ 2 miles (3 km) northwest of Anafonitria

Kerion
🗺 225 C1

Kithira
🗺 225 inset

Kithira Venetian Castle
✉ Kithira town

Agia Pelagia
✉ 12 miles (19 km) north of Kithira town

Cave of Agia Sofia
✉ 1 mile (1.6 km) east of Kithira town

Scientists measure a loggerhead turtle as part of the conservation program on Zakinthos.

TRAVELWISE

Planning Your Trip 236–238 • Getting Around 238–240 • Practical Advice 240–241 • Emergencies 241 • Hotels & Restaurants 242–260 • Shopping 261–262 • Entertainment 263–264 • Outdoor Activities 265

The sleek new Athens Coastal Tram runs from the center of the city to the beaches of Glyfada.

PLANNING YOUR TRIP

When to Go

Athens and the Greek islands are excellent year-round destinations, so you will enjoy your visit no matter when you travel. However, August is best avoided, not only because it is the peak vacation month—when space is limited in hotel rooms and on beaches—but also because temperatures can soar to well over 100°F (38°C), and Athens in particular can be very uncomfortable. In midwinter there may be rain and temperatures below 50°F (10°C), but equally you may get clear blue skies and temperatures of 20°F (-6°C)—and no crowds outside Athens and maybe Delphi.

The best times to visit are in the spring and the fall, when the weather is comfortably warm, there is little rain, and, since there are fewer vacationers, the naturally hospitable locals have time to talk to visitors. In the springtime wildflowers will be blooming on the islands and the landscape will be lush. If you wish to visit mountainous regions, for example on the islands of Egina or Crete, late May onward is when the snow starts to melt and paths become passable again.

An especially good time to visit is during Easter week, when there are many celebrations: Easter is the most important festival in the Orthodox Christian calendar, but it only occasionally coincides with the dates of Western Christian Easter.

What to Take

Greece is a casual country, and in only a handful of more formal restaurants would men need a jacket and tie in the evening. If you're traveling in summer, casual dress such as shorts and T-shirts are all you will need during the day, plus a swimsuit as one is never far from a beach, and light cotton clothing for the evenings. It remains warm enough to eat outdoors late at night during the summer, and even in spring and fall you would probably need to add only a sweater or light jacket. In summer it rarely rains in most of the Greek islands, and if it does, it will be in the form of a short, sudden shower. Rain is more common in the Ionian islands, where you are more likely to need a raincoat. In winter, a warm coat or jacket and a sweater are advisable in Athens and on the islands.

Mosquitoes occur in many places, especially in the greener Ionian and Sporades islands and on the mainland. They can be a minor nuisance almost anywhere and at any time of year, so carry plenty of bug spray. This can be purchased locally, along with the effective plug-in mosquito-repellent devices.

Most medical supplies are available unless you are traveling to an island with very little tourism. Drug stores are usually well stocked and the staff knowledgeable and English speaking. Make sure you have an ample supply of sunscreen—cooling breezes can be deceptive, and the Aegean sun is fierce.

Insurance

You are advised to take out full travel and medical insurance for a visit to Athens or the islands. Public medical care is pretty basic, and while there is plenty of private medical treatment available, it is costly. Drug stores or doctors' offices can deal with minor injuries.

Books About Athens & the Islands

There are numerous books, ancient and modern, to enrich a visit. The true classics cannot be ignored: Homer's *Odyssey* is a splendid adventure tale, while *The Histories* by Herodotus and the *Guide to Greece* by Pausanias will add background to visits to many of the classical sites. *The Greek Myths*, by Robert Graves, will illuminate the often complex world of Greek mythology, and A. R. Burn's *History of Greece* is a good all-around introduction to the world of the ancient Greeks.

To get a perspective on the amazing history of Athens, *The Archaeology of Athens*, by John M. Camp, is recommended. And to put the city in its national context, *Modern Greece: A Short History*, by C. M. Woodhouse, is a good way of bringing yourself up to date. The best of the 20th-century travelers' tales are those by Corfu writer Lawrence Durrell (*Prospero's Cell, Reflections on a Marine Venus*), his brother Gerald Durrell (*My Family and Other Animals*), Patrick Leigh Fermor (*Roumeli, Mani*), Henry Miller (*The Colossus of Maroussi*), and Patricia Storace (*Dinner with Persephone*).

Try reading any of the novels by Nikos Kazantzakis, particularly his most famous, *Zorba the Greek*. Other modern novels available in translation include Stratis Myrivilis's *The Mermaid Madonna*, portraying life in a Lesvos fishing village.

How to Get to Athens
By Air

Athens's international airport, Eleftherios Venizelos, is about 20 miles (33 km) east of the city. The national airline, Olympic Air *(tel 210/355 0500, www.olympicair.com)*, has scheduled flights from major cities all over the world.

Direct flights to Athens from the U.S. include twice a week from New York on Olympic Air, and Delta also has flights from New York to Athens. Other flights from major cities such as Chicago, Washington, D.C., Los Angeles, San Francisco, and Seattle are either through gateway cities in the U.S. or via European connections such as London (on British Airways, United, and others) or Amsterdam (on KLM).

From Athens there are numerous connecting flights to Greek airports on the mainland and throughout the islands. Olympic Air has had a virtual monopoly of the internal services, but several new carriers now offer a wider

service to major routes such as Crete and Rhodes.

By Rail

Greek trains are cheaper than buses but also tend to be slower. If you are planning a long stay in Europe, it is worth considering crossing the continent by train. The route goes through France, Switzerland, or Italy, and the journey takes about three days (you could stop off on the way). You can then cross by ferry from Italy to Patra in the Peloponnese and continue on to Athens.

By Sea

There are several ferry services from Italy (notably from Bari, Brindisi, Ancona, Trieste, and Venice) to Patra, which has a good rail link to Athens. A high-season journey between Italy and Greece costs from around $70 one-way for a foot passenger, up to around $150 for a car. Since agents normally only represent one ferry line, it is best not to consult them for general advice.

Entry Formalities
Passports & Visas

A valid passport is required for all visitors to Greece, entitling them to stay for up to 90 days. Visas are required for a visit of more than 90 days.

Drugs & Narcotics

Customs inspections are usually fairly informal affairs, but for anyone caught carrying drugs the penalties are severe. If you have prescription medicine, make sure to bring the prescription with you, both as a precaution at customs and in case you lose or use up your supplies. One anomaly is that codeine, which is widely available around the world as a painkiller, is illegal in Greece. You will not necessarily get into serious trouble for having it, but it may be confiscated.

Money
There is no limit to the amount of foreign currency and traveler's checks that you can bring into Greece.

GETTING AROUND
Traveling from Athens Airport
By Public Transportation
You can get from the new International Airport to Athens's city center (20 miles/33 km) by public transportation. Six express buses operate 24 hours a day. The cost is minimal and the journey time is between 70 and 90 minutes. Buy your ticket from the driver. The new Metro link is even quicker.

By Taxi
Do not take a taxi from solicitors inside the airport terminal building, but go outside and join the official line at the taxi rank. Check that the meter is switched on. If the meter is not working, you should know that the fare from the airport is approximately 20 euros for a 45-minute journey to downtown. Heavy traffic can slow that considerably. There is usually an additional charge for items of baggage. If you feel you are being overcharged, call the Tourist Police on 171.

Traveling in Athens
By Bus
The Athens bus network is extensive and cheap. That said, buses are invariably very crowded, hot in summer, and prone to cancellation. You will need a working knowledge of the city's layout and of the Greek alphabet (to understand the destination boards and route maps) if you plan to use buses. Within the

center, walking is usually the best option. If you do take a bus, note that tickets are bought in advance from kiosks near the major bus stops or from some stores. Stamp your ticket in a machine when you enter the bus.

By Subway
Athens has several Metro (subway) lines, the main one (Line 1) running from Kifissia in the north to Pireas in the south, with useful central stops at Omonoia and Monastiraki. A southeast–northwest line (Line 2) links Omonoia with Syntagma, and will eventually reach Glyfada on the coast. Line 3 starts in Egalio (western suburbs), connects Monastiraki and Syntagma, and links downtown with the airport. The subway is divided into zones, and you pay according to how many zones you cross. Buy your ticket at the station and then time-stamp it in the machine as you enter the platforms. The service is very cheap and trains are frequent, but you should check destination boards as not all trains run the full length of each line. Lines 2 and 3 are wonderfully modern. While Line 1 shows its age, its stations are slowly being renovated.

By Taxi
Taxis are a convenient way of getting around and are very cheap, provided you have some idea of what the fares should be. The cars are yellow, and you simply wave them down in the street, although there are also several official taxi ranks. The bottom of Syntagma Square is a good place to pick up a taxi. They are not supposed to stop there other than to drop off passengers, but drivers usually take the opportunity to pick up a fare.

Athenian taxis are shared, and the driver is entitled to pick up other passengers, and most will attempt to fill their vehicles; each person pays the fare on the meter. This arrangement counteracts a severe taxi shortage and boosts drivers' incomes without putting up individual fares.

By Train
With the exception of the Athens Coastal Tram, which runs from Syntagma Square to Glyfada, the aboveground train network in central Athens is of little practical use to the visitor. The mainline stations serve the distant suburbs and the rest of Greece.

Traveling Beyond Athens & to the Islands
By Air
Greece has a good internal flight network, though most flights are to and from Athens. It is often more convenient to fly into Athens and out again, as a way of getting from one island to another. Single fares are around 80–90 euros. Flights fill quickly during the summer months, so make advance reservations.

By Boat/Ferry
Greece has an excellent ferry service, as you would expect from one of the world's great maritime nations, although it can be somewhat erratic. There are numerous rival ferry companies, and schedules change constantly (an up-to-date schedule can be obtained from the Greek National Tourist Organization, www.greeka.com/greece/greece-ferries.htm). Boats may be canceled or delayed because of bad weather, so if you have a flight to catch allow an extra day in case of problems.

For travel between islands, or between the mainland and the islands, there are usually several choices. You will need to ask around to find out what these are, as travel agents often operate on behalf of one ferry line only. In addition to the slow and cheap regular ferries, there is a rapidly expanding network of hydrofoil services, which are much quicker but naturally much more expensive. If you get seasick, then you may feel the additional expense is worth it.

You will also find many small boats operating between neighboring islands or running excursion trips in the summer. Even if you don't want the full excursion these can sometimes be more convenient options than the larger commercial ferry services, and an individual running his own boat will be open to bargaining. Commercial fares are fixed, and tickets can be bought from a travel agent, sometimes from a table set up on the quayside or on the boat itself when it docks.

For most of the islands, the best ferry services are Hellenic Seaways, Blue Star Ferries, and Minoan Lines. Hellenic Seaways *(tel 210/419 9000, www.hellenicseaways.gr)* and Blue Star Ferries *(tel 210/414 5700, www.bluestarferries.com)* go to the Aegean islands, while Minoan Lines *(tel 210/414 5700)* is the best for Crete and the Ionian islands. Minoan ferries to the Ionian islands leave from the ports of Patra and Igoumenitsa. NEL Lines *(tel 210/412 5888, www.nel.gr)* also has regular routes from Pireas to Hios and Mytilini (on Lesvos).

There is a go-to site for all ferries *(www.ferries.gr)* if you want to book online and experiment with destinations and ferry services.

The Argo-Saronic Islands: Hellenic Seaways is the best option for the Saronic islands. Boats leave daily from Pireas year-round.

The Sporades: Hellenic Seaways has routes daily from Volos and Agios Konstantinos.

The Cyclades: Blue Star Ferries and Hellenic Seaways have boats that leave daily from Pireas.

Crete: Blue Star Ferries has boats leaving for Iraklio and Hania every day. Minoan Lines has boats daily to Iraklio.

The Dodecanese: Blue Star Ferries and Hellenic Seaways have boats that leave Pireas daily for Kos and Rhodes.

The Northeastern Aegean Islands: Hellenic Seaways have boats that leave Pireas daily for Hios and Mytilini (Lesvos). NEL Lines also has boats from Pireas to Hios and Mytilini three times a week.

The Ionian Islands: Minoan Lines has boats that leave daily from Patras for Corfu.

By Bus

Greece has an excellent and extensive bus system that is by far the most popular form of transportation for the Greeks themselves. There are few towns that don't have a busy bus station, and it can even be the simplest way of reaching some of the islands. For example, the Ionian islands have regular bus services to and from Athens, with the cost of the ferry included in the price.

Most rural areas are well served by buses, and the easiest way of traveling around many islands is by bus. On smaller islands, buses will frequently meet an incoming ferry to take passengers from the harbor to the main town. Rural bus journeys can be quite an experience, with passengers transporting all kinds of baggage and drivers carrying and delivering parcels for people and sometimes diverting from the route to do a favor for a friend. In addition to specific stops, most drivers will drop people off and pick them up anywhere that is convenient, so feel free to wave a bus down wherever you happen to be.

Tickets for the main intertown services (usually in reasonably comfortable air-conditioned buses) need to be bought in advance at the bus station; on local routes you may have to buy your ticket in a store near the main stop or on the bus itself. Schedules might be displayed on poles, placed in store windows, or pinned to walls, and may or may not be up-to-date and accurate. It is always best to check.

By Car

Car Rental: Renting a car in Greece is straightforward, although expensive. All the major names, such as Avis and Hertz, have offices in Athens, at Athens airport, and on the larger islands. The established international names are usually more reliable. Some of the smaller firms run their fleets throughout the year, giving minimal attention to servicing, in order to keep costs down. However, if you travel at a quiet time of year, you are more likely to be able to negotiate a better deal with an independent company than with one of the international chains, whose prices are fixed.

An ordinary national driver's license is all you need, and car rental agreements automatically include third-party insurance, which is a legal requirement. It would be wise to add personal accident insurance as accident rates here are among the highest in Europe. You must be at least 21 years of age, or 25 years for more powerful cars. There is a wide range of automobiles available. A credit card can be used as a deposit

Roads & Road Signs: The standard of Greek roads is improving all the time, thanks to generous grants from the European Union. Tolls apply on the expressways—but few are up to the standard of expressways in the U.S. Four lanes can become two without warning, and you may well encounter slow-moving farm vehicles. In rural areas a smooth-surfaced road can suddenly become a dirt track, with herds of animals a common hazard.

Road signs can be unreliable and are not consistently placed at junctions, making a decent map essential. A knowledge of the Greek alphabet is also vital: Main roads are usually marked in both Greek and Roman letters, but on side roads you may find signs in Greek only.

Regulations & Rules of the Road: In Greece driving is on the right, but in practice many drivers use the center of the road, especially when going around a corner, so be careful. Note that if a driver flashes his headlights at you, it is a warning that he is going ahead. Speed limits are 31 mph (50 kph) in built-up areas, 49 mph (80 kph) outside built-up areas, and 62 mph (100 kph) on divided highways. Seat belts must be worn, and drivers can be fined for not carrying a warning triangle, fire extinguisher, and first-aid kit.

Drunk driving (DWI) is a serious offense in Greece. One glass of wine or beer is probably enough to create a misdemeanor, and if you drink much more than that you will be committing a criminal offense leading to a possible prison sentence. Drivers should therefore observe complete abstinence.

Fuel: Unleaded gasoline is now available everywhere, at least in the busier places. In more remote areas, gas stations may be few and far between so try to keep your tank full or check where there are gas stations. In smaller towns and villages, stations will be family enterprises so they may

close on a Sunday, or you may find yourself being served by a small boy or girl who speaks no English. Many smaller stations don't accept credit cards so be sure always to have some cash with you.

Parking: Parking is straightforward, with only major cities having zones for which you need to buy a parking permit. Otherwise it is obvious that you either can or cannot park somewhere. If you do need a permit, there will be a notice in Greek and English on the street telling you where to obtain one.

Accident & Breakdown: In the event of an accident, for roadside assistance dial 10400, the call-out number for ELPA (the main Greek recovery service, like the AAA). If you have a rented car, you should have been given this or another emergency number to dial. It is an offense to drive away if you have been involved in an accident, which must be reported to the police. Do not sign any document that is written only in Greek.

Rental companies will tell you what to do in case of breakdown. They usually belong to one of the Greek equivalents of the AAA (ELPA, Hellas Service, or Express Service) and will give you a contact phone number in case of problems.

By Motorbike or Moped

Mopeds and motorbikes are usually available to rent in tourist centers and can be an excellent and economical way of getting around. Before taking to the road, be sure to check that the vehicle is in a safe condition. Although not mandatory, helmets are recommended. Be aware that accidents are common with inexperienced drivers.

By Train

Mainline stations connect Athens with Corinth, the northern Peloponnese, and with Halkida, on the island of Evia. Few of the other islands are large enough to need a railroad.

PRACTICAL ADVICE
Communications
Cell Phones & Telephones

A pre-paid cell phone card, or *kartokinito,* is the easiest way to call in and outside of Greece these days. You can buy a cheap cell phone in Athens or use one from abroad if it's tri-band or unlocked. Since July 2009, Greece has required those buying these types of phone cards to register them using a Greek ID card or, for foreign nationals, a foreign passport. You can buy a connection pack with a Greek SIM card for about 5 euros at *periptera* (kiosks), mini-markets, post offices, or directly from the stores of phone companies such as Vodafone, Cosmote, or WIND. You can also buy recharge, renewal, or "top-up" cards, at these outlets.

Vodafone, Cosmote, and WIND all offer generally the same prices for domestic and international calls and text messages, though the rates fluctuate slightly every month. International rates tend to be high, around 20 cents a minute.

You will see public pay phones on the street, at train and bus stations, in hotel receptions, and at offices of OTE (the Greek national telephone company). OTE offices can be found in most places, large or small, and are generally open from early morning until late in the evening, Monday to Saturday.

Post Offices

Post offices can be found practically everywhere in Greece. Even the smallest island has one, although it may also double as a bank or may be open only part-time. Major post offices, known as *tachydromeia*, are generally open Monday to Friday from 7:30 a.m. to 2 p.m., although some may stay open later on one night a week. Some also open on Saturdays until about noon. Parcels have to be sealed in front of the post office clerk, which is why you will see people standing in line with scissors and scotch tape. If you only want postage stamps, look for the sign saying *grammatosima*. Post offices no longer act as money exchanges due to the proliferation of ATMs.

Conversions

Greece uses the metric system. Weights are calculated in grams and kilograms (1 kg = 2.2 pounds), while liquids are usually given in liters (1 L= 0.2 gallon) or fractions of liters—it helps to remember that half a liter (500 mL) is equal to a little more than one pint. Distances are given in meters (1 m = 3.3 feet) and kilometers (1 km = 0.6 mile), while speed limits are given in kilometers per hour. Temperatures are given in degrees Celsius, a scale with a different zero point to Fahrenheit (0°C = 32°F). A quick way to convert one to the other is to double the figure in Celsius and add 30, so that, for example, 15°C converts to 60°F. This method is accurate to within a few degrees when converting the sort of temperatures you're likely to encounter in Athens.

Electricity

The electricity supply is 220 volts/50 Hz AC. North American appliances will need a transformer. The Greek electrical socket is a simple one with two round pins and occasionally three where devices need to be grounded. If you forget to take an adapter with you, it should be possible to buy one in most vacation areas in supermarkets or from electrical stores.

Money Matters

The Greek unit of currency is the euro. There are coins for 1, 2, 5, 10, 20, and 50 cents and 1 and 2 euros, with bills for 5, 10, 20, 50, 100, 200, and 500 euros.

Traveler's checks can be changed at most banks, hotels, and post offices on production of a passport, and in some stores and restaurants in tourist areas, although generally at a less favorable rate of exchange.

ATMs are widespread in cities, large towns, and major tourist resorts. Credit cards are widely accepted in the more expensive hotels, stores, and restaurants in popular areas. Do not assume, however, that you need only travel with "plastic." In Greece it is normal to settle even large transactions in cash. "No checks" is a common sign, even in some mid-range Athens hotels.

National Holidays

January 1   New Year's Day
January 6   Epiphany
February/March   Shrove Monday (41 days pre-Easter)
March 25   Independence Day
March/April   Good Friday, Easter Sunday, and the following Monday
May 1   Labor Day
June   Whitmonday (50 days after Easter)
August 15   Assumption of the Virgin
October 28   Ochi Day
December 25/26   Christmas

On national holidays you will find almost everything is closed, including historic sites, museums, banks, post offices, and some stores and restaurants. However, in tourist areas and major cities, you will have no trouble finding somewhere to eat and to buy provisions. Traveling can be difficult, so check before setting off.

Opening Times

Banks are generally open from 8 or 8:30 a.m. until 2 p.m. on weekdays only, and post offices from 7:30 a.m.–2 p.m. In larger towns, some banks and post offices may open on Saturday mornings.

Stores open from 8 a.m. to 2 p.m., when they close for the afternoon. They generally reopen at about 5, until 8 p.m., but some supermarkets and stores catering to visitors stay open much later. Opening and closing times may vary by an hour or so, but all stores will close for those few afternoon hours. Stores are generally closed on Sundays, except in tourist areas.

It is difficult to be precise about opening hours for museums and ancient sites as the hours change from winter to summer, and at some sites according to the mood of the keeper. Most are open year-round but, with the exception of major sites, are closed on Mondays and public holidays.

EMERGENCIES

Emergency calls are free from phone booths.

Medical emergency: In Athens dial **166**, or **171** for the Tourist Police. Elsewhere dial **166** for an ambulance *(asthenoforo)*, or **100**, which connects you to the branch of the police known as the *Ekato* (meaning "100"), who deal with fire and medical emergencies.

Fire *(fotyá):* **199**

Road assistance: 10400 (call-out number for ELPA, the main Greek breakdown and recovery service, see p. 240). There are emergency telephones at regular intervals on highways.

Hotels & Restaurants

The majority of accommodations in Athens and the islands are relatively inexpensive for the overseas visitor, with the exception of the top five-star hotels. Standards vary greatly, and while there is a Greek accommodations rating system (see below) it is not a perfect guide. Don't automatically dismiss hotels in the lower categories as many are spotlessly clean and beautifully located.

Hotels

The official government rating system classifies all hotels and other accommodations from A to E, which very roughly corresponds to five-star down to one-star in other ratings systems. There is also a Deluxe category. The rating dictates the price, and accommodations are inspected and graded annually. The grading is taken seriously, and all establishments must display in each room an official notice that tells the grade of the hotel, the rate for that room at different periods of the year and for different numbers of occupants, and whether the price includes breakfast or not. If there is no such notice for you to check then the establishment is breaking the law, but early in the year it is common to find the previous year's notice still displayed, until the new ones are available.

Checking in

If you are visiting a hotel without a reservation then it is the usual practice to ask to see the room before you take it. When you check in, you must give them your passport for the hotel's records, and this will normally be returned to you within a day.

Breakfast is sometimes included in the price and sometimes an optional extra. In more expensive hotels, breakfast is normally a generous buffet including juices, fresh fruit, yogurt and honey, cereal, eggs, cheeses, cold meats, and a variety of breads. In more basic places, you may be offered just a few slices of cold toast and coffee. You may find more choice in nearby cafés.

Most hotels will take major credit cards, but don't assume that you will always be able to pay by credit card. Some smaller family-owned places will take only one type of card or none at all, requiring checks, or travelers' checks, or even preferring cash.

Restaurants

Eating out is one of the great pleasures in Athens and the Greek islands. For much of the year it is warm enough to eat outdoors, and there is a ready supply of fresh fish and meat, which, simply grilled and then eaten at a table right by the water's edge, is a delightful way to spend an evening. The Greeks are also natural hosts, and most restaurants and tavernas have a great atmosphere. As with hotels, appearances can be very deceptive. You are just as likely to find good food in a tiny backstreet family taverna, where the husband waits on tables and his wife cooks in the kitchen, as in some seemingly classy restaurants that cater purely to the tourist trade and serve dishes adapted for it.

There is no rating system for Greek restaurants, and ordinary-looking places can be wonderful, while classy-looking ones can be dreadful. It is best to avoid any place that employs someone to stand outside and tempt you in, a ploy used only to inveigle overseas visitors who will probably never return, not Greek customers. Be cautious, although the rule is not infallible.

Many restaurants in tourist areas do not take reservations, so in some cases you will find no telephone number in the listings below. Most places are expandable; another table will be brought out unless they are absolutely at their maximum capacity, in which case you will be told how long you have to wait for a table. For this reason, the number of restaurant seats is not listed here as, for the vast majority of establishments, it simply does not apply.

There are several types of eating establishments in Greece. Restaurants (estiatorio) are classier, and tavernas more casual. In a taverna you may well have a paper tablecloth, and in more out-of-the-way places, the waiter might even use it to write the bill on at the end of the meal. An ouzerie is an old-fashioned bar serving ouzo as well as other drinks and snacks. There are also psarotavernes, which specialize in fish, and psistaries, which specialize in food cooked on a grill or spit roasted.

Greeks tend to eat late, like other Mediterranean people. Lunch is not normally served before about 2 p.m., and dinner may begin as late as 9 or 10 p.m. Most restaurants catering to overseas customers open much earlier to suit their different dining habits.

Few Greek restaurants have their own parking lots. In Athens it would be madness to drive anyway, so take a taxi or walk. On the islands, there is usually ample parking in streets nearby, and the Greeks take a relaxed attitude to parking. For these reasons, no indication is given in the restaurant listings as to parking availability.

Not all restaurants accept credit cards. As meals are generally inexpensive, this should not be a problem. Abbreviations used are AE (American Express), DC (Diners Club), MC (Mastercard), and V (Visa).

Few restaurants have customized facilities for customers with disabilities as most are long established in old buildings. Despite this, the Greeks are wonderfully helpful, and staff will always lend a helping hand. Simply telephone first and ask.

A fair number of restaurants, especially in Athens, close for August and sometimes longer in the summer. This is often to escape the summer heat, at a time when many of their Athenian customers leave the city for a break on the islands. Some restaurateurs have island restaurants, which they open up for the summer months, before returning to Athens for the winter. Many island restaurants are therefore closed all winter! Set dates cannot be given here, as they vary year by year according to the whim of the owner, but where possible a rough indication of major closings is given in the listings.

In the following selection, under each location hotels are listed first, grouped according to price and in alphabetical order within each group; they are followed by restaurants, which are similarly listed by price and by alphabetical order.
L = lunch   D = dinner

■ OLD ATHENS

As might be expected, there is greater dining choice in Athens than on the islands, with cuisines from all over the world as well as the best of Greek cooking. The Plaka is a popular eating area but has a number of poor places aimed purely at the passing foreign visitor trade, as well as some

excellent and authentic Greek establishments. Nearby, the Psirri district has a wide choice of truly Greek dining places, although you will certainly need your phrase book and menu reader.

HOTELS

SOMETHING SPECIAL

🏨 GRANDE BRETAGNE
$$$$$
SYNTAGMA SQUARE
TEL (210) 333 0000
www.grandebretagne.gr
Athens's landmark hotel right on Syntagma Square was built in 1864. It retains much of its old elegance, but inside are marbled interiors, a pool, modern business facilities, skyline city views, and a top restaurant. Illustrious guests have included Sir Winston Churchill, who stayed here in 1944 toward the end of World War II. Top-floor front rooms are in demand, with their spectacular Acropolis views. A magnificent spa has been installed, plus a lavish mosaic-tiled pool and *hamam* area, though treatments are, predictably, expensive.
🛏 341 🅿 🚇 Syntagma 🛗
🖥 🌐 All major cards

🏨 HILTON
🍴 $$$$$
VASILISSIS SOFIAS 46
TEL (210) 728 1000
www1.hilton.com
Recently renovated to its former landmark glory, with a fine restaurant and the popular Galaxy bar. Convenient for Syntagma, Benaki Museum, and National Gallery, but not the Plaka.
🛏 453 🅿 🚇 Evangelismos
🛗 🌐 🖥 All major cards

🏨 KING GEORGE PALACE
🍴 $$$$$

SYNTAGMA SQUARE
TEL (210) 322 2210
Recently renovated to a sumptuous standard, it now rivals its neighbor the Grande Bretagne as *the* hotel in Athens. It has a fabulous spa, comfortably designed rooms, and the Tudor Hall restaurant—whose Acropolis view is only matched by its superb food. The staff ooze relaxed friendliness.
🛏 102 🚇 Syntagma 🛗 🖥
🖥 🌐 🌐 All major cards

🏨 ST. GEORGE
🍴 LYKAVITTOS
$$$$$
KLEOMENOUS 2
TEL (210) 729 0711
www.sglycabettus.gr
Very convenient and comfortable luxury hotel in the fashionable Kolonaki district. It has a highly recommended rooftop restaurant with great views of the city at night.
🛏 153 🅿 🚇 Syntagma 🛗
🖥 🖥 🌐 All major cards

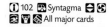

🖥 Elevator 🖥 Air-conditioning 🖥 Indoor Pool 🖥 Outdoor Pool 🖥 Health Club 🌐 Credit Cards

ATHENAEUM INTER-CONTINENTAL
$$$$
LEOFOROS SYNGROU ANDREA 89–93
TEL (210) 920 6000
www.ichotelsgroup.com
Superb hotel from the Inter-Continental chain, adapted to Greek style with paintings and sculptures by modern Greek artists in the public areas. Range of stores, bars, and restaurants. A short walk to downtown.

[i] 520 [P] [M] Sygrou-Fix
[S] [icon] [icon] [S] All major cards

DIVANI CARAVEL
$$$$
LEOFOROS VASILEOS ALEXANDROU 2
TEL (210) 720 7000
www.divanis.com
Very classy and modern hotel, much used by business travelers for its wide range of facilities, including a gym. Short walk or taxi ride to downtown.

[i] 471 [P] [M] Evangelismos
[S] [icon] [icon] [icon] [S] All major cards

DIVANI PALACE ACROPOLIS
$$$$
PARTHENONAS 19–23
TEL (210) 922 2945
www.divanis.com
Sitting in the shadow of the Acropolis in a quiet neighborhood, the hotel is convenient to downtown. Bland but large, comfortable rooms.

[i] 250 [P] [M] Akropoli
[S] [icon] [S] All major cards

O&B ATHENS BOUTIQUE HOTEL
$$$$
LEOKORIOU 7
TEL (210) 331 2950
This super-chic designer hotel offers personal services like free parking (a blessing in central Athens), DVD players,

a welcoming champagne drink, and the kind of personal attention that can be provided when there are just 22 rooms.

[i] 22 [P] [M] Thissio [icon] [S]
[S] All major cards

BABY GRAND
🍴 $$$
ATHINAS 65
TEL (210) 325 0900
www.culturehotels.com
Stylish and fun new hotel with a great restaurant and the first champagne bar in Athens. Some rooms are decorated by local artists—ask for the Spiderman room.

[i] 79 [P] [M] Omonoia
[icon] [S] [icon] [icon] [S] All major cards

DORIAN INN
$$$
PIREAS 15–17
TEL (210) 523 9782
www.dorianinnhotel.gr
Very classy hotel near Omonoia Square, recently improved with the opening of the new subway lines. Centrally located and handy for the National Archaeological Museum. Beautiful, 360-degree views of the Acropolis from the rooftop garden and pool.

[i] 146 [P] [M] Omonoia
[icon] [S] [icon] [S] All major cards

ELECTRA PALACE
$$$
NIKODIMOU 18–20
TEL (210) 324 1401
www.electrahotels.gr
Luxury option right in the Plaka, with rooftop pool and Acropolis views. All rooms have TV, phone, and minibar. Within walking distance of Syntagma and most of the main sights.

[i] 155 [P] [M] Syntagma [icon]
[S] [icon] [S] All major cards

HERODION
$$$
ROVERTOU GALLI 4
TEL (210) 923 6832
www.herodion.gr
Classy hotel on the south side of the Acropolis, away from the Plaka but with several highly recommended restaurants located nearby. All of the rooms have TV and telephone. Rooftop terrace has magnificent views of the Parthenon.

[i] 90 [M] Akropoli [icon] [S]
[S] All major cards

ROYAL OLYMPIC
$$$
ATHANASIOU DIAKOU 28-34
TEL (210) 928 8400
www.royalolympic.com
Conveniently located near the Acropolis and looking out over the ruins of the Temple of Olympian Zeus and Hadrian's Arch. The Olympic looks unimpressive, but its facilities are excellent and the rooms spacious.

[i] 304 [P] [M] Syntagma
[icon] [S] [icon] [S] All major cards

TITANIA
$$$
PANEPISTIMIOU 52
TEL (210) 332 6000
www.titania.gr
Huge hotel with high standards, close to Omonoia and within walking distance of the Plaka and the National Archaeological Museum. Well-equipped rooms; roof bar with view of the Acropolis.

[i] 396 [P] [M] Omonoia
[icon] [S] [S] All major cards

FRESH
$$–$$$
SOFOKLEOUS 26
TEL (210) 524 8511
www.freshhotel.gr
One of the new breed of Athens boutique hotels, with stark design, an exciting atmosphere, fashionable bar-

restaurant, and fabulous pool on the ninth floor.

133 **P** ▨ Omonoia 🔁 🅢 🌊 🔽 🅢 All major cards

🏨 ACROPOLIS VIEW
$$

GALLI AT WEBSTER 10
TEL (210) 921 7303
E-MAIL AV_HOTEL@OTENET.GR
www.acropolisview.gr
Affordable upscale option on south side of the Acropolis, in a quiet spot near Philopappos Hill, with wonderful views. Recently renovated rooms are small but pleasant.

32 ▨ Akropoli 🔁 🅢 🌊 AE, MC, Visa

🏨 ATHENS ACROPOLE
$$

PIREAS 1
TEL (210) 523 1111
E-MAIL AHOTEL@OTENET.GR
This large, moderately priced hotel close to Omonoia has been renovated and has clean rooms, all with telephones. The hotel has a bar, restaurant, and lounges.

167 **P** ▨ Omonoia 🔁 🅢 🔽 🌊 All major cards

🏨 EXARCHION
$$

THEMISTOKLEOUS 55
TEL (210) 380 0731
E-MAIL INFO@EXARCHION.COM
www.exarchion.com
Inexpensive option located close to the National Archaeological Museum in the lively student area of Exarcheia. Many rooms have a balcony, and there is also a rooftop dining area/bar.

49 ▨ Omonoia 🔁 🅢

🏨 MUSEUM HOTEL
$$

BOUBOULINAS 16
TEL (210) 323 8461
E-MAIL INFO@MUSEUM-HOTEL.GR
www.museum-hotel.gr

Behind the National Archaeological Museum but overlooking its gardens. Quiet and well maintained, this is a good affordable option if you want to be in this area. All rooms have a telephone.

93 **P** ▨ Omonoia 🅢 🌊 AE, DC, V

🏨 NEFELI
$$

YPERIDOU 16
TEL (210) 322 8044
www.hotel-nefeli.com
This is a small, family-run hotel that is inexpensive, friendly, modern, and spotlessly clean, although some of the rooms are small. It is convenient to both the Plaka and downtown.

18 ▨ Syntagma 🔁 🅢 🌊 AE, V

🏨 PLAKA
$$

KAPNIKAREAS 7
TEL (210) 322 2096
E-MAIL PLAKA@TOURHOTEL.GR
www.plakahotel.gr
Slightly pricier Plaka option, but chic, clean, modern, and bright in both the public areas and the rooms. Well located close to Mitropoleos. Some rooms have views of the Acropolis, as does the roof garden.

67 ▨ Monastiraki 🔁 🅢 🌊 All major cards

🏨 ACROPOLIS HOUSE
$

KODROU 6–8
TEL (210) 322 2344
E-MAIL HOTEL@ACROPOLIS HOUSE.GR
www.acropolishouse.gr
Inexpensive Plaka option in restored mid-19th-century mansion. Well maintained and family-run, it is a great place for those who prefer charm and character to modern conveniences.

19 ▨ Syntagma 🔁 🅢 🌊 V

🏨 ADONIS
$

KODROU 3
TEL (210) 324 9737
E-MAIL INFO@HOTEL-ADONIS.GR
www.hotel-adonis.gr
Good standard, economical hotel on pedestrianized street right on the edge of the Plaka and not far from Syntagma. Helpful staff; breakfast room/bar with Acropolis views.

20 ▨ Syntagma 🔁 🅢

🏨 CAROLINA
$

KOLOKOTRONI 55
TEL (210) 324 3551
E-MAIL INFO@HOTEL CAROLINA.GR
www.hotelcarolina.gr
A budget option that has seen better days but is perfectly acceptable if funds are limited. Some rooms are en suite and most are small, but they are kept clean and it is a convenient central base.

31 ▨ Monastiraki 🔁 🅢 🌊 AE, MC, V

🏨 CECIL HOTEL
$

ATHINAS 39
TEL (210) 321 7079
E-MAIL INFO@CECIL.GR
www.cecil.gr
Retro-style interiors with cage elevator. Roof garden has wonderful Acropolis views (plus four rooms). The hotel is run by two friendly brothers.

40 ▨ Monastiraki 🔁 🅢 🌊 All major cards

🏨 MARBLE HOUSE PENSION
$

ZINNI 35A
TEL (210) 923 4058
E-MAIL INFO@MARBLEHOUSE.GR
www.marblehouse.gr
Friendly, inexpensive small hotel in quiet location, a short

🔁 Elevator 🅢 Air-conditioning 🖭 Indoor Pool 🌊 Outdoor Pool 🔽 Health Club 🌊 Credit Cards

walk from the southern side of the Acropolis. Half the rooms are en suite, some have vine-covered balconies. Owners extremely helpful.

🛏 16 🚇 Sygrou-Fix 🚭
🚭 No credit cards

🏨 ORION
$
EMMANUEL BENAKI 105
TEL (210) 382 7362
www.orion-dryades.com
Very cheap but perfectly acceptable if you're traveling on a strict budget and don't mind a long walk to the near-est subway station (Omonoia). In the lively Exarcheia district, great for student nightlife and bars.

🛏 23 🚇 Omonoia 🚭 🚭
🚭 MC, V

RESTAURANTS

🍽 BOSCHETTO
$$$$
EVANGELISMOS PARK
TEL (210) 721 0893
This delightful Italian restau-rant, in Evangelismos Park on the edge of Kolonaki, serves fashionable food and fresh pasta, and uses ingredients popular in both Greece and Italy: e.g. squid, spinach, zuc-chini, and cheese.

🚇 Evangelismos 🕐 Closed Sun., L in winter, & 2 weeks in Aug. 🚭 🚭 All major cards

🍽 GB CORNER
$$$
GRANDE BRETAGNE HOTEL
PLATEIA SYNTAGMATOS
TEL (210) 333 0000
Part of the Grande Bretagne Hotel (see p. 243), this restaurant serves a variety of good Mediterranean cuisine and has a mouth-watering grill section.

🚇 Syntagma 🚭 🚭 All major cards

🍽 GEROFINIKAS
$$$
PINDAROU 10
TEL (210) 363 6710
Excellent food with a strong Middle Eastern influence. Chic and secluded.

🚇 Syntagma 🕐 Closed national holidays 🚭 🚭 All major cards

🍽 KONA KAI
$$$
SYNGROU 115
TEL (210) 930 0000
This restaurant in the Ledra Marriott Hotel specializes in Polynesian food (with decor as exotic as the dishes) but also has a Japanese menu. Very popular, so reservations are advisable.

🚇 Sygrou-Fix 🕐 Closed L Sun., & mid-Aug. 🚭 🚭 All major cards

🍽 L'ABREUVOIR
$$$
XENOKRATOUS 51
TEL (210) 722 9106
Upscale French restaurant in Kolonaki, where Pavarotti and other celebrities have dined. Elegant decor and equally elegant food: steaks a spe-cialty. Extensive and expensive wine list.

🚇 Syntagma 🚭 🚭 All major cards

🍽 PIL POUL
$$$
APOSTOLOU PAVLOU/POULO-POULOU
TEL (210) 342 3665
The Thissio and Psirri districts are the places to head for good modern Greek cooking, and this fashionable place also offers views of the Acropolis.

🚇 Thissio 🕐 Closed L & Sun. D 🚭 🚭 All major cards

🍽 BABY GRAND RESTAURANT
$$

<table>
<tr><td colspan="2">PRICES</td></tr>
<tr><td colspan="2">HOTELS</td></tr>
<tr><td colspan="2">An indication of the cost of a double room in the high season is given by $ signs.</td></tr>
<tr><td>$$$$$</td><td>Over $240</td></tr>
<tr><td>$$$$</td><td>$160-$240</td></tr>
<tr><td>$$$</td><td>$110-$160</td></tr>
<tr><td>$$</td><td>$70-$110</td></tr>
<tr><td>$</td><td>Under $70</td></tr>
<tr><td colspan="2">RESTAURANTS</td></tr>
<tr><td colspan="2">An indication of the cost of a three-course meal without drinks is given by $ signs.</td></tr>
<tr><td>$$$$$</td><td>Over $65</td></tr>
<tr><td>$$$$</td><td>$50-$65</td></tr>
<tr><td>$$$</td><td>$30-$50</td></tr>
<tr><td>$$</td><td>$20-$30</td></tr>
<tr><td>$</td><td>Under $20</td></tr>
</table>

BABY GRAND HOTEL
ATHINAS 65
TEL (210) 333 0000
Traditional taverna fare but with a 21st-century atmosphere and style, in this simple, fun, and inexpensive restaurant at the boutique Baby Grand Hotel (see p. 244).

🚇 Omonoia 🚭 🚭 All major cards

🍽 HERMION
$$
PANDROSSOU 7–15
TEL (210) 324 6725
Long-established restaurant just off the flea market, with both indoor seating and attractive courtyard dining area. Excellent service of good quality, moderately priced Greek favorites.

🚇 Monastiraki 🚭 🚭 All major cards

🍽 IDEAL
$$
PANEPESTIMIOU 46
TEL (210) 330 3000
Chic restaurant, with attentive service and an extensive

menu, including "drunkard's tidbits" (pork in a tomato sauce with olives, onions, mushrooms, and cheese) or shrimp with feta.
🚇 Omonoia 🕐 Closed Sun. 🅰️ 💳 All major cards

🍽 PRUNIER

$$

IPSILANTOU 63
TEL (210) 722 7379
This French bistro near the Hilton Hotel offers a romantic setting with typical bistro dishes, such as coq au vin and escargots. Some more exotic choices, too, like quail in oregano and lemon sauce.
🚇 Syntagma 🕐 Closed L & Sun. 🅰️ 💳 All major cards

🍽 SHOLARHIO

$$

TRIPODON 14
TEL (210) 324 7605
www.sholarhio.gr
This wonderfully simple place has no menu. Trays of meze are brought around, and you choose what you like the look of and pay accordingly. The drinks are equally simple. Inexpensive but oozing atmosphere—and the food is tasty.
🚇 Monastiraki 🅰️ 💳 All major cards

🍽 TO KAFENEIO

$$

LOUKIANOU 26
TEL (210) 722 9056
Chic but relaxed restaurant in Kolonaki, serving excellent Greek specialties such as spinach pie, baked eggplant with cheese, chicken in lemon sauce, and other dishes to an international clientele.
🚇 Syntagma 🕐 Closed Sun. 🅰️ 💳 All major cards

🍽 XINOS

$$

ANGELOU GERONTA 4
TEL (210) 322 1065

On a Plaka backstreet that few tourists find, this place is very popular with Athenians. Superior food, music late in the evening, and charming outdoor garden seating.
🚇 Syntagma 🕐 Closed L, Sat.–Sun., & winter 🅰️ 💳 All major cards

🍽 BAKALIARAKIA

$

KYDATHINAION 41
TEL (210) 322 5084
Simple Greek food in what claims to be the oldest taverna in Athens, established in 1865. Salt cod in garlic is the specialty that gives this basement place its name.
🚇 Monastiraki 🕐 Closed L midsummer 💳 No credit cards

🍽 BARBA YIANNIS

$

EMMANUEL BENAKI 94
TEL (210) 330 0185
This great favorite frequently has lines outside the door. Brisk service and a limited menu of good hearty Greek dishes. There is often impromptu music.
🚇 Omonoia 🕐 Closed Sun. D & Aug. 💳 No credit cards

SOMETHING SPECIAL

🍽 EDEN

$

PLAKA 12
TEL (210) 324 8858
This was the first purely vegetarian restaurant in Athens, and it serves food so tasty that meat eaters will not notice its absence. The bread is delicious, baked daily, and your coffee cup will be endlessly refilled.
🚇 Monastiraki 🕐 Closed Tues. 🅰️ 💳 All major cards

🍽 GURU

$

PLATEIA THEATROU 10, PSIRRI

TEL (210) 324 6530
On the ground floor, a Thai restaurant, known for good food and creative alcoholic concoctions, overlooks a lively bar area. Above, a laidback, Asian-style mezzanine lounge leads up to a late-night music club.
🚇 Monastiraki 🅰️ 💳 All major cards

🍽 KLIMATARIA

$

KLEPSIDRAS 5
TEL (210) 321 1215
Century-old tavern in the backstreets of the Plaka where the food is simple (chops, moussaka, stuffed vine leaves) but well prepared and very good value, and there's live music some nights, too.
🚇 Monastiraki 🕐 Closed L 💳 No credit cards

🍽 KOUKLIS

$

TRIPODON 14
TEL (210) 324 7605
Also known as To Yerani, this *ouzerie* is a well-established favorite, concentrating on hearty mezes such as *saganaki* (deep-fried cheese), *taramosalata,* fried fish, and sausages cooked in ouzo. Pleasant dining terrace, too.
🚇 Monastiraki 🅰️ 💳 All major cards

🍽 NEON

$

MITROPOLEOS 3
TEL (210) 322 8155
Neon is one of a chain of restaurants worth knowing about if you want somewhere a bit less formal and more cafeteria-style. Inexpensive, clean, lots of seating, and an international menu including pastas, steaks, chicken, and a range of simple Greek dishes.
🚇 Syntagma 💳 No credit cards

🛗 Elevator 🅰️ Air-conditioning 🏊 Indoor Pool 🏊 Outdoor Pool 🏋 Health Club 💳 Credit Cards

O PLATANOS

$

DIOGENOUS 4

TEL (210) 322 0666

An Athenian favorite that offers few concessions to tourism. It has one of the best locations in the Plaka, with tables outside in the summer under the plane tree that gives it its name.

🚇 Monastiraki 🕐 Closed Sun. 🚭 🚫 No credit cards

SAITA

$

KYDATHINAION 21

TEL (210) 322 6671

Unpretentious basement taverna, with wine from the barrel and murals on the walls. It has a standard menu that occasionally offers some delicious surprises, such as pork in a cream of celery sauce.

🚇 Syntagma 🕐 Closed L 🚭 🚫 No credit cards

SOMETHING SPECIAL

SIGALAS

$

PLATEIA MONASTIRAKI 2

TEL (210) 321 3036

For an authentic Athenian dining experience, Sigalas cannot be beaten. It is right on busy Monastiraki Square, with the bustle extending into the warren of the restaurant itself. Waiters in red sweaters rush about, some looking as if they have been there since the restaurant opened at the end of the 19th century. It is a casual place, where arguments and laughter rage, old photos plaster every wall, and the food comprises good, inexpensive examples of standard Greek taverna fare. On weekends, arrive early.

🚇 Monastiraki 🕐 Closed L 🚭 🚫 No credit cards

■ MODERN ATHENS & THE SUBURBS

HOTELS

PERISCOPE

$$$$

HARITOS 22

TEL (210) 729 7200

www.periscope.athenshotels.it

Yes, there is a periscope as you enter, one of the quirky stylish touches of this intimate boutique hotel in Kolonaki, every bit as chic as the neighborhood. It gets a lot of business travelers who want both character and high-tech facilities, and it raised the bar on hotel standards in Athens.

ⓘ 21 🚇 Evangelismos/Syntagma 🚭 🚭 🚫 All major cards

AIROTEL ALEXANDROS

$$$

TIMOLEONTOS VASSOUS 8, KOLONAKI

TEL (210) 643 0464

www.airotel.gr

Popular with business people, Airotel Alexandros is close to the U.S. embassy in one of the quietest neighborhoods in Athens. The modern decor is characterized by clean lines and pastel colors. The Don Giovanni restaurant offers quality Mediterranean food.

ⓘ 93 🅿 🚇 Megaro Moussikis 🚭 🚭 🚫 All major cards

CROWNE PLAZA

$$$

MICHALAKOPOULOU 50

TEL (210) 727 8000

www.hiathens.com

Located slightly away from downtown in the Ilisia district, this comfortable business hotel compensates by having all the facilities you might expect from a Holiday Inn, including a rooftop swimming pool and a choice of restaurants.

ⓘ 188 🅿 🚇 Evangalis-mos/Megaro Moussikis 🚭 🚭 🚫 All major cards

ILISIA BEST WESTERN

$$$

MICHALAKOPOULOU 25, ILISIA

TEL (210) 643 0464

www.ilisiahotel.gr

Set in a tranquil but relatively central location, the Ilisia offers value-for-money accommodations in a spacious modernized building overlooking a park. The hotel is a short walk from the subway, the Athens Concert Hall, and some of the city's principal museums.

ⓘ 90 🅿 🚇 Megaro Moussikis 🚭 🚭 🚫 All major cards

ZAPPION

$$

IRONDA 4, PANGRATI

TEL (210) 322 5891

In a residential street on which no traffic is allowed, the Zappion is a small, quiet hotel within walking distance of central Athens. This is a budget option whose rooms are small but comfortable and well maintained. The staff are friendly and helpful.

ⓘ 16 🚇 Syntagma 🚭 🚭 🚫 MC, V

IDEAL

$

NOTARA 142

TEL (210) 429 4050

www.ideal-hotel.gr

Hotels in Pireas can be expensive or seedy; the Ideal is neither. Near the international ferry ports; newly renovated. Worth making advance reservations if you need to spend a night in Pireas.

ⓘ 31 🚇 Pireas (long walk)/airport bus 🚭 🚭 🚫 AE, V

LILIA

$

ZEAS 131

TEL (210) 417 9108

E-MAIL INFO@LILIAHOTEL.GR
www.liliahotel.gr
Pleasant setting away from
the noisy waterfront; clean,
comfortable rooms. The closest harbor is Zea Marina, used
by hydrofoils and catamarans
to many destinations.
🛈 20 🚌 Pireas (taxi from
here advisable)/airport bus
🛗 ❄️ 💳 MC, V

RESTAURANTS

🍴 ALLI SKALA
$$$
SERIFOU 57, PIREAS
TEL (210) 482 7722
A distinguished restaurant
with a wonderful courtyard,
but not overpriced for Pireas.
Has a wider menu than just
seafood, including meats and
excellent examples of good
Greek homecooking.
🚌 Pireas ⏱ Closed L ❄️ 💳 All
major cards

🍴 DOURAMBEIS
$$$
AKTI PROTOPSALTI 29, PIREAS
TEL (210) 412 2092
A simple restaurant but with
outstanding—and expensive
—fresh fish dishes from the
Aegean Islands, including a
delicious crayfish soup. Established in 1932, this is
one of the best in Pireas.
🚌 Pireas ❄️ 💳 All major cards

🍴 ORIZONTES
(HORIZONS)
$$$
LYKAVITTOS HILL, KOLONAKI
TEL (210) 722 7065
Upscale dining atop Lykavit-
tos, the highest point above
the city. Reached by the
funicular on the corner of
Ploutarchou and Aristippou
(9 a.m.–midnight).
🚌 Evangelismos ❄️ 💳 All
major cards

🍴 VAROULKO
$$$
STRATIGOU PIREAS 80
TEL (210) 522 8400
www.varoulko.gr
Modern Greek and Continen-
tal cuisine, with an unusual
menu including such surprises
as grape leaves stuffed with
fish. Monkfish is the chef's
specialty. Reservations advised
for this Michelin-starred place.
🚌 Pireas ⏱ Closed L, Sun., &
Aug. ❄️ 💳 All major cards

🍴 ACHINOS
$$
AKTI THEMESTOKLEOUS 51
TEL (210) 452 6944
This split-level bar/restau-
rant has a stunning cliffside
location, like a Pireas version
of Santorini. The style is very
modern Mediterranean with
both simple and more creative
fish dishes. There's an impres-
sive wine list, too.
🚌 Pireas ❄️ 💳 All major cards

🍴 KOLLIAS
$$
STRATIGOU PLASTIRA 3
TEL (210) 462 9620
Renowned Pireas fish restaurant, with a menu that ranges
from the conventional (mac-
kerel, mussels, lobster) to the
unusual (shrimp and tomato
soup, scorpionfish).
🚌 Pireas ⏱ Closed Sun., Aug.,
& L summer ❄️ 💳 All major
cards

🍴 PLOUS PODILATOU
$$
AKTI KOUMOUNDOUROU 42,
MICROLIMANO
TEL (210) 413 7910
www.plous-podilatou.gr
Imaginative fresh seafood
served overlooking the water-
front at Microlimano. Great
selection of wines.
🚌 Pireas ❄️ 💳 All major cards

AROUND ATHENS

CORINTH

🏨 EFIRA
$
ETHNIKIS ANTISTASSEOS 52
TEL (27410) 24021
www.ephirahotel.gr
As in many of the mainland's
most popular spots, there
is a dearth of decent accom-
modations in Corinth, but the
Efira is an acceptable option.
It has typical clean and simple
Greek rooms and its own
restaurant.
🛈 45 🛗 ❄️ 💳 No credit
cards

DELPHI

🏨 PARNASSOS DELPHI
$$
V. PAVLOU 32, DELPHI
TEL (22650) 82321
www.parnassos.org
Centrally sited in the middle of
Delphi, Parnassos is a family-
run value-for-money option.
The rooms are not large but
well appointed, while three
suites have their own fire-
places. Handy for visiting the
area's historic sites, the hotel
is also handy for winter sports
visitors to Mount Parnassos.
🛈 30 🛗 ❄️ 💳 All major
cards

🏨 PITHO
$$
V. PAVLOU 40A, DELPHI
TEL (22650) 82850
Within a short distance of the
museum and the Sanctuary of
Apollo, this small family-run
hotel offers modern, comfort-
able accommodation. Enjoy
fine views from the verandah
and easy access to Mount
Parnassos ski center. Visitors
recommend this hotel for its
friendly, attentive service.
🛈 8 ❄️ 💳 All major cards

NAFPLIO

🏨 NAFPLIA PLACE
$$$

KASTRO ACRONAFPLIAS
TEL (27520) 28981
E-MAIL RESERVATIONS@
NAFPLIONHOTELS.GR
www.nafplionhotels.gr
This luxury hotel occupies a
prime position overlooking
Nafplio's harbor, the sea, and
across to the Peloponnese.
It's an easy stroll down into
the town, but a steep walk
back up again, so take a car or
a taxi. The 48 rooms, 3 suites,
and 33 villas all have lovely
sea views.

🛏 84 🚭 🅰 All major cards

SOUNION

🏨 GRECOTEL CAPE
SOUNION
$$$

AKRA SOUNION, NR. SOUNION
TEL (22920) 69700
www.grecotel.com
Superbly located five-star resort hotel, with its own beach
but backed by a pine forest on
the edge of a national park.
Lovely views of the Temple of
Poseidon, good food, health
club, and an outdoor pool;
some of the private villas have
their own swimming pools.

🛏 124 🅿 🚭 🏊 🍴 🅰 All
major cards

🍴 ILIAS
$$

AKRA SOUNION, NR. SOUNION
TEL (22920) 39114
An alternative to the eating
places outside the Temple of
Poseidon is this fish taverna on
the beach below. Less impressive view but slightly cheaper.
No surprises on the menu, but
lots of fresh fish.

🚭 🅰 No credit cards

VRAVRON

🏨 MARE NOSTRUM
$$$

ARTEMIDOS, VRAVRON
TEL (22940) 71000
www.mare-nostrum.gr
A large hotel in a relatively
isolated location away from
the crowds. This is a busy,
modern resort hotel with
many facilities, including a spa,
gym, tennis courts, pool, live
music, and conference rooms.
Comfortable rooms are well
furnished. Balconies along
the front have wide views of
the bay.

🛏 350 🅿 🚭 🏊 🍴 🅰 All
major cards

▪ THE NEAR ISLANDS

ALONISSOS

🍴 TO KAMAKI
$$

IKION DOLOPON, PATITIRI
TEL (24240) 65245
This *ouzerie* is the best eating
in town, a couple of streets
away from the waterfront. An
impressive menu of seafood
includes baked mussels and
stuffed squid. You can either
have them as mezes to whet
the appetite with an early-
evening ouzo, or even better,
spend the night there and
order several selections.

🕐 Closed Sept.–June 🚭
🅰 No credit cards

🍴 ASTROFENGIA
$

OLD ALONISSOS
TEL (24240) 65182
Wonderful views at this
popular restaurant, which is
about as high as you can go in
the Old Town. The evenings
get lively with a festive atmosphere in summer. The food
ranges from simple grilled fish
steaks and stuffed tomatoes

to the more sophisticated
artichoke hearts with a cream-
and-dill sauce.

🕐 Closed L 🚭 🅰 All major
cards

EGINA

🏨 EGINITIKO
ARCHONTIKO
$

EGINA TOWN
TEL (22970) 24968
Restored traditional mansion,
first built in 1820. Stronger
on atmosphere than quality
of rooms, but a perfectly
acceptable economic option
in the center of Egina town,
with its two courtyards and a
roof garden.

🛏 10 🚭 🅰 All major cards

🍴 TO STEKI
$$

PAN IRIOTI 45
TEL (22970) 23910
Some of the best eating in
Greece is in little meze places
like this, where they do simple
things like fried sardines, squid,

and octopus really well. It's right by the fish market and incredibly popular locally, so you know they're doing it right.
🔆 🅢 No credit cards

🍽 MARIDAKI AEGINA
$
DIMOKRATIAS, EGINA TOWN
TEL (22970) 25869
Lively waterfront restaurant/café where you can dine cheaply on salads or omelettes, moderately on grilled octopus or moussaka, or expensively on fresh fish.
🔆 🅢 No credit cards

IDRA

🏨 BRATSERA
$$$
TOMBAZI, IDRA TOWN
TEL (22980) 53971
E-MAIL BRATSERA@YAHOO
.COM
www.bratserahotel.com
Stay in this former sponge factory near the main harbor. Excellent conversion of the 1860 building with traditional island decor, pool, garden, and dining area.
ⓘ 26 🔃 🌊 🅢 🅢 All major cards

🍽 KONDYLENIA
$$
COAST ROAD W OF IDRA TOWN
TEL (22980) 53520
A short walk along the coast west of Idra is this wonderful taverna with terrific views across to the Greek mainland. It's a favorite place for watching the sunset. The menu is pretty impressive too, catering to the more sophisticated Idra palates with dishes such as spinach, squid, and shrimp casserole, although fresh fish simply grilled is also available.
🕓 Closed midwinter 🔆
🅢 No credit cards

🍽 TO STEKI
$$
MIAOULI, IDRA TOWN
TEL (22980) 53517
This taverna satisfies patrons all year in a pleasing setting with old murals on the walls, fresh fish on the menu, and a limited number of daily specials.
🔆 🅢 No credit cards

🍽 XERI ELIA
$
OFF MAIN SQUARE, IDRA TOWN
TEL (22980) 52886
www.xerielia-douskos.gr
Down the narrow street near O Kipos is this tucked-away traditional taverna, which has a garden dining area. Simple menu of meats and fish, but beautifully prepared and friendly service.
🔆 🅢 No credit cards

POROS

🍽 CARAVELLA
$
PARALIA
TEL (22980) 23666
Very friendly, busy waterfront taverna with a typical Greek menu prepared with care: moussaka, souvlaki, fish, octopus, stifado, vegetarian dishes.
🔆 🅢 All major cards

SKIATHOS

🏨 ATRIUM
$$$$
PLATANIAS
TEL (24270) 49345
E-MAIL INFO@ATRIUMHOTEL.GR
Stylish new hotel, in a wonderful setting on a wooded hill and with an Olympic-size pool looking out over the Aegean. The rooms are large, and they, too, have good views from their balconies. Restaurant, bar, and water sports available.
ⓘ 75 🔃 🔆 🌊 🎾 🅢 All major cards

🍽 KAMPOURELI OUZERIE
$$
PARALIA, SKIATHOS TOWN
TEL (24270) 21112
In the great bustling Greek ouzerie tradition, serving mezes (the Greek answer to the Spanish tapas)—a range of nibbles to eat with your ouzo, such as octopus, squid, and olives—and more substantial meals as well.
🔆 🅢 No credit cards

🍽 WINDMILL
$$
SKIATHOS TOWN
TEL (24270) 24550
www.thewindmillskiathos
.com
Right at the top of the eastern hill in the main town, this chic restaurant serves food just as special as the setting. Chicken with bourbon and chili is just one example of the unusual combinations. Desserts include poached pears.
🔆 🅢 No credit cards

SKIROS

🏨 NEFELI
$$
SKIROS TOWN
TEL (22220) 91964
www.skyros-nefeli.gr
This modern place, built in traditional fashion, is a mix of hotel rooms and larger apartments. At the edge of town, it's fairly quiet, but ask for a room with a view and make advance reservations. It is extremely popular.
ⓘ 14 🅿 🔆 🌊 🅢 All major cards

🍽 KRISTINA'S RESTAURANT
$$
SKIROS TOWN
TEL (22220) 91123
Austrian Kristina is trying to combine Greek traditions

with a more nouveau touch, such as a generous number of vegetarian dishes and a good variety of breads. Her specialty is chicken fricassee.

🕐 Closed Sun. 🚭 🚫 All major cards

SKOPELOS

🍴 ANATOLI OUZERIE
$

SKOPELOS TOWN
TEL (24240) 22851
This is a place aimed at Greeks, with live music late at night. Dine on a selection of their exceptionally good mezes. No address, so climb the hill and ask for Anatoli's. Locals will point the way.

🕐 Closed L & winter 🚭
🚫 All major cards

🍴 MOLOS
$

HARBOUR, SKOPELOS TOWN
TEL (24240) 22551
www.molos-skopelos.com
There are several restaurants on the waterfront offering good basic Greek food at inexpensive prices. Molos has fresh fish and grilled meats, as well as excellent casserole dishes.

🕐 Closed midwinter 🚭
🚫 No credit cards

🍴 TAVERNA T'AGNANTI
$

GLOSSA, SKOPELOS
TEL (24240) 33606
This little, family-run taverna is one of those unpretentious places that are a delight to find in the islands. It has a great atmosphere, friendly hosts, and inexpensive and well-prepared examples of standard Greek dishes: squid, grills, chops, and moussaka.

🚭 🚫 No credit cards

SPETSES

🏨 POSSIDONION

$$$
DAPIA WATERFRONT, SPETSES TOWN
TEL (22980) 72308
Poseidon himself would enjoy this, overlooking the harbor and across to the mainland. Delightfully old-fashioned hotel with slightly fading grandeur but great charm.

🛏 55 🕐 Closed winter 🚭
🚭 🚫 All major cards

🍴 LAZAROS
$$

KASTELLI
TEL (22980) 72600
This homely place serves its own retsina from the barrels on the walls, and there's a really lively atmosphere from the people who have climbed the hill behind the harbor to get here. It's worth it for delicious dishes like their goat in a lemon sauce, a popular local favorite.

🕐 Closed L, winter 🚫 No credit cards

🍴 LIRAKIS
$

MAIN HARBOR, SPETSES TOWN
TEL (22980) 72188
Above the Lirakis supermarket with a fine view of the harbor, the Lirakis has an eclectic menu ranging from omelettes and vegetarian dishes such as *briam* (very like ratatouille) to more sophisticated but traditionally Greek meat and fish choices.

🕐 Closed winter 🚭 🚫 All major cards

◼ THE CYCLADES

MIKONOS

🏨 MYKONOS GRAND HOTEL

$$$$
AGIOS YIANNIS
TEL (22890) 25555
E-MAIL INFO@MYKONOS

GRAND.GR
www.mykonosgrand.gr
Beautiful hotel, located directly above three sandy coves with stunning sunset views of Dilos island. Spa suites are designed for couples on their honeymoon.

🛏 111 🅿 🚭 🏊 🚻 🚭 🚫 All major cards

🏨 HOTEL BELVEDERE
🍴 $$$

HORA, ROCHARI
TEL (22890) 25122
E-MAIL CONTACT@BELVEDERE HOTEL.COM
www.belvederehotel.com
Ideal resort-style hotel in the main town, convenient for shopping, eating, and clubbing. Rooms are small but cozy. Features newly opened Nobu Japanese restaurant. American breakfast.

🛏 43 🚭 🏊 🚻 🚭 🚫 All major cards

SOMETHING SPECIAL

🍴 LA MAISON DE CATHERINE
$$$

NIKI AGIOS GERASIMOS, CHORA
TEL 22890 22169
In the Greek islands there are very few restaurants that can combine atmosphere and top-quality cooking, but this is one of those rarities. It brings French flair to Greek cooking, so while the menu may say coq au vin, it will be Greek chicken cooked in Greek wine with a result that would grace a Parisian restaurant. Be prepared to pay much more than average, and make a reservation ahead to guarantee a table in the intimate dining room.

🕐 Closed L 🚭 🚫 All major cards

🍴 LA TAVERNE
$$$

HOTEL CAVO TAGOO

MIKONOS TOWN
TEL (22890) 23692
Try and reserve a table
(advance reservations are
recommended) with a view
over the bay for this stylish
hotel restaurant, where haute
cuisine meets Greek menus
for delicious results such as
lamb chops with yogurt and
mint sauce.
🅢 🅢 All major cards

🍴 SEA SATIN
$$
MIKONOS TOWN
TEL (22890) 24676
The most fashionable place to
dine, beneath the windmills
and with a view of Little Venice
and the sea. Fresh fish and
vegetables are served with
laid-back but quick service. Bar-
becued T-bones are delicious.
🕒 Closed L

🍴 KIKI
$
AGIOS SOSTIS
The ultimate beach taverna.
There is no electricity and
no phone, so Kiki closes at
sundown. Juicy chops cooked
on charcoal, excellent salads
served in a shady courtyard.
🕒 Closed winter 🅢 No credit
cards

MILOS

🍴 PSARAVOLADA
$$$
AYIOS KIRIAKI
TEL (22870) 31050
www.psaravolada.gr
A warm welcome awaits visitors to this tastefully furnished
small resort of rooms, studios,
and apartments, perched
atop a hill. With a beautiful
sea view and a quiet location,
Psaravolada offers excellent
service, the privacy of your
own verandah, and a private
beach, down 250 steps to the
water's edge.
🅘 12 🅿 🅢 🅢 All major cards

NAXOS

🍴 ONIRO
$$$
PLATEIA BRADOUNA
NAXOS TOWN
TEL (22850) 23846
www.oniro-naxos.info
Probably the best restaurant
in town, Oniro commands
wonderful views from its
roof garden, the atmosphere
enhanced by the candlelit
tables and a peaceful court-
yard setting. The food matches
the mood, with a menu that
leans to the international but
does not exclude Greek dishes
such as lamb stuffed with
garlic and bacon and cooked
very slowly in the oven.
🕒 Closed L & winter 🅢
🅢 No credit cards

🍴 MANOLIS GARDEN TAVERNA
$
KASTRO, NAXOS TOWN
TEL (22850) 25168
www.manolisgardennaxos
.com
Right in the Old Town near
the castle, several restaurants
cater to the tourist trade, but
this delightful garden taverna
maintains its high reputation
by serving tasty traditional
Greek dishes such as mous-
saka, deep-fried eggplant,
and stuffed peppers and
tomatoes.
🕒 Closed winter 🅢 🅢 No
credit cards

🍴 NIKOS
$
PARALIA, CHORA
TEL (22850) 23153
Nikos is owned by fisherman
Nikos Katsayannis, so the fish
on the menu is guaranteed
fresh, and there are generally
several unusual varieties on
offer. Plenty of other choices
too, on a wide menu. The
wine list concentrates on
wines from Naxos and the

other Cycladic islands.
🅢 🅢 No credit cards

PAROS

🏨 ASTIR OF PAROS
$$$$
KOLYMBITHRES BEACH, NEAR
NAOUSSA
TEL (22840) 51976
www.astirofparos.gr
Paros's flagship hotel is almost
a Cycladic village in its own
right, with its own beach, small
golf course, and an art gallery.
The reception area displays
modern Greek art. Well worth
the outlay.
🅘 57 🅿 🕒 Closed winter
🅢 🅢 🅢 🅢 🅢 All major
cards

🍴 ALIGARIA
$
PLATEIA ALIGARI, PARIKIA
TEL (22840) 22026
This delightful little place is
run by a gifted cook, Elizabeth
Nikolousou. She knows how
to serve up old favorites
such as moussaka or stuffed
tomatoes with an attention to
detail that reminds you how
good they can be when done
properly.
🅢 🅢 No credit cards

🍴 LEVANTIS
$
PARIKIA
TEL (22840) 23613
The name of this friendly little
taverna, with its tables beneath
trailing vines, indicates a nod
toward the flavors of the
Middle East with the use of
yogurt, apricots, and nuts, and
tender chicken dishes.
🕒 Closed L & Tues. 🅢 🅢 All
major cards

SANTORINI

🏨 ASTRA APARTMENTS
$$$$$
IMEROVIGLI

TEL (22860) 23641
www.astra-apartments.com
Absolutely delightful small village-like complex of rooms, suites, and villas with their own pools. The Astra is stunningly located on top of cliffs, with heavenly sunset views, and is easily one of the most comfortable and relaxed places on the island.

☐ 85 P ☐ ☐ ☐ All major cards

🏨 VEDEMA HOTEL
🍴 $$$$
MEGALOCHORI
TEL (22860) 81796
E-MAIL INFO@VEDEMA.GR
www.vedema.gr
The Vedema features Cycladic-style villas in a converted wine merchant's mansion. An extensive selection of Greek and international wines is offered in the century-old restaurant. The Cocoon spa has massage tents on the nearby beach.

☐ 36 P ☐ ☐ ☐ ☐ All major cards

SOMETHING SPECIAL

🏨 VILLA RENOS
$$$$
THIRA, SANTORINI
TEL (22860) 22369
www.villarenos.gr
To enjoy a view to die for, look no farther than this beautifully decorated hotel. The deluxe rooms have their own jazuzzi, and every room has its own spacious balcony facing the stunning sea-filled volcanic caldera and the sunset for which the island is famous. Set on one of the highest spots on the island, this family run hotel attracts many return visitors, not least because of its faultless service.

☐ 7 ☐ ☐ ☐ All major cards

🍴 KATINA
$
OIA PORT
TEL 22860 71280
If you can face the trek down to the harbor at Oia—or rather face the climb back up again (though you can always phone for a taxi)—then Katina's is a great place for seafood, right by the sea.

☐ ☐ No credit cards

SERIFOS

🏨 RIZES
$$$–$$$$
SIMPOTAMA, SERIFOS
TEL 22810 52222
www.hotelrizes.gr
Opened in 2010, this small complex comprises spacious apartments and suites, each with a private terrace. Facilities include a restaurant, coffee bar, and a large pool, while each suite has a small private pool. The design incorporates traditional stone walls and high wooded ceilings; the furnishings are modern minimalist chic. The location is quiet, with wonderful sea views.

☐ 16 P ☐ ☐ ☐ All major cards

SIFNOS

🍴 TO LIOTRIVI
$$
ARTEMONA
TEL (22840) 32051
Sifnos is said to produce the best chefs in Greece, and the chef here, Yiannis Yiorgoulis, is said to be the finest one who has stayed on the island. Try a simple but unusual and delicious kaparosalata (caper salad), and I'll know why this place is so popular.

☐ ☐ No credit cards

🍴 CAPTAIN ANDREAS
$

BY THE BEACH, KAMARAI
TEL (22840) 32356
If your needs are simple—the best local fish, grilled—then this restaurant on the beach is the place to come. The eponymous owner catches most of the menu himself, buys the best from his fellow fishermen, and the taste and setting don't come any better.

☐ ☐ No credit cards

TINOS

🍴 TO KOUTOUKI TIS ELENI
$
G. GAGOU 5, PARALIA
TEL (22830) 24857
This is what Greek eating is all about. You may get the same dishes that are on every other menu (if there is a menu) along this back street packed with dining options, but the Koutouki serves everything with freshness and friendliness. Dishes like veal stew or chicken in lemon sauce are made to perfection.

☐ No credit cards

▓ CRETE

AGIOS NIKOLAOS

🍴 PELAGOS
$$
CORNER KORAKA & KATEHAKI STREETS
TEL (28410) 25737
Located in a two-story house, Pelagos offers a seductive choice of fresh seafood, including sea urchin salad. Outdoor street seating in addition to a secluded garden.
🚫 No credit cards

CHORA SFAKION

🍴 XENIA
$$
SFAKIA
TEL (28250) 91202
www.xeniacrete.com
Favored by return visitors, the hotel building is sympathetic to the surrounding traditional structures. The hotel has a popular taverna. Spacious rooms all offer wide views to the harbor, the open sea, or the mountains. There is easy access to beaches.
ℹ️ 19 🅿️ 🛗 ❄️ 🚫 All major credit cards

ELOUNDA

SOMETHING SPECIAL

🏨 ELOUNDA BEACH
$$$$$
ELOUNDA (1.2 MILES/2 KM NORTH OF CENTER)
TEL (28410) 63000
E-MAIL ELOHOTEL@ELOUNDA BEACH.GR
www.eloundabeach.gr
Easily the most luxurious hotel on Crete, and one of the finest in Europe, with room rates you might find in the center of New York or Paris. There are 301 rooms, some of which are actually private cottages with their own swimming pools,

rented out to the mega-rich who value their privacy. For other guests there are a pool, beach, water sports, miniature golf, sporting facilities, a sailing club, a health center, and an entertainment center.
ℹ️ 301 🅿️ 🏊 ❄️ 🚫 All major cards

🍴 VRITOMARTES
$
G. SFIRAKI WATERFRONT
TEL (28410) 41325
An unsophisticated and excellent taverna right on the harbor, where you dine gazing out over the sea. The fish on the menu was caught here just a few hours earlier, perhaps even by the owner himself. Meat and vegetable dishes are also available, but go for the fish every time.
🚫 Closed in winter ❄️ 🚫 MC, V

HANIA

🏨 VILLA ANDROMEDA
$$$
VENIZELOU 150
TEL (28210) 28303
E-MAIL VILANDRO@OTENET.GR
www.villandromeda.gr
This delightful, intimate hotel is in a restored neoclassical mansion from 1870. Its marble floors and elegant furniture give a grand impression, and rooms have views over sea and town, but can be noisy.
ℹ️ 8 ❄️ 🚫 All major cards

🏨 AMPHORA
$$
PARODOS THEOTOKOPOU-LOU 20
TEL 28210 93224
E-MAIL CONTACT@AMPHORA.GR
www.amphora.gr
First built around 1300, this restored mansion combines Venetian elegance, Turkish style, and modern comforts.

The roof terrace has a great view over Hania's beautiful harbor, and rooms are spacious, but there can be noise from the port.
ℹ️ 20 🛗 ❄️ 🚫 All major cards

🍴 TAMAM
$$
ZAMBELIOU 49
TEL (28210) 96080
www.tamamrestaurant.com
One of the best places in town, as you can usually tell by the queues, serving dishes that range across the Mediterranean, such as risotto or Greek baked red peppers, but combined with Middle Eastern influences.
🚫 All major cards

IRAKLIO

🏨 CANDIA MARIS
$$$
AMMOUDARA
TEL (28103) 314632
www.maris.gr
This luxury-class modern hotel was built in brick and marble using traditional Cretan styles, but the rooms (or rather cottages) all have modern facilities and sea views. The huge round swimming pool is an extra delight.
ℹ️ 534 🅿️ ❄️ 🏊 ❄️ 🚫 All major cards

🏨 LATO
$–$$
EPIMENIDOU 15
TEL (28120) 228103
www.lato.gr
This attractive hotel is simple and modern, but its friendly atmosphere and central location make it one of the best bets in the city. Some rooms have balconies overlooking the Venetian harbor, and the Archaeological Museum is close by.
ℹ️ 50 🛗 ❄️ 🚫 All major cards

KYRIAKOS
$$

LEOFOROS DIMOKRATIAS 53
TEL (28120) 222464
Some of the best food in
Iraklio, with traditional Cretan
dishes served with great style
and attention to detail. Formal
dress preferred, although it's a
remarkably friendly place. Try
the octopus with onions or the
house specialty: snails.
Closed Wed. & sometimes
in summer   All major
cards

KALYVES

KALYVES BEACH
$$–$$$

KALYVES APOKORONOU
TEL (28250) 31285
www.kalyvesbeach.com
Set beside a river and just
feet from a sandy beach, this
hotel has a pleasant location
in a quiet resort. All rooms
have balconies, some with
sea views. The hotel has two
beaches and two pools. The
decor is functional and some
rooms are small, but the staff
are helpful and the hotel offers
value for money.
150
All major cards

RETHIMNO

GRECOTEL CRETA PALACE
$$$$

MISIRIA BEACH
TEL (28310) 55181
E-MAIL CONTACT@GRECOTEL.GR
www.grecotel.com
Surrounded by lush gardens,
this modern resort hotel has
been built simply but stylishly
in traditional Cretan fashion.
In addition to the rooms
there are 204 cottages and
villas, with every facility. Three
restaurants, four bars, tennis
court, and scuba diving.

355   Closed winter
All major cards

DODECANESE & NORTHEASTERN AEGEAN

HIOS

GRECIAN CASTLE HOTEL
$$

HIOS TOWN
TEL (22710) 44740
E-MAIL INFO@GRECIANCASTLE
.GR
www.greciancastle.gr
Restored factory, tastefully
decorated and furnished, and
with lovely gardens. Located
on the seafront, it also offers a
restaurant and bar.
55   All major cards

TA PETRINA
$$

VOLISSOS
TEL (22740) 21128
www.tapetrina.gr
Charming rural hilltop hamlet
near beaches of northwest
coast. A British-Greek couple
have renovated the hotel to
incredibly high standards; the
terrace has barbecue facilities
and a great view.
5   No credit cards

TAVERNA HOTZAS
$

YIORYIOU KONDILI 3
HIOS TOWN
TEL (22710) 42787
The oldest taverna in town
and one of the best loved,
now in the fourth generation
of the same family. Hotzas is
an island institution and not to
be missed. It is tricky to find in
the backstreets, but everyone
knows its name. It has a lovely
garden eating area, which you
share with the taverna's cats
and hens.
Closed Sun. & L
No credit cards

KALIMNOS

PANORAMA
$

AMMOUDARA
TEL (22430) 23138
Slightly back from the busy
waterfront at the top of a
steep hill, this modern hotel
has very welcoming owners.
Some of the rooms have
terraces, and all have stunning
sea views and are beautifully
maintained.
13   No credit
cards

BARBA PETROS
$

PLATEIA DIAMANTIS, POTHIA
TEL (22430) 29678
Full of character, this restau-
rant at the north end of the
harbor offers fresh fish grilled
on olive-wood charcoal, along
with Greek island specialties
such as squid stuffed with
a delicious mix of spinach,
cheese, and herbs.
No credit cards

KARPATHOS

APOLIS
$$$$

KASTELIA, AMMOPI
TEL (22450) 81200
www.hotelapolis.com
A modern luxury hotel built to
form an ampitheater around
the pool in a scenic location.
The hotel is built of local
stone. The decor is elegant
and minimalist with exterior
earth-toned colors. A gourmet
restaurant overlooks the sea.
31   All major
cards

ALEX
$$

KARPATHOS TOWN
TEL (22450) 22004
www.alexhotel.gr
In a a quiet location dotted
with olive trees, this place

is a family-run hotel with a colorful garden and sea views. It offers value-for-money accommodations. The rooms, though small, have either a balcony or a verandah.

🛏 25 🅿 ♿ 🏊 🅾 All major cards

KOS

🏨 AFENDOULIS HOTEL
$
EVRIPILOU 1, KOS TOWN
TEL (22420) 25321
E-MAIL INFO@AFENDOUL ISHOTEL.COM
www.afendoulishotel.com
A friendly, family-run hotel, this is the kind of place that the Greek islands are all about. Simple but spotless, close to the town center and to the beach but in a quiet location. All rooms have balconies with views of the harbor.

🛏 23 ♿ 🅾 No credit cards

🍴 OLYMPIADA
$
KLEOPATRAS 2, KOS TOWN
TEL (22420) 23031
In a town that is full of below-average tourist tavernas, here is a treat. It's a genuine no-nonsense Greek restaurant serving good food at cheap prices. Try a simple souvlaki or one of the many vegetable dishes.

♿ 🅾 No credit cards

🍴 PLATANOS
$
PLATEIA PLATANOS, KOS TOWN
TEL (22420) 28991
With the best setting in town, the Platanos offers unusual Greek dishes such as octopus *stifado* and international variety such as Indonesian fillet steak. There's also live music on most evenings during the summer.

♿ 🅾 All major cards

🍴 TAVERNA MAVROMATIS
$
PSALIDI BEACH, KOS
TEL (22420) 22433
The Mavromati brothers who run this taverna take no easy options but cater to Greek palates as well as those of overseas visitors. The deep-fried cheese is delicious, as are the tender grilled meat dishes, and of course there is always fresh fish.

🕐 Closed winter, Mon., & Tues. ♿ 🅾 All major cards

LESVOS

🏨 OLIVE PRESS
$$
MOLIVOS BEACH, MOLIVOS
TEL (22530) 71646
www.olivepress-hotel.com
Set in a charming village, dominated by a castle, Molivos is an essential part of any visit to Lesvos, and you should try to reserve rooms here if you can. A traditional building right on the seafront, it really is where olives were pressed. There's a beautiful private courtyard and gardens too. Ask for a sea-view room.

🛏 53 ♿ 🅾 All major cards

🍴 VAFIOS
$$
VAFIOS, NEAR MOLIVOS
TEL (22530) 71752
www.taverna-vafios.gr
In the village of the same name, in the hills 3 miles (5 km) southeast of Molivos, the taverna Vafios is a popular drive out in the evenings. Locals know it has a good range of pies and grills. Wine from the barrel.

🕐 Closed winter ♿ 🅾 No credit cards

🍴 CAFENEON O ERMIS
$
KORNAROU 2, MITILINI
TEL (22510) 26232
This venerable *ouzerie* certainly oozes atmosphere, the interior being like a cross between an antique store and a bar. It is a very popular local hangout, good for a quick drink or a full meal. Choose from the tasty meze dishes, such as fried cheese or squid.

♿ 🅾 No credit cards

🍴 I SYKAMINIA
$
SKALA SYKAMINIAS
TEL (22530) 55319
A taverna in a quiet setting, right on the picturesque harbor of this little fishing village. A white church overlooks the harbor, and Turkey is just across the water. Take a table under the shade of the mulberry tree and sample the simple, delicious fish dishes such as squid or sardines. If there in late summer, try the regional dish of stuffed squash flowers.

♿ 🅾 No credit cards

LIMNOS

🏨 AKTI MYRINA
$$
MYRINA
TEL (22540) 22352
This resort hotel is about half a mile (1 km) west of the main town, with its own private beach, three restaurants, water sports, and tennis. The well-equipped rooms are actually stone cottages set in the attractive surroundings.

🛏 125 🕐 Closed winter 🅿 ♿ 🏊 🏋 🅾 All major cards

🍴 O PLATANOS
$
KYDHA, MYRINA
TEL (22540) 22070
Beautifully located on a little square just off the main street, O Platanos gets its name from

the two huge plane trees that it shelters beneath. The food is simple but very tasty country fare, such as meat casseroles and oven-baked lamb. Some vegetarian options, too.

🚭 🅰️ No credit cards

PATMOS

🏨 **AUSTRALIS**
$
SKALA
TEL (22470) 31576
www.patmosaustralis.gr
This family-run hotel, owned by a couple who used to live in Australia, is in a very quiet location and surrounded by beautiful gardens. Breakfast is served on a terrace overlooking the harbor.
🛏️ 18 🕐 Closed winter 🚭
🅰️ No credit cards

🍴 **VEGGHERA**
$$$
NEA MARINA, SKALA
TEL (22470) 32988
Vegghera is acknowledged as the best restaurant in town, set in an old mansion down at the marina. The owners combine Greek freshness with French flair and produce dishes like calamari in pesto, which brings a zing to an old standby. It's not cheap but it can justify the prices with the results.
🕐 Closed winter 🚭 🅰️ All major cards

RHODES

🏨 **HILTON RODOS RESORT**
$$$
LEOFOROS IALLYSOU, IXIA, RHODES TOWN
TEL (22410) 75000
E-MAIL GM.RHODES@HILTON.COM
www1.hilton.com
This excellent five-star hotel, with its own splendid gardens

and beach, is a few miles away from the noise of Rhodes town. Rooms are spacious and all have marble bathrooms, while facilities include restaurant, bar, sauna, tennis court, and Jacuzzi.
🛏️ 402 🅿️ 🚭 🅰️ 🏊 📺
🅰️ All major cards

🏨 **S. NIKOLIS HOTEL**
$$
IPPODAMOU 61
RHODES OLD TOWN
TEL (22410) 34561
www.s-nikolis.gr
An Old Town hotel that oozes history, incorporating stonework that goes back 800 years. Although some rooms are a little cramped, all of them are modern and have telephones. The owners also have rooms to rent nearby.
🛏️ 30 🚭 🅰️ All major cards

🍴 **ALEXIS4SEASONS**
$$$
ARISTOTELOUS 33
RHODES OLD TOWN
TEL (22410) 70522
One of the best fish restaurants in the Dodecanese. You will encounter seafood here not commonly seen on other menus (sea urchins, for example) and the best of the catch from the harbor. All vegetables are also organically grown by the owners.
🕐 Closed Sun. 🚭 🅰️ All major cards

🍴 **TA KIOUPIA**
$$
TREIS VILLAGE
RHODES TOWN
TEL (22410) 91824
Make sure you come here with an appetite. After a choice of soups you will be faced with a table full of tempting meze dishes and hearty main courses. Remember, too, that there is a big and mouthwatering dessert menu.

🕐 Closed L & Sun. 🚭 🅰️ All major cards

SAMOS

🏨 **FITO BUNGALOWS HOTEL**
$$
PITHAGORIA
TEL (22730) 61314
E-MAIL WELCOME@FITOBAY.GR
www.fitobay.gr
A peaceful, low-level hotel, with its bungalows nestling in well-tended lawns and gardens crossed by shady paths. Whitewashed walls and pine furniture create an air of comfortable simplicity.
🛏️ 87 🅿️ 🕐 Closed winter
🚭 🏊 🅰️ All major cards

🍴 **CHRISTOS**
$
PLATEIA AYIOU NIKOLAOU, SAMOS TOWN
TEL (22730) 24792
As simple as a Greek taverna can be, serving standard fare like chops, chicken, and fish, but all is well prepared and it

certainly keeps the locals happy.
🃏 No credit cards

SIMI

🏨 ALIKI
$$$
AKTI GENIMMATA, SIMI TOWN
TEL (22460) 71655
E-MAIL INFO@HOTELALIKI.GR
www.simi-hotel-aliki.gr
Although it has changed hands
in recent years, this venerable
hotel on a quiet part of the
Simi waterfront retains its
charm. A three-story neoclas-
sical mansion, it was built in
1895, and rooms have been
modernized so that they are
comfortable without being
stuffy. The best rooms are
those upstairs at the front,
with sea views and small
balconies.
ⓘ 15 🅢 🃏 No credit cards

SOMETHING SPECIAL

🍴 TAVERNA GEORGIOS
$
CHORIO, SIMI TOWN
There is no other restaurant
quite like this. It manages
to be chaotic yet produce
mouthwatering food night
after night. The eponymous
owner glides to and from the
kitchen, sometimes waiting
on diners or maybe taking his
bouzouki to entertain, as the
mood takes him. Don't be
slow to ask for service or the
bill. Wander into the kitchen
and ask to see what's cooking,
then grab a table, sit back, and
watch the drama unfold.
🕐 Closed L 🅢 🃏 No credit
cards

THASSOS

🏨 MAKRYAMMOS BUNGALOWS
$$$
MAKRYAMMOS
TEL (25930) 22101

E-MAIL INFO@MAKRYAMMOS-
HOTEL.GR
www.makryammos-hotel.gr
This resort hotel, with its own
bar, restaurant, and tennis
courts, is made up of cottages
plus ten luxurious suites
scattered around the lush
green grounds. It has its own
immaculate white sandy beach
and one of the best settings
you will find on Thassos.
ⓘ 206 🅿 🅢 🏊 🃏 AE,
MC, V

🍴 SIMI
$–$$
OLD HARBOR, THASSOS TOWN
TEL (25930) 22517
Sit at the front and watch the
boats in the harbor at this taverna. Popular with locals, this
place offers friendly service,
tasty food, and real value for
money. Try the seafood, the
kleftico, or meatballs. Because
Simi is small, bookings are
advisable in the high season.
🅢 🃏 No credit cards

TILOS

🏨 IRINI
$
LIVADIA
TEL (22410) 44293
Impeccably run family
hotel with attractive, well-
maintained gardens and a
peaceful location. Front rooms
have good sea views, and the
breakfasts are generous. Nothing is too much trouble for the
owners.
ⓘ 23 🅢 🏊

■ CORFU & THE IONIANS

CORFU

🏨 HOLIDAY PALACE CORFU
$$$$
NAUSICAS 2, KANONI
TEL (26610) 36540

E-MAIL RESERVATIONS@
CORFUHOLIDAYPALACE.GR
www.aquisresorts.com
Luxury resort hotel close to
the airport and a taxi (or bus)
ride away from Corfu town.
Two restaurants, several bars,
snack bars, two pools, and a
casino are among the facilities.
ⓘ 256 🅿 🅢 🏊 🃏
🃏 All major cards

🏨 CAVALIERI
$$$
KAPODISTRIOU 4, CORFU TOWN
TEL (26610) 39041
E-MAIL INFO@CAVALIERI-HOTEL
.COM
www.cavalieri-hotel.com
This is almost on the water-
front, and upper front rooms
have good views of the Old
Fort and the sea. It's in an
old mansion that has been
restored without losing the
traditional style. The rooms are
a little spartan but do have all
modern conveniences.
ⓘ 50 🅢 🅢 🃏 All major cards

SOMETHING SPECIAL

🏨 BELLA VENEZIA
$$
ZAMPELI 4, CORFU TOWN
TEL (26610) 46500
E-MAIL BELVENHT@HOL.GR
www.bellaveneziahotel.com
This refurbished hotel has
a charm and character all
its own. The building is a
19th-century neoclassical
mansion that has been lov-
ingly restored, with spacious,
high-ceilinged rooms. There is
also a beautiful garden. It is on
a quiet street a few minutes'
walk from the center of
town. Staff are noted for their
friendliness.
ⓘ 31 🅢 🅢 🃏 All major cards

🍴 LA CUCINA
$$–$$$
GUILDFORD 15, CORFU TOWN
TEL (26630) 45029
An elegant restaurant offering

Greek and international cuisine and a large wine list. Expect to pay more than in most other places in Corfu town, but the options are worth it. Try the Exotica salad, a mix of avocado, mango, and shrimp, or the pizzas, king crab legs, or juicy steaks.

⊕ Closed midwinter 🅢
🅢 All major cards

🍴 REX
$$
PODISTRIOU 66, CORFU TOWN
TEL (26610) 39649
www.rexrestaurant.gr
For real Greek food try Rex, which has been in business since 1932. The restaurant is decorated with local paintings, and the service is friendly. Choose from a wide variety of tasty dishes.
🅢 🅢 Major credit cards

KEFALONIA

🏨 WHITE ROCKS
$$$$$
PLATYS YIALOS, LASSI, ARGOSTOLI
TEL (26710) 28332
One of the best hotels on the island, with its own private beach and another public beach nearby. It has good facilities and is not too far from Argostoli. In addition to the rooms it has 60 cottages.
ⓘ 102 🅿 ⊕ Closed winter
🅢 🅢 🅢 🅢 All major cards

🍴 EMELISSE ART HOTEL
$$$
FISKARDO, KEFALONIA
TEL (26740) 412000
www.arthotel.gr
Stylish Balinese furniture adorns these bungalows strewn over a peninsula. Wonderful homemade breakfasts.
ⓘ 63 🅿 ⊕ Closed Nov.–Apr. 🅢 🅢 🅢 All major cards

🍴 OLD PLAKA
$
METELAS, ARGOSTOLI
TEL (26710) 24849
Typical open-all-hours Greek place, but a dressier clientele comes in the evenings. Reasonably priced but tasty Greek fare. Pork stuffed with garlic is a succulent house specialty.
🅢 🅢 All major cards

LEFKADA

🍴 MEGANISSI
$$
KATOMERI, NR. LEFKADA TOWN
TEL (26450) 51639
Unwind in this idyllic spot, about a 15-minute walk uphill from the port of Lefkada town. Choose a middle or upper story superior room with a good-size terrace rather than the smaller ground floor accommodations. This place has better food than many tavernas.
ⓘ 14 🅢 🅢 🅢 No credit cards

PAXI

🍴 VASSILIS
$
WATERFRONT, LONGOS
TEL (26620) 31587
Right on the picturesque little harbor at Longos, this restaurant looks very ordinary but serves up the best food on the island, backed by an extensive wine list. Best to reserve a table at busy times of the year.
⊕ Closed some days L (phone to check) 🅢 🅢 All major cards

🍴 VONTZA
$
PAXOS CLUB HOTEL ROAD, GAÏOS
TEL (26620) 32172
Simple and charming, Vontza

is appreciated by locals for delicious food and genuine friendly service. The menu may be limited but the portions are not. This place offers value-for-money real Greek cooking.
🅢 No credit cards

ZAKINTHOS

🏨 NOBELOS HOTEL
$$$
VOLIMES
TEL (26950) 27632
E-MAIL INFO@NOBELOS.GR
www.nobelos.gr
Four romantic suites—with traditional furniture and antiques—overlooking the sea. Greet the dawn with homemade breakfast.
ⓘ 4 🅿 🅢 🅢 All major cards

Shopping

Many shops sell ceramics and a range of knickknacks. By looking around it is possible to find more unusual items, such as handmade puppets, made by craftspeople rather than settling for mass-produced goods. Leather is a good buy, as is gold and silver jewelry, for which the Greeks have a fine reputation. And look out for traditional regional produce: Many of the islands have their own specialty foods and drinks.

Generally Greek food and wine don't travel well, although some brand-name spirits are good bargains and so is the virgin olive oil. Also look for delicate embroidery and handwoven items, lace, cotton skirts, and blouses.

Where to Go

If you are keen on ceramics, the best examples are available on the islands of Rhodes, Sifnos, and Skiros, though you will find good work for sale almost anywhere in the country. Athens and Rhodes are both good for gold, but prices are high. Quality leatherwork is widely available, but the finest examples are available on Crete, and in particular the town of Hania. Quality embroidery can be found on the Ionian islands, especially Kefalonia and Zakinthos.

Haggling

Haggling is acceptable in certain circumstances, notably in tourist areas such as the Plaka in Athens. Here, store owners will start you off on the process anyway by immediately quoting you a price less than the one on the ticket. Don't just accept this as a bargain, but consider if the price might come down further: It usually will. There is often room for maneuvering in jewelry and craft shops.

▨ OLD ATHENS

Antiques, Arts, & Crafts

Art Foundation, Normanou 5 Square 3, tel (210) 323 8757. Part gallery, part theater space, part bar, this is often called, simply,

Taf, and is one of the hottest places to talk about art in Athens. It opened in 2008 in a renovated building in Monastiraki.

Cheapart, Thermistokleous and A. Metaxa 25, tel (210) 323 3740. This energetic gallery and art store in Exarcheia was started in 1995 by George and Dimitris Georgakopoulos. The space now represents more than 450 artists. You can see the latest in contemporary art and buy works directly from the artist.

Greek Women's Institution, Kolokotroni 3, tel (210) 325 0524. This outlet highlights the Greek embroidery tradition, providing the more remote rural and island communities with some financial benefit from the country's popularity as a tourist destination—which they would not otherwise receive. A cause worth supporting.

Kostas Sokaras, Adrianou 25, tel (210) 321 6826. Embroidery, jewelry, Greek folk costumes, and puppets from the traditional Greek art of the shadow theater.

Martinos, Pandrossou 50, tel (210) 321 3110. There are some genuinely good antiques shops in among the Plaka's souvenir shops, and this is one of the best.

Books

Compendium, Nikis 28, tel (210) 322 1248. English-language books, magazines, guides, fiction, books about Greece, maps, and

a large secondhand section for exchanging your used paperbacks. There are sometimes readings from local or visiting authors—check the notice board for details.

Pantelides, Amerikis 11, tel (210) 362 3673. This sells everything from popular blockbuster paperbacks to obscure specialist works.

Clothes

The car-free Ermou Street (connecting Syntagma and Monastiraki Metro stations) has a range of international clothing stores such as Benetton, Lacoste, and Marks & Spencer, as well as many Greek equivalents.

Stavros Melissinos, Pandrossou 89, tel (210) 321 9247. Now a Plaka institution, Stavros Melissinos has been making sandals and writing poetry since the 1960s. He made sandals for John Lennon and will do the same for you.

Food & Drink

Visit the **Central Market** south of Omonoia on Athinas to buy herbs, spices, nuts, olives, cheeses, and other delicacies.

Aristokratikon, Karayioryi Servias 9, tel (210) 322 0546. Greeks like really sweet candy, and this upmarket store has been supplying the city with chocolates and other indulgences for decades.

The Mastihashop, Panepistimiou Street/Kriezotou Street, tel (210) 363 2750. This lovely little shop near Syntagma sells everything made from the mastic plant—which grows on the island of Hios—including sweets, juices, cosmetics, and medicines, all said to be health-giving.

Jewelry

Marathianakis, Voukourestiou 21, tel (210) 362 7118. Stunning Greek gold pieces based on Byzantine designs.

Zolotas, Stadiou 9, tel (210) 322 1222. One of Greece's leading jewelers, with work worth seeing in its own right, whether you buy or not. Also has a store in the Plaka at Pandrossou 8.

■ MODERN ATHENS & THE SUBURBS

Kolonaki

Artisti Italiani, Kanari 5, tel (210) 363 9085. Italian designs for women and men, and appropriately priced.

Borell's, Ypsilandou 5, tel (210) 721 9772. Antique and modern jewelry just off Kolonaki Square.

Pireas

Chios Shop, Fokionos 4/Gounari, tel (210) 412 1222. Traditional food and drink, including wine, from the island of Hios.

■ AROUND ATHENS

Nafplio

To Enotio, Staikopoulos 40, Old Town, tel (27520) 21143. The Greeks have a great tradition of shadow puppet shows, and you can buy examples of the puppets here, both old and new.

■ THE NEAR ISLANDS

Egina

Elefteris Diakoyiannis, Vas-Georgiou 39, Egina town, tel

(22970) 24593. A good selection of ceramics from all over Greece.

Skiros

Andreou's, Agoras, tel (22220) 92926. This woodcarving workshop sells hand-crafted furniture in time-honored Skyrian style, along with kitchen utensils and smaller household items.

■ THE CYCLADES

Andros

Batsi Gold, Bats, tel (22820) 41575. Find a good collection of jewelry inspired by ancient Greek myths and legends: bracelets, earrings, necklaces, pins, and rings.

Santorini

Canava Roussos, Kamari, tel (22860) 31278. Here is a chance to sample Santorini wine at source and buy a few bottles at reasonable prices.

■ CRETE

Eleni Kastrinoyanni, Ikarou 3, Iraklio, tel (28210) 26186. Exclusive store selling modern examples of Cretan weaving, embroidery, pottery, and jewelry.

Elixir, Koundourou 15, Agios Nikolaos, tel (28410) 82593. Stocks fine Cretan produce such as olive oil, soap, and honey.

Leather Alley, Odos Skridlof, Hania. Close to the market, the street known as Leather Alley is lined with stores selling leather goods, including sandals, boots, handbags, belts, and wallets.

■ DODECANESE & NORTHEASTERN AEGEAN

Lesvos

The Lesvos Shop, Pavlou Kountourioti 22, tel (22510) 26088.

This shop is a community project that helps keep island traditions alive by selling local ouzo, olive oil, soaps, and ceramics.

Rhodes

Ministry of Culture Museum Reproduction Shop, Ippitou, Rhodes Old Town. Official government shop where you can pick up top-quality reproductions of statuary and other items on display in Greek museums.

Simi

Aegean Sponge Center, Harbor, Yialo. There are thousands of sponges for sale on an island that once made part of its wealth from sponge fishing. Learn about the life of a sponge fisherman.

■ CORFU & THE IONIANS

Corfu

Mavromatis Distillery, 8 miles (13 km) from Corfu town on road to Palaiokastritsa, tel (26630) 22174. See how brandy, ouzo, and the unique local kumquats liqueur are made. A chance to buy them, too, of course.

Symposium, Near Nisaki, tel (26630) 91094. As you enter Nisaki, look for this wonderful food store, stocking the best food and drink products. Food lovers' eyes will light up.

Kefalonia

Alexander's, Vergoti, Argostoli, tel (26710) 23057. Varied collection of Greek handicrafts, including jewelry, ceramics, dolls in island costumes, and embroidery.

Zakinthos

Handicraft Cooperative, Lombardou 42, Zakinthos town. This excellent store sells island-made products including rugs, clothing, embroidery, and tablecloths.

Entertainment

Entertainment is often impromptu: Someone is inspired to get up and sing or dance In a bar or taverna; there's a party to mark one of the many feast days scattered throughout the Greek calendar; or maybe it's someone's name day (the Greek equivalent of a birthday), when everyone sharing the same name will jointly host a party. However, there are also some more organized events and festivals.

■ OLD ATHENS

Arts & Music Festivals
Folk Dance
Dora Stratou Theater
Filoppapou Hill, Athens
Tel (210) 324 4395
Dora Stratou was a renowned dancer and enthusiast for Greek music and culture, and the dance troupe she founded performs nightly from May to the end of September in this delightful open-air theater.

Hellenic Festival
Herodes Atticus Theater, Athens
Tel (210) 322 1459 or (210) 323 2771
An annual festival of music, dance, drama, and other arts held throughout the months of June–late September or early October.

Jazz & Blues Festival
Lykavittos Hill, Athens
Held in June each year.

Sound & Light Show
Pnyka Hill, Athens
Tel (210) 322 1459
Held in a great setting—Pnyka Hill is opposite the Acropolis—from April to October. There are different language shows each evening, so check the current program.

■ MODERN ATHENS & THE SUBURBS

Feasts
Blessing of the Waters
Pireas Port

January 6 is a national holiday, the Feast of the Epiphany, but it is also the day for the Blessing of the Waters (see p. 118), to bring good fortune to this maritime nation for the forthcoming year. This is done at Pireas (and elsewhere in Greece).

Independence Day
March 25 is **Independence Day,** when Athens hosts parades and other special festivities to celebrate the 1821 War of Independence against the Turks.

■ AROUND ATHENS

Arts Festivals
Epidavros Drama Festival
Epidavros Ancient Theater, Epidavros
Tel (210) 322 1459
Held in conjunction with Athens's Hellenic Festival, this festival of drama in the stunning setting of Epidavros's ancient theater runs throughout the summer. Performances are not held every night, so obtain a current program.

Nafplio Festival
Municipality of Nafplio, Trion Navarhou Square 21, Nafplio
Tel (27520) 27153
The festival features classical music, drama, and other arts in the charming town of Nafplio every summer.

Feasts
Feast of St. George
Arachova, near Delphi
Celebrated with traditional

music, dancing, and costumes in the mountain village of Arachova on April 23.

Feast of Profitis Ilias
Mount Taygettus, near Sparta
From July 18 through July 20, this feast is celebrated with services and festivities at many monasteries throughout Greece. However, the biggest celebration takes place on the high peak of Mount Taygettus, near Sparta (see p. 131).

■ THE NEAR ISLANDS

Feasts
Feast of Agios Riginos
Skopelos
The island's patron saint is commemorated on February 25.

Independence Day
Idra
March 25—Independence Day—is celebrated with particular fervor and exuberance on Idra.

Feast of St. George
Skiros
This island's patron saint's day, April 23, is marked enthusiastically with music and feasting.

Battle of the Straits of Spetses
Harbor, Spetses town
There is a reenactment of the battle (in which the combined forces of Spetses and Idra defeated the Ottoman fleet in 1821) on September 8.

THE CYCLADES

Feasts

Apeiranthos Festival
Apeiranthos, Naxos
On the last Sunday of Lent, villagers in Apeiranthos blacken their faces and challenge each other in improvizing satirical couplets called *kotsakia*.

Feast of St. Pelagia
Tinos town, Tinos
The healing icon from Panagia Evangelistria church is paraded through the streets of Tinos town on July 23 in honor of St. Pelagia. Music and fireworks entertain the crowds late into the night.

St. Elias's Day
Santorini
This saint's day is celebrated on July 20. Traditional pea and ham soup is served, followed by walnut and honey dessert—and folk dancing.

CRETE

Arts Festivals

Iraklio Arts Festival
Iraklio, Crete
This features drama, dance, and music concerts with international names as well as Greek stars. It is held each August.

Renaissance Festival
Rethimno, Crete
Tel (28310) 22245 or (28310) 53583
Held every August/September, this includes lively music and theater.

Feasts

Blessing of the Sheep
Assi Gonia, Crete
This unusual feast on April 23 involves thousands of sheep being blessed at the church of St. George, before their milk is distributed to the villagers. Music, dance, and food follows.

Wine Festival

Rethimno Wine Festival
Rethimno, Crete
An annual event, usually held throughout July.

DODECANESE & NORTHEASTERN AEGEAN

Arts & Music Festivals

Rhodes Folk Dance
Nr. Plateia Arionos, Rhodes town, Rhodes
Tel (22410) 20157
Nightly performances during the week, from May to October (currently 9:15 p.m. Mon., Wed., & Fri.), by the Nelly Dimoglou Company.

Sound & Light Show
Municipal Garden, Rhodes town, Rhodes
Tel (22410) 21922
From April to October. Shows are in different languages.

Feasts & Festivals

Burning of Judas Iscariot
Panagia, Thassos
On Easter night, an effigy of Judas Iscariot is burned in the village.

Feast of Agia Marina
Agia Marina, Kasos
July 17 is a big day in the village of that name on Kasos.

Feast of Agia Paraskevi
Agia Paraskevi, Lesvos
This takes place on July 26.

Feast of the Assumption
Agiasos, Lesvos
This feast, on August 15, is widely celebrated, but on Lesvos it is best observed in the village of Agiasos.

Feast of the Assumption
Olympos, Karpathos
If you are on Karpathos on August 15, join the ceremony in this lovely mountain village.

Feast of Profitis Ilias
Profitis Ilias Monastery, near Kameiros, Rhodes
Celebrations are particularly colorful here.

Feast of St. George
Most islands
Celebrated widely on April 23. On Kos and Limnos there is traditionally horse racing.

Ikaria Panayiri
Ikaria
These fiestas take place throughout the summer, some lasting for three days.

History Festival

Medieval Rose Festival
Rhodes town, Rhodes
Tel (22410) 74405
www.medievalrose.org
A festival of medieval culture, which attracts hundreds of historical reenactors from across Greece and Europe. Held in late June.

CORFU & THE IONIANS

Arts & Music Festivals

Corfu Festival
Corfu town, Corfu
A celebration of orchestral and choral performances, drama, and art in September.

Sound & Light Show
Old Fortress, Corfu town, Corfu
Tel (26610) 37520
From May until late September.

Feasts

Unification of the Ionian Islands
Corfu town, Corfu,
This feast, on May 21, is celebrated throughout the island group, but especially in and around Corfu town.

Outdoor Activities

Greece offers a wide array of activities, with water sports featuring prominently. Most resorts have a choice of sports available, such as windsurfing, waterskiing, pedaling boats, jet skiing, and paragliding. Activities such as walking, mountain trekking, and cycling tend to be unorganized and left to the individual. Tennis, soccer, and basketball are popular, and there are a few golf courses.

Golf

Glyfada Golf Club
Konstantinou Karamanli
Glyfada, Athens
Tel (210) 894 6459
A 150-acre (60 ha), 18-hole, par-72 course. The best in Greece, with a clubhouse and full facilities.

Afandou Golf Course
Afandou, Rhodes
Tel (22410) 51451
www.afandougolfcourse.com
An 18-hole, par-73 course. Designed by Donald Harradine and in a particularly lovely setting.

Corfu Golf Club
Ropa Valley, Corfu
Tel (22610) 94220
www.corfugolfclub.com
An 18-hole, par-72 course, suitable for all levels. Coaching is given, there is a restaurant, and the shop has equipment for rent.

Crete Golf Club
Hersonissos, Crete
Tel (28970) 26000
www.crete-golf.com
An 18-hole, par-70 course, overlooking stunning Cretan landscape. Restaurant and clubhouse facilities.

Horseback Riding

Hellenic Riding Club
Paradisou 18, Maroussi, Athens
Tel (210) 681 2506
The sport is not very big in Greece, but this organization has details of riding clubs in Athens and around the country.

Marathon Running

SEGAS
Syngrou 137, Athens
Tel (210) 933 1113
www.athensclassicmarathon.gr
The original marathon route is run twice a year (see p. 137). Details of how to enter are available from SEGAS.

Mountaineering

Hellenic Federation of Mountaineering Clubs
Milioni 5, Kolonaki, Athens
Tel (210) 364 5904
There are numerous mountaineering clubs around Greece that can provide information on activities, mountain trails, and the many mountain huts and refuges that can be reserved through them. The Hellenic Federation will have up-to-date information.

Halkida Alpine Club
Angeli Gouviou St. 22
Halkida, Evia
Tel (22210) 25230
For information on good climbs on Egina (see p. 153).

Sailing

Hellenic Professional Yacht Owners Association
A8–A0 Zea Marina, Pireas
Tel (210) 452 6335
Has general information on sailing conditions in Greek waters.

Scuba Diving

Diving is permitted only in certain areas during daylight hours, so check locally. There are 68 diving centers in Greece, mostly on the islands, including Corfu, Crete, Hios, Idra, Kos, Lefkada, Lesvos, Mikonos, Naxos, Paros, Rhodes, Samos, Thassos, and Zakinthos. For details, contact: **Union of Greek Diving Centers**, tel (210) 922 9532.

Spectator Sports

Soccer remains Greece's sporting obsession, though in recent years this passion has been matched by a love of basketball. It may be hard to get served in a bar or taverna when all eyes are glued to a match on TV. For those who want to watch a less popular spectator sport, there is now a cricket festival during the summer months, with matches played on Corfu and other Ionian islands. Check with the website of the **Hellenic Cricket Federation** (www.festival.cricket.gr) for more information.

Waterskiing

Hellenic Water Ski Federation
Thrakis St. 50, Ilioupolis, Athens
Tel (210) 994 4334
Has general information on Athens-area facilities.

Windsurfing

Experienced windsurfers who want the best facilities should look to the Ionian Islands (Corfu, Lefkada, and Zakinthos in particular) and to Kos, Lesvos, Naxos, Paros, and Samos. For more information, contact: **Hellenic Windsurfing Association**, Filellinon St. 4, 10533 Athens, tel (210) 323 3696.

INDEX

ILLUSTRATIONS CREDITS

National Geographic
TRAVELER
Athens & the Islands

Published by the National Geographic Society
John M. Fahey, Jr., *Chairman of the Board, and Chief Executive Officer*
Tim T. Kelly, *President*
Declan Moore, *Executive Vice President; President, Publishing*
Melina Gerosa Bellows, *Executive Vice President; Chief Creative Officer, Books, Kids, and Family*

Prepared by the Book Division
Barbara Brownell Grogan, *Vice President and Editor in Chief*
Jonathan Halling, *Design Director, Books and Children's Publishing*
Marianne R. Koszorus, *Director of Design*
Barbara A. Noe, *Senior Editor*
Carl Mehler, *Director of Maps*
R. Gary Colbert, *Production Director*
Jennifer A. Thornton, *Managing Editor*
Meredith C. Wilcox, *Administrative Director, Illustrations*

Staff for This Book
Caroline Hickey, Lawrence M. Porges, *Project Editors*
Kay Kobor Hankins, *Art Director*
Mary Stephanos, *Copy Editor*
Al Morrow, *Design Assistant*
Michael McNey, David Miller, *Map Production*
Rachael Jackson, Linda Makarov, Julie Woodruff, *Contributors*

Manufacturing and Quality Management
Christopher A. Liedel, *Chief Financial Officer*
Phillip L. Schlosser, *Senior Vice President*
Chris Brown, *Technical Director*
Nicole Elliott, *Manager*
Rachel Faulise, *Manager*
Robert L. Barr, *Manager*

Windmill Books Ltd.
Lindsey Lowe, *Editorial Director*
Tim Harris, *Managing Editor*
Jeni Child, *Design Manager*
Supriya Sahai, *Senior Designer*
Joan Curtis, *Designer*
Sophie Mortimer, *Picture Manager*
Martin Darlison, *Cartographer*
Clive Carpenter, Joe Fullman, Alastair Gourlay, Leon Gray, Ben Hollingum, Sally McFall, *Contributors*

National Geographic Traveler:
Athens & the Islands
ISBN 978-1-4262-0823-2

The National Geographic Society is one of the world's largest nonprofit scientific and educational organizations. Founded in 1888 to "increase and diffuse geographic knowledge," the Society works to inspire people to care about the planet. National Geographic reflects the world through its magazines, television programs, films, music and radio, books, DVDs, maps, exhibitions, live events, school publishing programs, interactive media and merchandise. *National Geographic* magazine, the Society's official journal, published in English and 33 local-language editions, is read by more than 40 million people each month. The National Geographic Channel reaches 370 million households in 34 languages in 168 countries. National Geographic Digital Media receives more than 15 million visitors a month. National Geographic has funded more than 9,600 scientific research, conservation and exploration projects and supports an education program promoting geography literacy.

For more information, please call 1-800-NGS LINE (647-5463) or write to the following address:

National Geographic Society
1145 17th Street N.W.
Washington, D.C. 20036-4688 U.S.A.

Visit us online at www.nationalgeographic.com

For information about special discounts for bulk purchases, please contact National Geographic Books Special Sales: ngspecsales@ngs.org

For rights or permissions inquiries, please contact National Geographic Books Subsidiary Rights: ngbookrights@ngs.org

The information in this book has been carefully checked and to the best of our knowledge is accurate. However, details are subject to change, and the National Geographic Society cannot be responsible for such changes, or for errors or omissions. Assessments of sites, hotels, and restaurants are based on the author's subjective opinions, which do not necessarily reflect the publisher's opinion.

Printed in China

11/TS/1

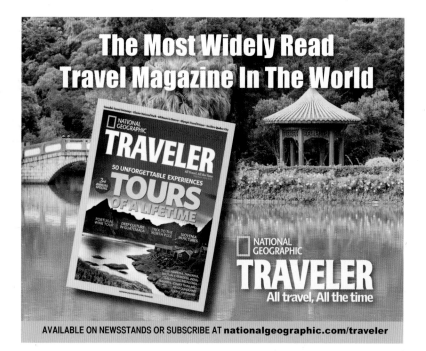